✶ *The Confederate General* ✶

Volume 6

✴ *The Confederate General* ✴

Volume 6

Steuart, George H. to Zollicoffer, Felix K.

William C. Davis, Editor

Julie Hoffman, Assistant Editor

A Publication of the
National Historical Society

Library of Congress Cataloging-in-Publication Data
The Confederate General / William C. Davis,
    editor; Julie Hoffman, assistant editor.
        p. cm.
        ISBN 0-918678-68-4 (v. 6) : $29.95
        Contents: v. 6. Steuart, George to Zollicoffer, Felix.
        1. United States—History—Civil War, 1861-1865—
Biography. 2. Confederate States of America. Army.—Biography. 3.
Generals—Confederate States of America—Biography. 4.
Generals—Southern States—Biography. 5. Generals—United States
—Biography.
I. Davis, William C., 1946-   .   II. Hoffman, Julie.
    E467.C76   1991
    973.7'42'0922 [B]   91-8508

Editorial Assistant, Eleanor Mauck
Designed by Art Unlimited
Printed in the United States of America

✴ Contents ✴

✶ *George Hume Steuart* ✶

An excellent post-March 1862 full-length portrait of Steuart in which his buttons and braid match his rank, except the colonel's stars on his collar. (Campbell-Colston Papers, Southern Historical Collection, University of North Carolina, Chapel Hill)

George H. Steuart was born in Baltimore, Maryland, on August 24, 1828. Enrolling at the United States Military Academy at the age of sixteen, Steuart was graduated in 1848, ranking thirty-seventh in a class of thirty-eight members. Assigned to the cavalry, he served on the western frontier in Texas, Kansas, Nebraska, and Colorado. He was promoted to 1st lieutenant on March 3, 1855, and to captain on December 12, 1855. When the Civil War began, Steuart resigned his commission on April 22, 1861, and accepted a captaincy in the Confederate army.

Steuart had reported for duty at Harpers Ferry, Virginia, by June 1. Brigadier General Joseph E. Johnston assigned him to command of Maryland troops, and on June 26, when the 1st Maryland was organized, Steuart was appointed lieutenant colonel and Arnold Elzey colonel. At First Manassas, while Elzey commanded a brigade, Steuart led the regiment. For his performance in the battle Steuart received his colonelcy, to rank from July 21, and command of the regiment. The troops welcomed his promotion, for Steuart had earned a reputation as a fair but firm disciplinarian and a capable and brave officer in combat.

On March 18, 1862, Steuart was promoted to brigadier general, to rank from March 6, and assigned to a brigade in the division of Major General Richard S. Ewell. During the 1862 Shenandoah Valley Campaign Steuart directed both infantry and cavalry. In the early stages of the operations he commanded his infantry brigade, which consisted of the 1st Maryland and the 44th, 52d, and 58th Virginia. On May 24th Major General Thomas J. "Stonewall" Jackson transferred him to command of the 2d and 6th Virginia Cavalry. But his performance with the mounted units at Winchester displeased Jackson, and on June 2 Steuart returned to his brigade. Six days later, at Cross Keys, the Marylander was severely wounded in the shoulder by shellfire.

The wound disabled Steuart for nearly a year. Returning to the army in May 1863, Steuart assumed command of a brigade—2d Maryland; 1st and 3d

North Carolina; and 10th, 23d, and 37th Virginia—in the division of Major General Edward Johnson. At Gettysburg on July 2 and 3 Steuart's brigade fought in the vicious struggle on Culp's Hill, capturing a line of breastworks, a number of prisoners, and a battleflag. Its losses in the two-day fighting amounted to nearly seven hundred.

Steuart served under Johnson throughout the operations of the fall and winter of 1863. At Spotsylvania on May 12, 1864, a Union assault crushed the so-called "Mule Shoe" salient, wrecking Johnson's division and capturing hundreds of its members, including Steuart. During his imprisonment Steuart was sent to Hilton Head, South Carolina, where Union commanders placed him and other officers under the fire of Confederate cannon.

Exchanged several months later, Steuart assumed command of a brigade in the division of Major General George Pickett. The brigade, comprised of the 9th, 14th, 38th, 53d and 57th Virginia, served in the trenches north of the James River during the Petersburg Campaign. Steuart's brigade fought at Five Forks on April 1, 1865. Five days later at Sayler's Creek Pickett's division was shattered with only a remnant of eight hundred men with the army at Appomattox.

Steuart returned to his native state after the war, buying a farm in Anne Arundel County. He was active in veteran affairs for many years, serving as commander of the Maryland Division of the United Confederate Veterans. The capable if undistinguished brigadier died at South River, Maryland, on November 22, 1903, and was buried in Green Mount Cemetery, Baltimore.

Jeffry D. Wert

Goldsborough, W.W., *The Maryland Line in the Confederate Army, 1861–1865* (Baltimore, 1900).

Johnson, Bradley T., *Maryland*, Vol. II in Evans, *Confederate Military History*.

Tanner, Robert G., *Stonewall in the Valley* (Garden City, N.Y., 1976).

A bust portrait of Steuart taken at approximately the same time as the standing view. (Museum of the Confederacy, Richmond, Va.)

✴ *Clement Hoffman Stevens* ✴

Stevens was born on August 14, 1821, in Norwich, Connecticut, where his father was serving in the United States Navy. The elder Stevens soon resigned from the navy and moved his family to Florida. With the outbreak of the Seminole War in 1836, the family moved to Pendleton, South Carolina. Clement Stevens acted as private secretary to two naval officers for several years but he left the navy in 1842 to go to work at the Planters and Mechanics Bank in Charleston. By 1861 he had become cashier of that institution. Stevens invented an ironclad battery and constructed one at Cummings Point on Morris Island. Historians regard this as the first armored fortification ever built, and some writers call it the prototype for the ironclad ram *Virginia*. The battery played an important role in the bombardment and reduction of Fort Sumter. Stevens also invented a portable oven that his troops later put to excellent use in baking bread.

He served as a volunteer aide on the staff of Brigadier General Barnard E. Bee, his brother-in-law, at the First Battle of Manassas, July 21, 1861, and received a severe wound. Returning to Charleston to recuperate, Stevens took command of a militia regiment and acted as volunteer aide-de-camp to Brigadier General Roswell S. Ripley. In late January 1862 Stevens assisted in organized an attack on Edisto Island, where armed blacks had attacked Confederate pickets. He and Ellison Capers raised the 24th South Carolina Infantry Regiment, of which they were commissioned on April 1, 1862, as colonel and lieutenant colonel, respectively. Stationed initially on Cole's Island, the regiment soon received orders to go to Secessionville on James Island. The men saw some skirmishing with Union gunboats along the Stono River in May. Stevens commanded the picket force on the island, consisting of portions of his own and two other regiments, on June 16. His line was attacked by the Federals at the commencement of the Battle of Secessionville that day. Receiving reinforcements from Colonel Johnson Hagood, Stevens was able eventually to repulse the enemy assault. The 24th South Carolina remained on James Island through the summer and fall.

From time to time Stevens held command of all of the troops in the vicinity of Secessionville, and he sat on a court of inquiry called to investigate the death in a duel of Colonel Ransom Calhoun at the hands of Major Alfred Rhett, both of the 1st South Carolina Artillery. The court condemned dueling, but Rhett remained in service. Stevens took his regiment with several others to Pocataligo, South Carolina, on October 22 to retake a portion of railroad from a Federal force that had advanced from Port Royal Ferry. The troops saw some light skirmishing but returned to James Island on October 24. On December 14 Stevens was assigned to command a brigade of South Carolina regiments sent to Wilmington, North Carolina, in response to a Union raid. The troops did outpost duty and erected earthwork fortifications during the next month or so before

No wartime uniformed portrait of Clement Stevens has surfaced. This is a prewar civilian view. (Evans, *Confederate Military History*)

returning to James Island. During the Union naval attack on Fort Sumter on April 7, 1863, Stevens commanded the Eastern Division of James Island, but few of men were engaged in the firing on the enemy gunboats.

About May 3 Stevens' regiment was placed in Brigadier General States Rights Gist's brigade, which had received orders to reinforce General Joseph E. Johnston's army in Mississippi. Stevens was delayed at Charleston for a few days and reached the army too late to participate with his men in the Battle of Jackson on May 14. The regiment followed Gist's brigade in all of its campaigns in Mississippi that summer and fall, including the Siege of Jackson, July 9–16. With Major General William H.T. Walker's division, Gist's brigade reinforced the Army of Tennessee at Chattanooga in late August. The brigade was detached at Rome, Georgia, and missed the first day of fighting in the Battle of Chickamauga, September 19–20. Stevens' troops could not leave Rome because the engineer of their train had killed its fire and had gone to sleep. Stevens and two others found the engineer, and Stevens threatened to shoot the man. Eventually he found a man in his regiment who could fire up the boiler, and the officers forced the engineer into the cab so that he could direct the train toward the battlefield. In an attack the next morning Stevens had two horses killed under him and was severely wounded. Gist referred to him as "iron-nerved" and recommended him for his "distinguished gallantry." Walker praised him also for his "capacity as an officer,…gallantry on the field, and…his devotion to the cause" and recommended him for promotion.

Stevens was made a brigadier general February 1, 1864, to rank from January 20, and received command of the Georgia brigade formerly commanded by Claudius C. Wilson in Walker's division. The brigade participated in all of the marches of the division during the opening stages of the Atlanta Campaign, but the men saw only minor skirmishing in a few engagements. Nevertheless, Stevens soon earned the nickname "Rock" from his troops. On July 18 he sent a letter to General Joseph E. Johnston expressing the brigade's confidence in him and its sorrow at their separation. Stevens' brigade was in the charge on the Union earthworks at the Battle of Peachtree Creek on the afternoon of July 20. Stevens was mortally wounded by an artillery round in the assault. His horse was also fatally wounded by the same shot but made its way to the front of the line of battle before collapsing.

Stevens died on July 25 in Atlanta. General Braxton Bragg called his death "a most serious loss." Stevens was buried in Pendleton, South Carolina.

Arthur W. Bergeron, Jr.

Capers, Ellison, *South Carolina*, Vol. V in Evans, *Confederate Military History*.

"Extracts from the Diary of Lieutenant-Colonel John G. Pressley, of the Twenty-Fifth South Carolina Volunteers." *Southern Historical Society Papers*, XIV (1886), pp. 35–62.

Hagood, Johnson, *Memoirs of the War of Secession* (Columbia, S.C., 1910).

"Operations Before Charleston in May and July, 1862," *Southern Historical Society Papers*, VIII, (1880), 541–47.

Tucker, Glenn, *Chickamauga: Bloody Battle in the West* (Indianapolis, 1961).

⋆ *Walter Husted Stevens* ⋆

Walter H. Stevens was born in Penn Yan, New York, on August 24, 1827. An 1848 graduate of the United States Military Academy, ranking fourth in the class, Stevens was brevetted a 2d lieutenant of engineers. For the next dozen years Stevens served primarily in Louisiana and Texas on various engineering duties. He inspected lighthouses along the Gulf Coast, surveyed rivers, and worked on projects in New Orleans, earning promotion to 1st lieutenant in 1855. During these years he married the sister of future Confederate general Louis Hébert of Louisiana.

When the Civil War began, Stevens embraced the Southern cause. He submitted his resignation, but the War Department refused to accept it and dismissed him on a technicality on May 2, 1861. Stevens accepted a captaincy of engineers and was assigned to the staff of General P.G.T. Beauregard. During the early operations in northern Virginia Stevens oversaw the construction of works near Fairfax Court House. Beauregard praised Stevens for this work, stating that he had "shown himself to be an officer of energy and ability." Stevens served under Beauregard at First Manassas.

When General Joseph E. Johnston assumed command of Confederate forces after the battle, he appointed Stevens chief engineer of the army, with the rank of major. Under Stevens' direction the Confederate army built extensive works around Centreville throughout the fall. Stevens remained on the staff of Johnston throughout the Peninsula Campaign of May 1862. When Johnston fell wounded at Seven Pines on May 31, General Robert E. Lee assumed command of the army. Stevens, with the rank of colonel, was assigned to the defenses of Richmond.

For the next two years Stevens directed the construction of the extensive fieldworks and forts that encircled the Confederate capital. He was an excellent engineering officer and erected a formidable series of works.

In the spring of 1864 Lee appointed Stevens chief engineer of the Army of Northern Virginia. Promoted to brigadier general September 2, to rank from August 28, 1864, Stevens again rendered valuable service as the Confederate army behind its breastworks withstood the siege of Petersburg for nearly ten months. When Petersburg fell and Richmond was abandoned in April 1865, Stevens was reportedly the last uniformed man to cross the Mayo Bridge during the evacuation of the capital. A trusted aide and friend of Lee, Stevens surrendered with the army at Appomattox.

Stevens fled the country after the war, accepting a position of engineer of the Imperial Railroad in Mexico from Maximilian. He died in Vera Cruz on November 12, 1867, at the age of forty. His remains were returned to the United States and buried in the Hollywood Cemetery, Richmond, the former citadel of the Confederacy whose existence owed much to the skill of Walter Stevens.

Jeffry D. Wert

Hotchkiss, Jedediah, *Virginia*, Vol. III in Evans, *Confederate Military History*.

Only two uniformed portraits of General Walter Stevens have come to light. This one was taken after August 1864. (Campbell-Colston Papers, Southern Historical Collection, University of North Carolina, Chapel Hill)

Stevens as he appeared earlier in the war while an officer on Lee's staff. (Library of Congress)

⋆ *Carter Littlepage Stevenson* ⋆

The only known wartime uniformed photo of Stevenson does not offer sufficient clues to guess at its date, or whether he was a colonel or brigadier at the time of the sitting. (Alabama Department of Archives and History, Montgomery)

Born near Fredericksburg, Virginia, on September 21, 1817, Carter Littlepage Stevenson graduated from West Point in 1838. He ranked forty-second out of the forty-five graduates and received a commission as a 2d lieutenant in the 5th Infantry. Stevenson was serving in Florida when he was promoted to 1st lieutenant on September 22, 1840. He then served in Wisconsin and in Michigan before participating in the Mexican War. While serving as aide-de-camp to Brigadier General Hugh Brady during that conflict, he distinguished himself at Palo Alto and at Resaca de la Palma. Promoted to captain on June 30, 1847, Stevenson remained on the Texas frontier following the Mexican War and participated in railroad explorations and in skirmishes against the Indians. During 1856 and 1857 he fought the Seminoles in Florida, and in 1858 he participated in the Utah Expedition.

Stevenson remained in Utah until he submitted his resignation on June 6, 1861, and departed on a leave of absence with the intention of offering his services to his native state. His commanding officer, who departed later that day for the same purpose, failed to forward Stevenson's resignation, and Stevenson was dismissed from the U.S. Army on June 25, 1861, "it having been ascertained, to the satisfaction of the War Department, that he had entertained and expressed treasonable designs against the Government of the United States."

In June of 1861 Stevenson entered the Confederate Regular Army as a major of infantry. Although promoted to lieutenant colonel in that organization in July, before the end of that month he had received a commission as colonel in the provisional army and had been assigned to command the 53d Virginia Infantry Regiment. When General Pierre G.T. Beauregard was preparing to leave Virginia for Tennessee in February of 1862 he recommended that Stevenson be promoted to brigadier general and that he be posted to the Western Theater. Stevenson received the promotion on March 6, to rank from February 27, but when orders were issued for him by the War Department on March 15 he was ordered to report to Major General Benjamin Huger for duty on the Weldon Railroad in southeastern Virginia. However, these orders were changed almost immediately and Stevenson was transferred to the Department of East Tennessee.

Upon his arrival in Knoxville Stevenson was assigned to command the troops in that region including the garrison at Cumberland Gap. In June, numerically superior Federal forces succeeded in outflanking the Southerners at Cumberland Gap and thereby forcing the Confederates to abandon that position in order to avoid being cut off. The garrison then united with other detached units to form a brigade under Stevenson. When Major General Edmund Kirby Smith invaded Kentucky in August, Stevenson was elevated to division command, and he and his division were left behind in East Tennessee to threaten Cumberland Gap from the south. After his maneuvering eventually forced Union Brigadier General George W. Morgan to evacuate Cumberland Gap, he entered Kentucky. Stevenson and his division saw no action because they arrived too late to reach Perryville before the fighting had ended there. Nevertheless, Stevenson was promoted to major general on October 13, to rank from October 10, before he and his division accompanied the Confederate withdrawal to Knoxville via Cumberland Gap.

Stevenson was given a division in General Braxton Bragg's army, but was ordered to take his division to Mississippi before the Battle of Murfreesboro. On December 30, Stevenson arrived at Chickasaw Bluffs, just north of Vicksburg, in time to witness the withdrawal of the Federals after their having been repulsed on the preceding day. Although new to the area of operations, he was placed in command of the troops at Chickasaw Bluffs because of his seniority as major general.

When Union Major General Ulysses S. Grant crossed the Mississippi River below Vicksburg in the spring of 1863, Stevenson commanded a division in the field under Lieutenant General John C. Pemberton. Stevenson's division bore the brunt of the fighting at Champion's Hill on May 16, where it was outflanked and forced to retreat. Following their defeat on May 17, the Confederates were forced to withdraw from the Big Black River. Stevenson personally commanded what remained of Pemberton's field army on its retreat to Vicksburg, Pemberton having hastened to Vicksburg to organize its defense prior to the arrival of his troops. During the siege of Vicksburg Stevenson commanded

the right wing of the land defenses. When Pemberton surrendered on July 4, every officer and man in the garrison was paroled.

In early September Stevenson and the members of his division were declared exchanged, an action which Federal authorities claimed was a violation of the cartel. Nonetheless, by the end of the month Stevenson had his men deployed about Lookout Mountain, on the outskirts of Chattanooga. On November 24 Union forces under Major General Joseph Hooker attacked Stevenson's position. Assaulted in front and flank by vastly superior numbers, Stevenson's men finally had to withdraw to the safety of Missionary Ridge.

Following the fighting at Chattanooga Stevenson participated in every battle fought by the Army of Tennessee, except for the Battle of Franklin. During the Atlanta Campaign in 1864 Stevenson distinguished himself at Resaca on May 15 and at Kennesaw Mountain on June 27. When General John Bell Hood assumed command of the army, Stevenson temporarily commanded the corps until Lieutenant General Stephen D. Lee replaced him. Stevenson missed the Battle of Franklin on November 30 because his division and one other were left on the south side of the Duck River to demonstrate against Major General John M. Schofield while Hood made his flanking movement with the balance of his army. During the Battle of Nashville, Stevenson stubbornly defended Overton Hill in the center of the Confederate line until forced to retreat by overwhelming numbers. When Lee was wounded at Winstead Hill on December 17, Stevenson again assumed command of the corps. Also, he personally commanded the infantry division that covered the Confederate withdrawal from Tennessee. Stevenson led his division at Bentonville, March 19–21, 1865, and received his parole at Greensboro, North Carolina, on May 1.

After the war, Stevenson worked as a civil and mining engineer in Caroline County, Virginia, until his death on August 15, 1888. He was buried in Fredericksburg.

Lawrence L. Hewitt

Heitman, Francis B., *Historical Register and Dictionary of the United States Army, From Its Organization, September 29, 1789, to March 2, 1903* (Washington, 1903), Vol. I.

Hotchkiss, Jedediah, *Virginia*, Vol. III in Evans, *Confederate Military History*.

⋆ *Alexander Peter Stewart* ⋆

The only known wartime photo of General Stewart, probably taken after his June 1863 promotion to major general. (Museum of the Confederacy, Richmond, Va.)

Of all of the many men who commanded corps in the troubled Army of Tennessee, few if any could claim to be more obscure than the one whose men called him "Old Straight," Alexander P. Stewart. Neither flamboyant nor retiring, he simply did his job well.

Born October 2, 1821, in Rogersville, Tennessee, Stewart secured an appointment to the Military Academy at West Point, and graduated in the class of 1842, standing a respectable twelfth out of fifty-six graduates, among them his sometime roommate James Longstreet. Soon afterward brevet 2d lieutenant Stewart joined the 3d U.S. Artillery, but was soon recalled to the Military Academy to teach mathematics. It seems to be there that his nickname first attached itself to him. In 1845 he resigned, deciding that he preferred teaching to soldiering, and took the chair of mathematics and natural and experimental philosophy at Lebanon, Tennessee's Cumberland University. In the 1850s he moved on to Nashville University, serving on the same faculty as future General Bushrod Johnson.

Stewart was an old line Whig, and therefore opposed to secession in the political crisis of 1860–61. Nevertheless, when Tennessee voted to secede, Stewart put down his books and took up his sword, accepting a commission as major in the artillery. His first assignment was the construction and management of the batteries on the "Iron Banks" of the Mississippi at Columbus, Kentucky. During the Battle of Belmont on November 8, 1861, he commanded those batteries in the bombardment that supported the Confederate counterattack across the river. Not only did his service here commence an association with Leonidas Polk that would last until Polk's death, but it also resulted in his appointment as brigadier general on that same date, to rank from November 8. Indeed, Stewart's appointment may have been decided before the battle, for General Albert Sidney Johnston had been trying to secure him such an appointment for at least a month, having it in mind to put Stewart in command of Forts Henry and Donelson.

General Stewart was assigned command of a brigade in Polk's I Corps of the Army of Mississippi, consisting of the 13th Arkansas, and the 4th, 5th, and 33d Tennessee, along with Stanford's Mississippi Battery. His first action with them would be Shiloh, and an exceptionally bloody maiden contest at that. In the confusion of the morning of April 6, Johnston ordered Stewart forward, but when the brigadier arrived on the scene, he found no orders and no superior to give him direction. Then other officers ordered one or more of his regiments away without telling him; in the confusion Tennessean fired upon Tennessean. Then William T. Sherman's Federals opened a devastating fire on the remainder of the brigade, and soon afterward Stewart's men opened fire on another Confederate brigade by mistake. Despite these costly confusions, Stewart later played a good supporting role in the attack on the Hornet's Nest, but by the next day his brigade was exhausted, disorganized, and almost disintegrated.

At Stones' River that winter, Stewart's brigade had grown to include the 4th, 5th, 19th, 24th, 31st, and 33d Tennessee, and the Mississippi Battery, and he led it with a skill that showed he had learned lessons at Shiloh. Late on the morning of December 31, it was Stewart whose attack finally broke down Sheridan's heroic stand in the face of Bragg's onslaught against Rosecrans' crumbling right flank. In recognition of his performance, Stewart would be appointed a major general on June 5, to rank from June 2, 1863. He took over the division composed of the brigades of William B. Bate, John C. Brown, and Henry D. Clayton. Operating along the Duck River line in the pre-Chickamauga operations, he served in Simon Buckner's Corps in Longstreet's Left Wing during that great Rebel victory. At the head of his so-called "Little Giant" division, Stewart broke the Federal line briefly on the first day of the fight, and was almost at the head of the attack the next day that shattered the Federal army. In the subsequent Chattanooga operations,

Stewart led his division on Breckinridge's Corps, where he held the left of the line atop Missionary Ridge.

During the Atlanta Campaign, Stewart was distinguished in the Dallas and New Hope Church fighting, and then when Polk, his corps commander once more, was killed on June 14 on Pine Mountain, Bragg gave the corps to Stewart. A few days later, on June 23, 1864, the President ratified the move with a promotion to lieutenant general, effective from June 2. For the rest of the war Stewart was at the head of his corps. He urged Joseph E. Johnston not to relinquish command when Davis relieved him in July, then performed well at Peachtree Creek and Ezra Church. Army commander Hood held him in high regard especially admiring the way Stewart spoke to his men before a battle, riding among them and giving them cheer. In the Battles of Franklin and Spring Hill, Stewart received bumbling instructions from Hood that neutralized his effectiveness, and at Nashville similar mismanagement by Hood led to Stewart being nearly overwhelmed. The following spring, with the Army of Tennessee only a remnant about four thousand strong, Stewart, as senior corps commander, was given command, and joined with other small "armies" under Hardee and Bragg to form the command led by Johnston in the Battle of Bentonville. As usual, Stewart performed ably; Hardee and Bragg did not. It was to be "Old Straight's" last battle. In May 1865 he gave his parole at Greensboro along with the rest of Johnston's army.

Stewart returned to education after the war, first at Cumberland University, and then in 1874 he accepted the chancellorship of the University of Mississippi. He remained there until 1886, meanwhile serving on the advisory commission of Federal and Confederate veterans who were responsible for the development and marking of what is now the Chickamauga and Chattanooga National Park. He died on August 30, 1908, in Biloxi, Mississippi, and was buried in St. Louis, Missouri, where he had family and business ventures intermittently after the war. Unfailingly able and dependable, "Old Straight" Stewart was the last surviving "commander" of the Army of Tennessee, and, indeed, of all Confederate army commanders.

William C. Davis

Connelly, Thomas L., *Autumn of Glory* (Baton Rouge, La., 1971).
Tucker, Glenn, *Chickamauga* (Indianapolis, Ind., 1961).

✳ *Marcellus Augustus Stovall* ✳

Stovall, whose grandfathers were both revolutionary war officers, was born at Sparta, Georgia, on September 18, 1818. His father, an Augusta merchant, sent him to school in Massachusetts. When he was seventeen, Stovall returned to Augusta and enlisted in the Richmond Blues. He was then the youngest member of that company of volunteers, and while serving with that unit, he saw action in Florida during the Seminole uprising of 1835. He received an appointment to the U.S. Military Academy in 1836, but after he had spent only one year at West Point, he was invalided out of the Cadet Corps because of rheumatism. Next, he toured Europe and then returned to Augusta, where he established himself as a merchant and, simultaneously, involved himself in the affairs of the local militia. In 1846 he removed to Floyd County, Georgia, where he settled on an estate near Rome and became active in a volunteer company of artillery. Stovall was serving as captain of this unit, the Cherokee Artillery, when Fort Sumter was fired upon in April of 1861.

The Civil War began and immediately Stovall was made colonel of artillery in the Georgia state militia because of his military education and experience. He served locally in that capacity until October, at which time he was commissioned lieutenant colonel of the 3d Georgia Infantry Battalion in the C.S. Provisional Army, to rank from October 6, 1861. Initially, Stovall was posted to Lynchburg, Virginia, and then to Goldsboro, North Carolina; in both instances he served in garrison. That he possessed superior organizational skills and leadership qualities was evident by the discipline and morale displayed by his men. His battalion consistently reported a higher percentage of its men fit for duty at muster than did any of the other units with which it was associated.

The battalion was still in Lynchburg on September 25 and it was ordered to Bristol, Tennessee, on November 11, so the stay at Goldsboro must have been brief. In East Tennessee, Stovall's men guarded railroad bridges and protected Southern sympathizers in that Unionist region. Following the evacuation of Cumberland Gap in June of 1862, Stovall's unit was assigned to Brigadier General Carter L. Stevenson's brigade. On July 3, Stevenson was put in charge of a division, and his brigade was taken over by Colonel James G. Rains. Two days later, Stovall apparently saw his first action in the affair at Waldron's Ridge. Detached from Stevenson's division, Stovall's battalion repeatedly thrilled local citizens with their evolutions during parades. The battalion rejoined Stevenson's division prior to the Confederate withdrawal from Kentucky.

In December, Stovall's battalion again formed part of a brigade under Brigadier General Rains in Major General John P. McCown's division, which was transferred to the Army of Tennessee. On December 31, during the Battle of Murfreesboro, Stovall distinguished himself during the Confederate attack through a dense cedar thicket which was directed against the Union right flank.

The only known wartime uniformed portrait of General Stovall, dating from after January 1863. (Museum of the Confederacy, Richmond, Va.)

Although Rains was killed in that battle, his brigade was assigned to Brigadier General William B. Bate. Stovall had to await promotion to brigadier general until April 23, 1863, to rank from January 20. On May 25, Stovall was ordered to report to Major General John C. Breckinridge to take command of Brigadier General William Preston's brigade. Breckinridge's division promptly departed for Mississippi, and by June 3, Stovall's troops were guarding the roads southwest of Jackson. His brigade consisted of the 1st, 3d, and 4th Florida, and the 60th North Carolina Infantry Regiments and Captain J.W. Mebane's Tennessee battery. Ordered to Clinton on June 30, the division returned to Jackson on July 5. During the middle of that month, the brigade, augmented by the addition of the 60th North Carolina, participated in the siege of Jackson.

The division returned to the Army of Tennessee in September, where it arrived in time to participate in the Battle of Chickamauga. Breckinridge praised Stovall's performance during that engagement, where he led his five regiments in an assault with one other brigade that gained the Union left flank and rear, thereby contributing greatly to the Confederate victory. Breckinridge reported: "To Brigadier-General Stovall...[and two others] the country is indebted for the courage and skill with which they discharged their arduous duties." Colonel W.L.L. Bowen of the 4th Florida remarked: "Much of the credit and success accorded the Fourth Florida regiment is ascribed to General Stovall and staff for the efficient and prompt manner in which he conducted his brigade."

After Chickamauga, Stovall was given command of an all-Georgian brigade in Major General Alexander P. Stewart's division, which he led throughout the fighting at Chattanooga in November. In 1864, Stovall distinguished himself in the Atlanta Campaign, and on July 22 during the Battle of Atlanta, his brigade penetrated the Federals' fortifications and captured a battery. Unfortunately, the hard-pressed Georgians were unable to secure the guns, and Stovall was absent, sick. In fact, Stovall was ill during much of the campaign, being absent from his command from May 15 until June 1. On July 27, General Braxton Bragg reported the "sickness and inefficiency, indeed, incapacity of Stovall, who is absent..." Stovall did lead his brigade during the Battle of Jonesboro on August 31 and in the invasion of Tennessee later that year. Although he missed the Battle of Franklin because his division had been left on the south bank of the Duck River, his brigade was one of the few that survived the Battle of Nashville with its efficiency level sufficient to participate in rear guard actions. In the closing months of the war, he served in the Carolinas. On February 27, 1865, his brigade of four regiments had only 378 men effective for duty, which made it the third largest brigade in Lieutenant General Stephen D. Lee's corps. Stovall participated in the Battle of Bentonville, March 19–21, and surrendered on April 26.

Officially paroled on May 9, 1865, Stovall returned to Augusta, where he became a cotton broker and manufactured fertilizers. He organized and operated the Georgia Chemical Works. On August 4, 1895, he died at Augusta and was buried there.

Benjamin E. Snellgrove

Derry, Joseph T., *Georgia*, Vol. VI in Evans, *Confederate Military History*.

An almost forgotten portrait of Otho Strahl taken in June 1863 or later. (*Confederate Veteran*, IV)

✶ *Otho French Strahl* ✶

Otho French Strahl was born June 3, 1831, at McConnelsville, Morgan County, Ohio; he matriculated at Ohio Wesleyan University at Delaware. One of his friends there was a man with whom he would serve in first the Army of the Mississippi and then the Army of Tennessee, the future brigadier general Daniel H. Reynolds. Strahl read law with Reynolds at Somerville, Tennessee, and was admitted to the bar in 1858. They then went their separate ways, the former establishing his office in Dyersburg, Tennessee, and the latter in Lake Village, Arkansas.

In the weeks following the firing on Fort Sumter and President Abraham Lincoln's call for seventy-five thousand volunteers, Tennessee moved toward secession, and Strahl made his decision. He would stand with his adopted state. In early May, he was elected captain of the Dyer Guards. They were ordered into camp at Germantown where, along with nine other companies, they were organized as the 4th Tennessee Volunteer Infantry Regiment and mustered into the Provisional Army of Tennessee on May 15. Strahl, on the same day, was elected the regiment's lieutenant colonel, while Rufus P. Neely was chosen colonel. The regiment was immediately ordered to Randolph, on the Mississippi, some fifty river miles above Memphis, and assigned to the River Brigade. Strahl and the regiment were sent to Fort Pillow on July 18, where on August 16 they were transferred to Confederate service. Here the 4th was brigaded with the 12th Louisiana, the brigade commanded by Colonel Neely. As senior officer, Strahl led the regiment when, on September 5, it went into camp at Columbus, Kentucky.

The regiment spent the autumn and first winter of the war posted in and around Columbus as one of the units assigned to Brigadier General John P. McCown's division. Strahl and his comrades of the 4th were sent across the Mississippi on November 7. He reinforced Brigadier General Gideon J. Pillow and his men battling the Yanks at Belmont, but arrived too late to participate in the fighting. After the loss of Fort Donelson

(February 16, 1862), the Confederates evacuated Columbus on March 3, and the 4th Tennessee—512 strong—went into camp at Corinth, Mississippi. The regiment was bloodied at Shiloh (April 6–7), suffering two hundred and nineteen casualties, more than fifty percent of those engaged. It entered the battle as a unit in Brigadier General A.P. Stewart's brigade, Major General Leonidas Polk's corps. On the 6th the regiment led by Colonel Neely and Strahl charged and captured a Union battery supported by Ohio and Illinois troops from Brigadier Generals W.T. Sherman's and John A. McClernand's divisions, earning a commendation from General Stewart.

During the Corinth siege (April 28–May 30), Neely died. When the Army was reorganized in accordance with the "Bounty and Furlough Law," Strahl was elected colonel to rank from April 24, 1862.

On the night of May 29 the Confederates evacuated Corinth and withdrew to Tupelo. An army reorganization on July 8 found Stewart's brigade—now composed of the 4th, 5th, 24th, 31st, and 33d Tennessee Infantry Regiments and Stanford's Mississippi Battery—assigned to Major General Benjamin Franklin Cheatham's Tennessee Division. Beginning in mid-July, General Braxton Bragg employed the iron horse to win the race to Chattanooga, and on August 17 the campaign that was to carry the Confederates deep into Kentucky began. Strahl and his regiment marched by way of Pikesville, Sparta, and Gainesboro, and were at Munfordville, Kentucky, on September 17. The battle for Kentucky took place at Perryville on October 8 and Strahl's unit, along with Stewart's other regiments, crossed Doctor's Fork. The savage fighting cost the 4th Tennessee nearly half its strength but crushed Union Brigadier General James S. Jackson's division. Bragg, however, had botched a campaign that had opened with great promise and that night the Confederates abandoned the field and began a long and bitter retreat back through Cumberland Gap into Tennessee.

At Murfreesboro on December 29, the 4th and 5th Tennessee were consolidated under Strahl's command

A better-known view, apparently from a separate sitting.
(U.S. Army Military History Institute, Carlisle, Pa.)

and on December 31 he led his men against the Federals at Stones' River. After much desperate fighting, they helped drive Philip H. Sheridan's battered division from the cedar glades west of Van Cleve Lane and north of Wilkinson Pike. General Stewart cited Strahl's conduct at Stones' River as "beyond praise."

Some eight weeks following the army's January 5 retreat from Murfreesboro to Tullahoma and Shelbyville, Strahl, as senior officer, assumed command of the brigade upon Stewart's reassignment to lead John McCown's division. Strahl's brigade (the 4th, 5th, 19th, 24th, 31st, and 33d Tennessee Infantry Regiments and Stanford's Mississippi Battery) were pelted by torrential rains and muddy roads, but saw no fighting during the Tullahoma Campaign (June 23—July 4). On July 29, 1863, he was promoted brigadier general.

Strahl led one of Cheatham's five brigades at Chickamauga and entered the fight at 1 P.M. on September 19. He battled Union soldiers of Palmer's and Van Cleve's divisions in the woods near Winfrey's fields. On the 10th Strahl and his men were in reserve and accordingly did not suffer as heavy casualties as many of the other infantry brigades in the West's bloodiest battle.

An army reorganization aimed at breaking up Cheatham's division found Strahl and his Tennesseans reassigned to General Stewart's division. At Missionary Ridge on November 25, Strahl was first compelled to abandon the rifle-pits at the foot of the ridge and then the crest as the troops to his right and left scattered. Strahl spent the winter of 1863–64 in and around Dalton, Georgia, where on February 20, Cheatham's division was reconstituted to include Strahl's brigade and assigned to Lieutenant General William J. Hardee's corps.

Strahl and his brigade took the field on February 20. Rushed by rail and boat to western Alabama they reinforced Lieutenant General Leonidas Polk, whose small army, confronted by Major General William T. Sherman's columns, had abandoned Jackson and Meridian, Mississippi, and retreated eastward to Demopolis, Alabama. Strahl and his troops reached Demopolis to find Sherman en route back to Vicksburg. Strahl's Tennesseans then returned to Dalton.

The next time Strahl met Sherman there was no respite. Sherman's "army group" advanced and engaged the Army of Tennessee, now led by General Joseph E. Johnston, on May 7. From May 9 until the end of August, Strahl was never far from the enemy. He and his troops were under fire during sixty of the next seventy-one days, at such places as Rocky Face's Dug and Mill Creek Gaps (May 8-12), Resaca (May 14–15), Adairsville (May 17), Ellsbury Mountain (May 26–June 2), and Kennesaw Mountain (June 27), where they were posted one-half mile south of the Dead Angle. Strahl was at the Battle of Atlanta (July 22), but missed the fight at Jonesboro (August 31–September 1) that led to the evacuation of Atlanta by the Army of Tennessee, which since July 18 had been led by General John Bell Hood.

Strahl rejoined his brigade by September 20 and, with John C. Brown now leading the Tennessee Division and Cheatham the corps, he recrossed the Chattahoochee River in late September. The last days of November found Strahl back in Middle Tennessee. He was at Spring Hill on the 19th and, on the 30th, he was one of the six Confederate generals killed or mortally wounded in the Franklin holocaust. An eyewitness described his death: "I was near General Strahl, who stood in the ditch and handed up guns to those posted to fire them. I had passed to him my short Enfield about six times. The man who had been firing, cocked it and was taking deliberate aim when he was shot, and tumbled down dead into the ditch upon those killed before him. When the men so exposed were shot down their places were supplied by volunteers until these were exhausted, and it was necessary for General Strahl to call for others. He turned to me, and though I was several feet back from the ditch, I rose up immediately, and walking over the wounded and dead took position, with one foot upon the pile of bodies of my dead fellows and the other upon the embankment, and fired guns which the general himself handed up to me, until he, too, was shot down." The general was not instantly killed, but soon after received a second shot and then a third, which finished him.

He was initially buried nearby at Columbia, then at St. Johns Church, Ashwood, Tennessee, along with Generals P.R. Cleburne and H.B. Granbury. At the turn of the century his remains were removed and reinterred at Dyersburg, his former home.

Edwin C. Bearss

Porter, James D., *Tennessee*, Vol. VIII in Evans, *Confederate Military History*.

A little-known portrait of Stuart as a major general, taken between July 1862 and May 1864. (Cook Collection, Valentine Museum, Richmond, Va.)

* *James Ewell Brown Stuart* *

James Ewell Brown "Jeb" Stuart was born in Patrick County, Virginia, on February 6, 1833. After attending Emory and Henry College for two years, Stuart entered the United States Military Academy in 1850, graduating four years later, and ranking thirteenth in the class. Brevetted a 2d lieutenant in the Mounted Rifles, he was assigned to Texas. In the spring of 1855 Stuart was promoted to 2d lieutenant and reported the the 1st U.S. Cavalry at Fort Leavenworth, Kansas. For the next four years Stuart served with the regiment on the frontier in campaigns against the Indian tribes. On November 11, 1855, he married Flora Cooke, daughter of Phillip St. George Cooke, future Union cavalry brigadier. Several weeks later, on December 20, Stuart received his promotion to 1st lieutenant.

Stuart's rapid promotions in the peacetime army indicated that the War Department appreciated his talent and promise. The department granted Stuart a six-month leave of absence in 1859 to travel to Washington, D.C., and to obtain a patent for his saber hook, a device he invented to allow a cavalryman to rapidly remove his saber and scabbard from his belt. Stuart secured the patent and sold the rights to the government for $5,000. While Stuart was in the capital, John Brown raided the government arsenal at Harpers Ferry in western Virginia, in October. Stuart served as a volunteer aide to Colonel Robert E. Lee, whose troops captured Brown and his men. Returning to Kansas in 1860, Stuart remained at his post until March 4, 1861, when he secured a two-month leave. En route eastward, Stuart learned of Virginia's secession and resigned his commission on May 3. A week later he was appointed lieutenant colonel of the Provisional Army of Virginia.

Stuart reported for duty at Harpers Ferry, where Colonel Thomas J. Jackson assigned him to command of several cavalry companies. From the outset Stuart demonstrated his marked ability for outpost and reconnaissance duty. On July 16 twelve companies were organized into the 1st Virginia Cavalry with Stuart as colonel. Five days later at First Manassas Stuart led the regiment in a mounted charge that scattered a Union regiment.

Following the Confederate victory, Stuart established a string of outposts across northern Virginia outside of the Federal capital. His vigilance and information earned the praise of superiors. On August 10 Brigadier General Joseph E. Johnston wrote to President Jefferson Davis, urging Stuart's promotion: "He is a rare man, wonderfully endowed by nature with the qualities necessary for an officer of light cavalry. Calm, firm, acute, active, and enterprising, I know of no one more competent than he to estimate the occurrences before him at their true value. If you add to this army a real brigade of cavalry, you can find no better brigadier-general to command it."

Davis agreed and on September 24 Stuart was awarded a brigadiership to rank from that date, and command of six regiments, the entire cavalry force of Johnston (by now a full general). During the fall and winter of 1861–62 Stuart's mounted units guarded the advance positions of the army. When Johnston withdrew toward Richmond in March, Stuart covered the rear. On June 1 Lee (now too a full general) replaced a wounded Johnston and on the 10th Stuart proposed a raid behind the Union army on the Peninsula. Two days later with twelve hundred troopers Stuart began a four-day "ride" around the entire Federal force, supplying Lee with valuable intelligence. Stuart had become a Southern hero.

During the Seven Days' Campaign, June 25-July 1, Stuart's horsemen led the infantry units, scouted, and raided the abandoned Union base at White House. For his performance Stuart earned a major-generalcy, on July 25, to take effect immediately, and three days later Lee reorganized the cavalry into a two-brigade division under Stuart.

Stuart's prowess as a cavalry commander increased during the campaigns of summer and fall. On August 22–23, he raided in the rear of Major General John Pope's Union army at Catlett's Station, capturing Pope's uniform

Stuart's best-known pose, in full finery. (Cook Collection, Valentine Museum, Richmond, Va.)

and dispatch books, hundreds of thousands of dollars, supplies, and three hundred prisoners. At Second Manassas he guarded the army's flanks; at Sharpsburg on September 17 his artillery assisted the infantry in repulsing Federal assaults. On October 10–13 his cavalrymen raided northward to Chambers-burg, Pennsylvania.

On November 10 Lee again reorganized the cavalry giving Stuart four brigades and a battalion of horse artillery. At Fredericksburg on December 13 the cavalry guarded the army's right flank, and Stuart directed the fire of Major John Pelham's horse artillery. Then at month's end Stuart undertook a fourth raid, the so-called Dumfries Raid, into northern Virginia.

By the end of 1862 Stuart's fame rivaled that of "Stonewall" Jackson's. Throughout the Confederacy he was known simply as "Jeb." With hard work, tirelessness, training, and organization he had welded his cavalry units into the finest mounted force in the Confederacy. He believed that cavalry's primary mission was reconnaissance—cavalry should provide a screen for its army while securing information about enemy movements. In this role Stuart was a matchless horse soldier.

Stuart also relished the pageantry of mounted warriors. He was a cavalier who was ambitious and savored the fame accorded him. Stuart surrounded himself with similar spirits who made his headquarters perhaps the liveliest in the army. Despite the showmanship and pomp Stuart was a brilliant cavalry officer.

By the spring of 1863, however, the nature of mounted warfare in the East was changing. Union horsemen, superior in equipment, horseflesh, and numbers, were improving. For Stuart and his legions, their dominance of 1862 gave way to a parity with their opponents.

At Chancellorsville in May 1863 the cavalry provided Lee with the intelligence that resulted in Jackson's flank attack against the Federal army. When Jackson fell mortally wounded on May 2, Lee assigned Stuart to command of the II Corps, which he led in assaults on May 3. Although Stuart wanted promotion to lieutenant general and command of the infantry corps, Lee returned him to the cavalry.

A month later, on June 9, Federal cavalry surprised and attacked Stuart's horsemen at Brandy Station. The battle lasted all day as the opponents launched successive attacks and counterattacks against each other.

At a single sitting Stuart posed for three variant portraits. The twinkle in his eye betrays the smile usually lurking beneath his beard. (Cook Collection, Valentine Museum, Richmond, Va.)

Only the position of Stuart's hands gives away the subtle difference in this portrait and the one that follows. (Cook Collection, Valentine Museum, Richmond, Va.)

The last pose from the sitting. (Cook Collection, Valentine Museum, Richmond, Va.)

Stuart handled his units with skill, and his men held the field at the conclusion. But Brandy Station was an embarrassment for Stuart while marking the arrival of the Union mounted arm.

Brandy Station signaled the opening operations of the Gettysburg Campaign. June 19–21 in a series of engagements at Aldie, Middleburg, and Upperville Stuart's troopers screened Lee's army beyond the Blue Ridge by repulsing the Union probes. Five days later with discretionary orders from Lee Stuart embarked on another ride around the Federal army. From the 15th until July 2 Stuart was beyond contact with Lee's army that was marching into Pennsylvania. As a result, Lee's advance elements stumbled into the Battle of Gettysburg. On July 3 Stuart's cavalrymen clashed with Federal horsemen and were repulsed. Lee stated in his report that the army's movements before the battle "had been much embarrassed by the absence of cavalry." For Lee it was a strong censure but deserved.

On September 9 Lee reorganized the cavalry into a two-division corps. Stuart, however, was not promoted to lieutenant general. During the fall and the winter of 1864 Stuart's corps performed its usual duties but undertook no raids.

During the Overland Campaign of May 1864 Union cavalry under Major General Philip H. Sheridan raided toward Richmond. On May 11 Stuart met Sheridan at Yellow Tavern less than six miles from the Confederate capital. In the swirling combat a Federal trooper shot Stuart in his right side under the rib cage. Stuart was taken into the city, where he died the next evening, May 12. When Lee learned of Stuart's death, he said: "He never brought me a piece of false information." It was a fitting epitaph for the Confederacy's cavalier knight.

Jeffry D. Wert

Blackford, W.W., *War Years With Jeb Stuart* (New York, 1945).

McClellan, J.B., *The Life and Campaigns of Major-General J.E.B. Stuart* (Boston and New York, 1885).

Thomas, Emory M., *Bold Dragoon: The Life of J.E.B. Stuart* (New York, 1986).

A very fine portrait of Taliaferro, post-March 1862. (William A. Turner Collection)

Yet another variant, and almost certainly taken at the same time. (U.S. Army Military History Institute, Carlisle, Pa.)

A variant pose, possibly taken at the same sitting. (Library of Congress)

⋆ *William Booth Taliaferro* ⋆

William Taliaferro was born at "Belleville" in Gloucester County, Virginia, on December 28, 1822. A member of an aristocratic family, Taliaferro was graduated from the College of William and Mary in 1841 and then studied law at Harvard. During the Mexican War he was appointed a captain of the 11th United States Infantry on February 23, 1847. Promoted to major of the 9th Infantry on August 12, Taliaferro mustered out a year later. From 1850 to 1853 he served in the Virginia House of Delegates. By 1861 Taliaferro held the rank of major general in the state's militia.

When the Old Dominion seceded in April, Taliaferro's militia forces occupied Norfolk and Gloucester Point. A month later Taliaferro was appointed colonel of the 23d Virginia, which was accepted into Confederate service on July 1. Authorities assigned the regiment to the command of Brigadier General Robert S. Garnett in western Virginia, where it fought in the engagements of Rich Mountain and Corrick's Ford during the fall. By year's end Taliaferro was commanding a brigade—comprised of the 3d Arkansas, 1st Georgia, 2d and 37th Virginia—in Brigadier General W.W. Loring's Army of the Northwest.

Taliaferro was an unpopular officer with the men and a difficult subordinate with superiors. His strict discipline so alienated the troops that on one occasion a drunken Georgian assaulted him. Then in January 1862, when Loring's command was stationed in Romney by Major General Thomas J. "Stonewall" Jackson, he, Loring, and other officers protested to the War Department about Jackson. Taliaferro even relinquished his command to travel to Richmond in an effort to utilize his political connections against Jackson. Although he failed, Taliaferro was promoted to brigadier general on March 6, 1862, effective March 4.

A month later Taliaferro was assigned to a brigade under Jackson, who officially protested the appointment, asserting that Taliaferro had allowed his former brigade to become "demoralized." While neither officer welcomed the assignment, Taliaferro served under Jackson throughout the Shenandoah Valley and Seven Days' campaigns. At Cedar Mountain on August 9 Taliaferro assumed command of Jackson's former division when Brigadier General Charles Winder was killed. Taliaferro led the division during the early operations of the Second Manassas

Campaign. At Groveton on August 28 he fell seriously wounded.

Taliaferro had returned to command of the division by December. At Fredericksburg on the 13th he suffered a slight wound as the division acted in a reserve role, losing less than two hundred men. After the battle when he failed to receive a promotion to major general, Taliaferro requested a transfer and was assigned to General P.G.T. Beauregard's command at Charleston, South Carolina.

In July 1863, Taliaferro's thirteen-hundred-man command defended Battery Wagner on Morris Island against a combined Union force of warships and army troops. For over a week Taliaferro's troops withstood the firestorm and attacks, including the famous assault of black troops of the 54th Massachusetts. A month later Beauregard assigned Taliaferro to command of a division on James Island.

On February 2, 1864, Taliaferro assumed command of the District of East Florida. He held this post for less than a month, returning then to James Island. In May he took command of the Seventh District of South Carolina. At year's end he led a three-brigade division in the operations at Savannah, assisting in the evacuation of the city before the advance of Major General William Sherman's Union armies. At the war's end he commanded a division under General Joseph E. Johnston in North Carolina. Taliaferro received a parole at Greensboro on May 2, 1865.

Taliaferro resumed his legal and political career after the war. He served in the legislature 1874–79, and as a judge in Gloucester County 1891–97. He was also a member of the boards of the Virginia Military Institute and the College of William and Mary. The former Confederate brigadier and antagonist of Stonewall Jackson died at his estate, "Dunham Massie," in his native county on February 27, 1898. He was buried in Ware Church Cemetery.

Jeffry D. Wert

Hotchkiss, Jedediah, *Virginia*, Vol. III in Evans, *Confederate Military History*.

Krick, Robert K., *Stonewall Jackson At Cedar Mountain* (Chapel Hill and London, 1990).

Tanner, Robert G., *Stonewall in the Valley* (Garden City, N.Y., 1976).

✳ *James Camp Tappan* ✳

The only known wartime uniformed photo of General Tappan is this post-November 1862 portrait. (*Confederate Veteran*, XXXIX)

James Camp Tappan, whose mother was James Madison's niece, was born in Franklin, Tennessee, on September 9, 1825. Tappan had strong ties to New England, the birthplace of his parents, and attended Exeter Academy in New Hampshire. In 1845 he graduated from Yale University in the same class as future Confederate General Richard Taylor. After studying law in Vicksburg, Mississippi, Tappan passed the bar in 1846 and opened a law practice in Helena, Arkansas. Becoming active in state politics, he twice was elected to the state legislature and served as speaker during his last term. He also was elected circuit judge and served as the receiver of the Helena land office.

In 1861 Tappan first was elected captain of an infantry company and then, despite his Northern heritage, was elected colonel of the 13th Arkansas Infantry in May. His first taste of battle was at Belmont, Missouri. In command of Camp Johnston, he formed his men in line of battle on November 7 when he received word of the approaching enemy under Brigadier General U.S. Grant. Brigadier General Gideon J. Pillow soon arrived with reinforcements and assumed command of the combined force. Grant attacked, drove Tappan and Pillow back to the Tennessee River, and burned Tappan's camp. When Brigadier General Benjamin F. Cheatham crossed the river with more men, Tappan's regiment led the counterattack on Grant's flank that forced the Federals to withdraw. Tappan lost eighty-two men in the fight, but his actions were praised by the local commander, Major General Leonidas Polk.

By April 1862 the 13th Arkansas was in General Albert Sidney Johnston's army approaching Shiloh,

Tennessee. Although some sources claim Tappan led the regiment in action against the "Hornets' Nest" on April 6, official records show that he was absent sick until April 7. He managed to arrive on the field from Corinth, Mississippi, that morning and after some difficulty found the regiment on the army's left. Tappan joined his men there and fought with them during the withdrawal.

After serving in the Kentucky Campaign that autumn, Tappan was promoted to brigadier general on November 5, 1862, to rank from that date. Transferred to the Trans-Mississippi Department, he took command of an Arkansas cavalry brigade in Major General Sterling Price's army in February 1863. In June his cavalry was sent to join Major General John G. Walker's division, which was on a raid through northeast Louisiana breaking up Union leasee plantations. Tappan rejoined Price in Arkansas at the end of the summer and went with Brigadier General Thomas James Churchill to help Major General Richard Taylor during the Red River Campaign in early 1864.

Tappan was placed in command of a division of Arkansas infantry and marched forty-five miles in thirty-six hours to join Taylor at Pleasant Hill, Louisiana. On April 9 Taylor sent Churchill on a maneuver to turn Major General Nathaniel Banks' left flank. The Confederates failed to get behind the flank, however, and attacked obliquely along Banks' front. Tappan's division managed to break through one Federal line and engaged in hand-to-hand combat with the enemy. The attack then was repulsed by a second, stronger line, and the Confederates were forced to retreat. Losses were heavy, and Tappan wrote that the fight was as fierce as any he had experienced.

After Pleasant Hill Tappan moved swiftly with Churchill back to Arkansas to help stop Major General Frederick Steele's Camden Expedition. On April 30 at Jenkins' Ferry Tappan was back in command of his brigade. By that time Steele was in retreat, trying to cross the Saline River at the ferry. Tappan's men led the Confederate attack as skirmishers, but after a brisk fight Steele managed to cross the river to safety. Tappan's last active campaign was with Price on his Missouri Raid in late 1864.

After the war Tappan returned to Helena to reopen his law practice and return to politics. He again was elected to the legislature but twice declined to run as the Democratic gubernatorial candidate. He became the dean of the state bar, was a delegate to the 1884 Democratic National Convention, and was appointed to the United States Military Academy's board of visitors in 1885. Tappan died at Helena on March 19, 1906, and was buried in Maple Hill Cemetery.

Terry L. Jones

Harrell, John M., *Arkansas*, Vol. X in Evans, *Confederate Military History*.

The only known wartime uniformed photo of Lieutenant General Richard Taylor, taken probably after July 1862. (Alabama Department of Archives and History, Montgomery)

✴ Richard Taylor ✴

The only son of Zachary Taylor, Richard Taylor was born on January 17, 1826, near Louisville, Kentucky. Named for his grandfather, a Virginian who had served under George Washington as a revolutionary war officer, young Taylor shunned his father's "Rough and Ready" image. He always sought to recapture the family's heritage among Virginia's colonial elite, which included ties to the Madisons and the Lees. Often absent from his son while stationed at various frontier military posts, Zachary Taylor sent him to private schools in Kentucky and Massachusetts before securing his admittance to Yale College in 1843. Graduating two years later, Taylor had gained no scholastic honors but instead had concentrated on reading widely in classical and military history. Unable to settle on a career, he visited General Taylor's camp at Matamoros in June of 1846, early in the Mexican War. Finally he agreed to manage the family cotton plantation in Jefferson County, Mississippi, and in 1850 he persuaded his father, who had been elected president in 1848, to purchase "Fashion," a large sugar plantation in St. Charles Parish, Louisiana.

After Zachary Taylor's sudden death in July of 1850, Taylor inherited Fashion, expanded its acreage, and saw its labor force grow to nearly two hundred slaves, making him one of the richest men in Louisiana. But the freeze of 1856 ruined his crop, forcing him into heavy debt (with a large mortgage on Fashion), a fragile condition underwritten largely by his generous mother-in-law Aglae Bringier, a wealthy French Creole matriarch whose daughter, Myrthe, Taylor had married in 1851. Yet he still projected an image of aristocratic affluence, racing Thoroughbred horses, frequenting the gaming tables at the exclusive Boston Club in New Orleans, and thus falling deeper into debt.

Elected to the Louisiana senate in 1855, Taylor was first a Whig, then a Know-Nothing (American Party), and finally a Democrat, veering toward a strong anti-Republican, proslavery position, although always distrustful of Southern fire-eaters' radical demands for disunion. As a delegate from Louisiana to the 1860 national Democratic Convention in Charleston, he witnessed the party's fatal splintering along sectional lines. There he attempted, but failed, to forge a less radical course for Southerners by proposing a compromise between moderates and implacable fire-eaters. Viewing disunion and war as inevitable, Taylor served as a delegate to the Louisiana secession convention in January of 1861 and voted with the majority for immediate secession. Yet his prophetic proposals to protect the state from military invasion went largely unheeded by overconfident fellow secessionists.

Retiring in disgust to his plantation, Taylor recognized the Confederacy's lack of unity and even predicted eventual defeat, but he remained willing to serve if called. Unwittingly elected colonel of the 9th Louisiana Infantry, Taylor assumed command in July and took the regiment to Virginia. Surprisingly, in late October he received promotion to brigadier general by order of President Jefferson Davis (his brother-in-law by Davis' first marriage to one of Taylor's sisters). Although devoid of formal military training or combat experience, Taylor at least enjoyed his brigade's strong respect along with a reputation as a consummate student of military history, strategy, and tactics. "Dick Taylor was a born soldier," asserted a close friend. "Probably no civilian of his time was more deeply versed in the annals of war." Placed in command of the Louisiana Brigade, which included Major Chatham Roberdeau Wheat's notorious battalion of "Louisiana Tigers," Taylor proved vital to Major General Thomas J. "Stonewall" Jackson's brilliant campaign in the Shenandoah Valley during the spring of 1862. At Winchester on May 25, and again at the climactic battle of Port Republic on June 9, he led the Louisianans in timely assaults against fortified enemy positions. "To General Taylor and his brigade belongs the honor of deciding two battles, that of Winchester and this one [Port Republic]," affirmed Major General Richard S. Ewell, his immediate superior.

Promoted at Jackson's behest to major general on July 25, 1862, at thirty-six years of age Taylor was the youngest officer to attain such rank to date and one of only a few who were non-West Pointers. Suffering terribly from chronic rheumatoid arthritis, however, he was transferred upon Davis' recommendation back to Louisiana in August to take command of the District of West Louisiana. From the beginning he feuded with his superior, General Edmund Kirby Smith, commander of the Trans-Mississippi Department, regarding Taylor's need for troops to defend Louisiana's civilian population against Federal forays. Smith also thwarted Taylor's abiding desire to free New Orleans from Federal occupation, an objective that received emphatic, although temporary, encouragement from Confederate Secretary of War George W. Randolph.

During 1863 Taylor directed a resourceful and effective series of clashes with Federal forces over control of lower Louisiana, most notably at Forts Bisland and Franklin (April 13–14), Brashear City (June 23), and Bayou Bourbeau (November 3). In the spring of 1864, after withdrawing up the Red River Valley in the face of Major General Nathaniel P. Banks' huge invasion force, Taylor became appalled at the devastation of total war inflicted by the enemy upon Louisiana's heartland. On April 8, with an army of no more than nine thousand men, mainly Louisianans and Texans, he ignored Smith's explicit instructions to delay, attacking Banks' disorganized column a few miles below Mansfield near Sabine Crossroads, routing it, and pursuing it southward to Pleasant Hill. There, the next day, the Federals withstood Taylor's poorly executed assaults and forced him to retire, but Banks' generals had lost all confidence in him, compelling him to withdraw to Alexandria.

Outraged when Smith detached John G. Walker's Texas Division for unnecessary and haphazard fighting against a separate enemy column in Arkansas, Taylor was left with only about five thousand men to harass Banks. Taylor repeatedly demanded Walker's Division in order to crush Banks and liberate New Orleans, but Smith stubbornly refused. Convinced of Smith's arrogant ambition and incompetence, Taylor exploded with a series of insulting and insubordinate diatribes against Smith. He submitted his resignation from the service after Banks escaped Alexandria on May 13 and abandoned the Red River Valley. Although unwilling to admit his strategic blunder in failing to allow Taylor to keep Walker's Division,

Smith harbored no personal grudge in the controversy. Taylor, however, never forgave Smith. Despite the fact that Taylor had saved both Louisiana and Texas from enemy conquest, he viewed the campaign as a grave disappointment.

Preferring to ignore the Taylor–Smith feud, on July 18 President Davis placed Taylor in command of the Department of Alabama, Mississippi, and East Louisiana and promoted him to lieutenant general, making him one of only three non-West Pointers to achieve such high rank in the Confederate army. From the autumn of 1864 to the end of the war Taylor directed the defense of his department, receiving scant cooperation from state governors and legislatures and struggling with Jefferson Davis' poor coordination of the Confederacy's departmental system. Fortunately, Taylor could rely on Nathan Bedford Forrest's superb cavalrymen to resist Federal incursions and support the embattled Army of Tennessee by raiding enemy supply lines in Tennessee. Forrest consistently demonstrated his admiration for Taylor's leadership, remarking candidly, "He's the biggest man in the lot. If we'd had more like him, we would have licked the Yankees long ago."

In January of 1865 Taylor briefly assumed command of the shattered Army of Tennessee after General John Bell Hood's catastrophic defeats at Franklin and Nashville. As the Southern military effort rapidly disintegrated during the spring, Taylor saw his own department crumble at the hands of Union Brigadier General James H. Wilson's massive cavalry raid through Alabama and Major General Edward R.S. Canby's triumphant siege of Mobile. Taylor had "shared the fortunes of the Confederacy," as he later recalled, having "sat by its cradle and followed its hearse." The war inflicted harsh personal sacrifices upon him: he lost his plantation to enemy devastation and occupation; his two young sons died of scarlet fever as wartime refugees; and his wife suffered so severely that she lapsed into a long decline that ended with her premature death in 1875.

After surrendering his department to Canby on May 4, 1865, Taylor returned to New Orleans and set out to revive his blighted finances by securing a lease of the New Basin Canal from the state. He also garnered support and friendship from a wealthy New York City attorney, Samuel Latham Mitchell Barlow, one of the Democratic Party's most powerful leaders. On Barlow's behalf, Taylor negotiated with Presidents

Andrew Johnson and Ulysses S. Grant and lobbied members of Congress in a sustained attempt to obtain lenient treatment for the South. Deeply distrustful of Radical Republicans, Taylor considered Reconstruction an increasingly loathsome evil, pushing him toward a reactionary position that gave tacit approval to the violent backlash by Southern white Democrats against blacks' efforts to assert their new voting rights under Republican sponsorship. Intimately involved in Samuel J. Tilden's Democratic presidential campaign in 1876, Taylor influenced maneuverings in Congress in the wake of the disputed election returns, a sectional crisis finally diffused by the Compromise of 1877, the formal demise of Reconstruction. On April 12, 1879, at barely fifty-three years of age, Taylor died at Barlow's home in New York City, succumbing to severe internal congestion resulting from his continual battle with rheumatoid arthritis. He was buried in a family crypt in Metaire Cemetery, New Orleans. Shortly before his death he published his personal memoirs, *Destruction and Reconstruction*, one of the most valuable primary accounts of the Civil War era.

T. Michael Parrish

Parrish, T. Michael, *Richard Taylor: Soldier Prince of Dixie* (Chapel Hill, 1992).

Taylor, Richard, *Destruction and Reconstruction: Personal Experiences of the Late War* (New York, 1879).

✮ *Thomas Hart Taylor* ✮

Thomas H. Taylor, taken after his November 1862 appointment to brigadier. (Cook Collection, Valentine Museum, Richmond, Va.)

Taylor was born in Frankfort, Kentucky, on July 31, 1825. He received his education at Kenyon College in Ohio and Centre College in Danville, Kentucky, graduating from the latter in 1843. Taylor studied law and practiced the profession briefly. At the outbreak of the war with Mexico he enlisted as a private in the 3d Kentucky Infantry. His service during the conflict led to his promotion to the rank of 1st lieutenant, and he sometimes exercised command of his company. Taylor made two trips across the Plains to California in 1852 and 1853, driving cattle herds to the new state. After his return to Kentucky he operated a farm and lumber business in Hickman County. A flood wiped him out, and he became a businessman in Memphis.

Taylor entered the Confederate army as a captain of cavalry in the regular service. On April 13, 1861, Adjutant General Samuel Cooper ordered him to go through Memphis and Nashville to Kentucky and examine the possibility of establishing recruiting stations at those points. He eventually made his way to Louisville and began enlisting men.

On May 24 Cooper issued orders recalling Taylor to Nashville to assume charge of the depot there. Taylor soon went to Virginia. Just prior to the battle at Manassas in July General Pierre G.T. Beauregard sent Taylor through the lines with messages from Jefferson Davis to Abraham Lincoln. General Joseph E. Johnston organized his separate Kentucky companies into the 1st Kentucky Infantry in early August, and Taylor was appointed colonel of the unit. Taylor's men were involved in an engagement at Dranesville on December 20 under Brigadier General James E.B. Stuart. Taylor's role was less than glamorous and demonstrates the confusion that existed on many Civil War battlefields. Stuart reported, "Colonel Taylor became separated from his regiment in passing from its left to its right and found himself beyond the enemy's lines, but by great coolness and presence of mind he extricated himself and joined his regiment that night."

On March 17, 1862, Taylor was placed in command at Orange Court House and was named provost marshal for the vicinity. The regiment subsequently was moved to the Peninsula, where it was mustered out in May. Taylor received orders to report to Major General Edmund Kirby Smith in eastern Tennessee. Several days later Smith planned to send the brigade to Chattanooga in response to a threat against that city, but the movement of another Union force toward Cumberland Gap caused him to retain Taylor's men near Knoxville. Smith reorganized his army in early July, and Taylor's brigade became a part of Brigadier General Carter L. Stevenson's division. Taylor lost his Georgia regiment but gained another Alabama and two more Tennessee regiments.

When Kirby Smith's army marched into Kentucky in mid-August, Stevenson's division moved to besiege Cumberland Gap. Taylor's men participated in the month-long operation against that place and were the first troops into the post after the Federals evacuated it on September 17 The division then joined Kirby Smith in Kentucky but saw no fighting while the Confederates were in that state. Taylor received command of a new brigade of Georgia regiments after the division returned to eastern Tennessee. He was appointed a brigadier general, effective November 4, 1862, but Davis never forwarded his nomination to that grade to the Confederate Senate. Taylor and his men accompanied Stevenson's division to Vicksburg in December, arriving after the Battle of Chickasaw Bluffs. After occupying the entrenchments there for a few days, Taylor's brigade moved to Jackson for several weeks. Taylor brought his men back to Vicksburg toward the end of January 1863 and put them in camp south of the city. The troops did picket and guard duty for the next several months.

On March 29 he assumed command of the troops in the river batteries and on the Vicksburg waterfront in addition to his own brigade. Because Taylor had never been confirmed as a brigadier, the War Department found another commander for his brigade. Brigadier General Alfred Cumming was sent from Mobile to replace Taylor, which he did on May 13. Major General John C. Pemberton was instructed to "make such other disposition of Colonel Taylor" as he thought proper. Later General Joseph E. Johnston instructed Pemberton to retain Taylor on duty in his army. Taylor served on the latter's staff and carried orders for him during the Battle of Champion's Hill (Baker's Creek) on May 16. After the Confederate defeat Taylor helped in trying to rally retreating

troops at Edwards Depot. The next day he placed four artillery pieces on the west side of Big Black River Bridge. He again tried to rally fleeing soldiers after the disaster in that battle but soon returned to the artillery position, where he remained until the army was ordered to fall back into the Vicksburg entrenchments. During the siege Taylor served as Pemberton's inspector general and as post commander. Pemberton reported that "in both capacities [he] rendered most valuable service."

Taylor went to Montgomery, Alabama, after the surrender of the Confederate garrison. He saw duty at Mobile in early 1864. On March 5 he was assigned to command of the District of South Mississippi and East Louisiana in the Department of Alabama, Mississippi, and East Louisiana. In that capacity he had few troops to protect the region from enemy incursions and faced civilian discontent with government seizures of supplies. Colonel John S. Scott relieved Taylor as district commander on April 28, and Taylor reported to department headquarters in Demopolis, Alabama. On June 24 he was named provost marshal general of the department with headquarters at Meridian, Mississippi. He had moved to Mobile by November 1 and become post commander there. As post commander he had a few units of reserve and local defense troops to preserve order. Taylor retained this position until the evacuation of the city on April 11, 1865. As a part of that evacuation he had charge of the destruction and removal of cotton located in Mobile. Lieutenant General Richard Taylor named him as his commissioner to parole troops at Jackson, Mississippi, when the Department of Alabama, Mississippi, and East Louisiana was surrendered.

Taylor ran a business in Mobile until 1870 and then returned to his native state. He served as a deputy United States marshal for five years. In 1881 he was elected police chief of Louisville and filled that office for eleven years. Taylor also acted briefly in the 1880s as superintendent of the Louisville and Portland Canal. He died on April 12, 1901, in Louisville and was buried in that city's State Cemetery

Arthur W. Bergeron, Jr.

Johnston, J. Stoddard, *Kentucky*, Vol. IX in Evans, *Confederate Military History.*

✯ *James Barbour Terrill* ✯

The only known uniformed portrait of Terrill, taken probably in 1863 when he was colonel of the 13th Virginia. (U.S. Army Military History Institute, Carlisle, Pa.)

James Barbour Terrill was born at Warm Springs, Bath County, Virginia, on February 20, 1838, into a prominent local family. After graduating from the Virginia Military Institute in 1858, Terrill studied law in Lexington before opening a legal practice in his hometown. When Virginia seceded in April 1861, the Terrill family split, with James embracing the Confederate cause and his brother, William, a West Point graduate, remaining loyal to the Union. William rose to the rank of brigadier general and was killed at Perryville in October 1862.

James Terrill was elected major of the 13th Virginia at its organization in May 1861. The regiment, under Colonel A.P. Hill, was present at First Manassas, serving in a support role. When Hill was promoted to brigadier general in February 1862, Colonel James A. Walker assumed command of the regiment, and Terrill was promoted to lieutenant colonel. During the 1862 Shenandoah Valley Campaign the regiment served in the brigade of Arnold Elzey. At Cross Keys on June 8 Walker replaced a wounded Elzey, and Terrill commanded the regiment.

The officers and men of the 13th Virginia continued to distinguish themselves throughout the operations of 1862. The regiment served under Elzey during the Seven Days' Campaign, but when he fell seriously wounded again, Jubal Early succeeded to command of the brigade. At Cedar Mountain on August 9 Terrill earned the praise of Early, who wrote that Terrill and several other officers "acquitted themselves with great gallantry." Three weeks later at Second Manassas Terrill commanded half of the regiment in the two-day Southern victory.

After missing the Maryland Campaign in September, Terrill returned to the 13th Virginia later that fall and commanded it at Fredericksburg on December 13. With Walker elevated to brigade command, Terrill led the regiment at Chancellorsville and Gettysburg in May and July 1863, respectively. He was promoted to colonel on May 15, 1863. For two years under Hill, Walker, and Terrill, the 13th Virginia had fashioned as fine a combat record as that of any regiment in the army. Early stated that the 13th "was never required to take a position that they did not take it, nor to hold one that they did not hold it."

During the Wilderness and Spotsylvania campaigns in May 1864 Terrill and the regiment served in the brigade of John Pegram. Terrill once more rendered distinguished service and was recommended for promotion to brigadier general. On May 30 at an engagement at Bethesda Church Terrill was killed and buried on the field by Federal troops. Two days later he was promoted and confirmed a brigadier, to rank from May 31.

James Terrill was one of the finest regimental commanders in the Army of Northern Virginia. After the war his father erected a monument to him and his brother, who was buried at West Point. The inscription read: "This monument erected by their father. God only knows which was right."

Jeffry D. Wert

Hotchkiss, Jedediah, *Virginia*, Vol. III in Evans, *Confederate Military History.*

✶ *William Terry* ✶

A previously unpublished, and only known uniformed portrait, view of William Terry, taken when he was colonel of the 4th Virginia, probably in late 1863. (William A. Turner Collection)

William Terry was born in Amherst County, Virginia, on August 14, 1824. An 1848 graduate of the University of Virginia, Terry briefly taught school before studying law. Admitted to the bar in 1851, he opened a practice in Wytheville. Terry did confine himself to the legal profession but acted as editor of the local newspaper, the *Telegraph*, and served as a lieutenant in the Wytheville Grays, a militia company. When Virginia authorities hanged John Brown for treason in December 1859, the Wytheville Grays and other militia units guarded the abolitionist.

The spark struck by Brown engulfed the nation, and when Virginia seceded on April 17, The Grays volunteered. Nine days later the Grays were organized as Company A, 4th Virginia, with Terry as 1st lieutenant. At First Manassas on July 21 the 4th Virginia and the 2d, 5th, 27th, and 33d Virginia won enduring fame under Brigadier General Thomas J. "Stonewall" Jackson. Their association continued with Jackson until the latter's death in May 1863.

Terry was promoted to major on April 22, 1862, and fought with the regiment in the Shenandoah Valley and Seven Days' campaigns. At Second Manassas in August he suffered a wound that necessitated weeks of recovery. Returning to the regiment in the fall, Terry led the 4th Virginia at Fredericksburg on December 13 when Lieutenant Colonel Robert Gardner fell wounded. His performance elicited official praise from E.F. Paxton, the brigade commander.

Terry continued in command of the regiment throughout the operations of 1863. He led it at Chancellorsville in May and at Gettysburg in July. In the latter battle on July 3 the Stonewall Brigade charged up the rugged slopes of Culp's Hill. Terry's Virginians advanced almost into the Federal works on the slope before being repulsed. Brigade commander James A. Walker cited Terry in his report for "gallant and efficient conduct." Terry received his colonelcy in September.

On May 12, 1864, at Spotsylvania a massive Union assault crushed the so-called "Mule Shoe" salient and ravaged the Stonewall division. On May 20 Terry was promoted to brigadier general, to rank from May 19, and assigned to command of the remnants of the famous unit. He led the command during the 1864 Shenandoah Valley Campaign and during the Petersburg Campaign in the winter of 1865. On March 25, 1865, during the Confederate assault on Fort Stedman Terry suffered a severe wound and was incapacitated during the conflict's final two weeks.

Terry resumed his legal practice in Wytheville after the war. He served two terms in the United States House of Representatives, 1871–73 and 1875–77. On September 5, 1888, while attempting to ford a swollen Rock Creek, Terry fell into the waters and drowned. One of the finest combat officers in the famous Stonewall Brigade, he was buried in Wytheville.

Jeffry D. Wert

Hotchkiss, Jedediah, *Virginia*, Vol. III in Evans, *Confederate Military History*.

✦ *William Richard Terry* ✦

William R. Terry as a captain early in the war. (Museum of the Confederacy, Richmond, Va.)

William R. Terry was born at Liberty, Bedford County, Virginia, on March 12, 1827. He was graduated from the Virginia Military Institute in 1850 and then attended the University of Virginia. Returning to his hometown, Terry there became a merchant. When Virginia seceded in April 1861, Terry organized a company of cavalry in Bedford County, was elected captain, and reported for service at Lynchburg.

Within a month Terry's company was posted near Fairfax Court House. On June 16 in a skirmish at Vienna, Terry and his mounted unit distinguished themselves. Colonel Maxcy Gregg, commanding the Confederate forces, reported that Terry and Captain Dulany Ball and their cavalrymen "commanded my entire confidence by their bearing, and only needed opportunity for more effective action." A month later, on July 21 at First Manassas Terry's troopers guarded artillery and participated in the pursuit of the routed Federal army, capturing about eighty prisoners and two battleflags.

In September Jubal Early, recently promoted to brigadier general and the officer to whom Terry had reported at Lynchburg, recommended Terry for the colonelcy of the 24th Virginia, Early's former regiment. Terry received the promotion and command on September 21 and for the next two years led the regiment in most of the major campaigns of the Army of Northern Virginia.

On May 5, 1862, at Williamsburg the 24th Virginia and the 5th North Carolina of Early's brigade attacked a Union force and, in the words of Major General D.H. Hill, division commander, "were pressing on vigorously through the heavy ground, exposed to a most murderous fire, but not halting or faltering for a moment." The 24th Virginia lost 190 officers and men in the assault, including Terry, who suffered a serious wound. Major General James Longstreet praised Terry and several other officers for discharging "their difficult duties with marked skill and fearlessness."

The wound incapacitated Terry for three months, but he returned to the regiment to lead it at Second Manassas, August 29–30. The regiment now belonged to the brigade of James Kemper, commanded by Colonel Montgomery D. Corse, who described the unit and its commander as "the steady veteran Terry, with the gallant Twenty-fourth." When Corse suffered a slight wound, Terry assumed command of the brigade. Kemper soon returned to the brigade, and Terry led the regiment at Sharpsburg in September and at Fredericksburg in December.

As a part of Major General George Pickett's division, Kemper's brigade operated in southeastern Virginia during the spring of 1863, missing the Battle of Chancellorsville in May. Two months later at Gettysburg Pickett's command achieved enduring fame.

In the July 3 assault the 24th Virginia held the right of the division's front. As Kemper's Virginians neared the Union line, a brigade of Vermonters enfiladed the Confederates' right flank. "Old Buck" Terry, as his men called him, refused the 24th and part of the 11th to the right and, in the opinion of Colonel Joseph Mayo, who replaced a fallen Kemper, saved the brigade from annihilation. Although some sources list Terry as wounded, he emerged from the repulse unscathed.

In the fall of 1863 Terry assumed temporary command of the brigade. In the spring of 1864 Pickett's division served in the Department of North Carolina and southern Virginia, participating in the operations around New Berne, North Carolina. Returning to Virginia in May, the division fought in the Bermuda Hundred Campaign. At Drewry's Bluff on the 16th Terry led the brigade in a spirited assault, capturing Union Brigadier General Charles A. Heckman. Terry received his promotion to brigadier general on June 10, to date from May 31.

Terry commanded the brigade throughout the Petersburg Campaign. On March 31, 1865, at Dinwiddie Court House he suffered his final wound of the war. Because of the wound he was not with the army when it surrendered at Appomattox nine days later.

Terry had a varied postwar career. He served eight years in the state senate and for a number of years as superintendent of the state penitentiary. From 1886 to 1893 he was superintendent of the Confederate Soldiers' Home in Richmond. He resigned the latter position because of ill health, having suffered a paralytic stroke. The excellent regimental commander and capable brigadier died in Chesterfield County, on March 28, 1897. He was buried in Hollywood Cemetery.

Jeffry D. Wert

Georg, Kathleen R. and Busey, John W., *Nothing But Glory: Pickett's Division at Gettysburg* (Hightstown, N.J., 1987).

Hotchkiss, Jedediah, *Virginia*, Vol. III in Evans, *Confederate Military History*.

Robertson, William Glenn, *Back Door to Richmond: The Bermuda Hundred Campaign, April–June 1864* (Newark, Del., 1987).

✦ *Allen Thomas* ✦

Thomas was born on December 14, 1830, in Howard County, Maryland. He graduated from Princeton University in 1850 and studied law in Ellicott City. After practicing law for several years in Howard County, Thomas moved to Louisiana in 1857, having married the sister of future Confederate General Richard Taylor's wife. He established a plantation in St. Landry Parish and became an officer in the state militia.

When the Civil War began, Thomas organized a battalion for state service and took it to New Orleans in the spring of 1862. His men evacuated the Crescent City just prior to its fall to Federal forces and moved to Camp Moore near Tangipahoa, Louisiana. There on May 3 five independent companies were added to his battalion, and he became colonel of the 29th Louisiana Infantry (sometimes mistakenly referred to as the 28th Louisiana).

The regiment left for Vicksburg, Mississippi, on May 20 and arrived there the next day. During the first Union campaign against Vicksburg, Thomas' men were stationed near Warrenton with several other regiments to dispute any land advance by the enemy. The regiment continued to do picket and guard duty near Vicksburg through the summer and fall of that year. In response to Major General William T. Sherman's threat on the Yazoo River north of Vicksburg in December, Thomas and his men marched to support the troops in that vicinity. They became part of Brigadier General Stephen D. Lee's brigade. Thomas exercised temporary command of a demi-brigade composed of his own and four other regiments during portions of the subsequent operations. The 29th

Louisiana was engaged in some skirmishing at Chickasaw Bayou on December 27 and about dark that day relieved the 17th Louisiana Infantry in an advanced position near Mrs. Lake's Plantation. Thomas and his men were attacked by some of Sherman's troops the next morning. They held the enemy in check until noon, when overwhelming numbers forced them to retreat back to the main line. Thomas' losses were only forty-three men killed, wounded, missing, and deserters. The regiment fell back in good order and occupied entrenchments on the left flank of Lee's lines. When Sherman's army assaulted the earthworks on December 29, Thomas' troops repulsed all attacks on their front. Major General John C. Pemberton praised Thomas and his men for their action in the campaign. Lee wrote that Thomas "exhibited great gallantry and with his regiment did splendid service."

The 29th Louisiana remained in that area until the spring of 1863. Lee took the regiment with several others to oppose the Union Steele's Bayou Expedition in March 1863. By the time Major General Ulysses S. Grant's Federal army launched its campaign against Vicksburg in May, Thomas' regiment had been transferred to Brigadier General Francis A. Shoup's brigade of Major General Martin L. Smith's division. On May 20, after Vicksburg had been besieged, the regiment was sent by Shoup to reinforce the trenches held by Brigadier General William E. Baldwin's brigade.

The only known wartime photo of General Allen Thomas, taken after February 1864. (Albert G. Shaw Collection Virginia Historical Society, Richmond)

Baldwin was wounded during the Union attack on May 22, and Thomas took temporary command of the brigade. He held command until his regiment was ordered back to Shoup's brigade the next day. The 29th Louisiana occupied the entrenchments on the center of Shoup's line for the remainder of the siege. Thomas exercised temporary command of the brigade late in the siege. In his battle report Shoup said that Thomas "was constantly at his post. He was vigilant and energetic."

With the remainder of the Vicksburg garrison, Thomas and his men were paroled after Pemberton's surrender. Rather than remain in parole camps near Enterprise, Mississippi, the men returned to their homes in Louisiana. By January 1864 Thomas was in south Louisiana trying to collect deserters and to reorganize his command. He was promoted to brigadier general on February 17, effective February 4, to replace Henry W. Allen in command of a brigade of Louisiana regiments that had been captured at Vicksburg. The Union Red River Campaign, which began the next month, interrupted Thomas' efforts to get the men of the brigade into camp for reorganization and to await exchange. At the end of the campaign Thomas established a camp at Pineville, where he was to collect all of the exchanged Vicksburg and Port Hudson prisoners in the state.

On June 8 Major General Richard Taylor requested permission to add Thomas' brigade to Major General Camille J. Polignac's division. Taylor had orders to take Polignac's and Major General John G. Walker's divisions across the Mississippi River with him to Mississippi. He wanted to take Thomas' men with him so that the men could be rearmed and could perform active duty. Lieutenant General Edmund Kirby Smith felt that the brigade was too weak and disorganized to be effective and decided to retain it near Alexandria until all of its men could be gathered together. Taylor's attempt to take these divisions across the Mississippi failed, but Thomas' brigade was assigned to Polignac's division as the 1st Louisiana Brigade. The men remained in camp at Pineville when Polignac's division marched into Arkansas in September.

Lieutenant Colonel Wright C. Shaumburg of Kirby Smith's staff inspected Thomas' brigade in November and had some serious criticism of it and its commander. He wrote: "Too little care is taken by the brigade commander to render his troops efficient, either by drill or enforcement of discipline. He does not give that personal attention to the wants and exercises of

his command which is absolutely necessary. I do not consider him a competent officer as a disciplinarian, drill officer, or administrative. His knowledge of orders and regulations might be greatly increased, to the good of his command and himself." Schaumburg recommended the employment of Thomas' men in erecting earthwork fortifications around Alexandria, which Kirby Smith subsequently ordered.

On January 1, 1865, Thomas was placed in command of all front line forces in the District of Western Louisiana. Several weeks later the brigade formerly commanded by Brigadier General Henry Gray was joined to Thomas' to make Thomas a division commander. A third brigade, composed of recently dismounted Louisiana cavalrymen, was added to the division in mid-March. Despite his inspector general's report in November 1864, Kirby Smith pronounced Thomas "an efficient division commander" shortly after the addition of this brigade. In April 1865 Major General Harry T. Hays was placed in charge of the division, and Thomas revered to brigade command. Thomas went on sick leave in May and was paroled at Natchitoches on June 8.

After the war Thomas became a planter in Ascension Parish. He was a Democratic presidential elector for Horace Greeley in 1872 and for Winfield S. Hancock in 1880. He declined a nomination for the U.S. Congress in 1876. In 1882 he was named to the Louisiana State University board of supervisors and taught agriculture there from 1882 to 1884. President Grover Cleveland appointed Thomas as coiner of the United States Mint in New Orleans, but he moved to Florida in 1889. From 1894 until 1897 he was consul and minister to Venezuela. Thomas resumed his residency in Florida until 1907, when he purchased a plantation near Waveland, Mississippi. He died there on December 3 of that year and was buried in an unmarked tomb in the Bringier family vault in the Ascension Catholic Church Cemetery, Donaldsonville, Louisiana.

Arthur W. Bergeron, Jr.

Bartlett, Napier, *Military Record of Louisiana* (Baton Rouge, 1964).

Bergeron, Arthur W., Jr., *Guide to Louisiana Confederate Military Units, 1861–1865* (Baton Rouge, 1989).

Dickinson, J.J., *Florida*, Vol. XI in Evans, *Confederate Military History*.

Dimitry, John, *Louisiana*, Vol. X in Evans, *Confederate Military History*.

★ Bryan Morel Thomas ★

Born near Milledgeville, Georgia, on May 8, 1836, Thomas first attended Oglethorpe University in Georgia and then won an appointment to the United States Military Academy. He entered West Point in 1854 and graduated twenty-second of twenty-seven in the class of 1858. Upon graduation, he was brevetted a 2d lieutenant in the 8th Infantry and assigned to Fort Columbia in New York, where he did garrison duty. He later transferred to the 5th Infantry and took part in the Indian fighting on the frontier. He participated in the Utah Expedition and as a member of the Navajo expedition, he also saw service in New Mexico.

On April 6, 1861, after his home state of Georgia had seceded from the Union he resigned his commission as a 2d lieutenant in the U.S. Army and accepted a commission as a lieutenant in the regular service of the Confederate States. He was assigned to Mobile, Alabama, as an ordnance officer on December 20, 1816.

Thomas joined Brigadier General Jones M. Withers as a member of his staff on March 18, 1862. He fought at the Battle of Shiloh on April 6–7, performing the duties of chief of ordnance and artillery, although he had been assigned as Withers' adjutant and inspector general on March 26. Withers wrote in his report that "Lieut. B.M. Thomas discharged his duties on both days of the battle with active zeal and gallantry." Advanced to captain and then to major he remained on Withers' staff during the Kentucky campaign and at Murfreesboro. Major General Withers stated in his

report on the Battle of Murfreesboro: "Maj. B.M. Thomas, adjutant and inspector general, reported on the field from sick leave on the morning of [January] 2d, and immediately entered on the discharge of his duties with intelligence and efficiency." He continued to serve under Withers as one of his staff officers throughout 1863.

On March 8, 1864, Lieutenant General Leonidas Polk recommended to the War Department that Thomas be promoted to colonel and assigned to command a cavalry regiment that had been organized in Alabama by Brigadier General James H. Clanton. Thomas was transferred to Clanton's command but he was not promoted to colonel. Polk also suggested that Thomas recruit a cavalry brigade in Alabama. Acting upon Polk's suggestion, Thomas did undertake the task of recruiting a brigade, but because previous demands had already seriously depleted the state's manpower reserve he was able to recruit a total of only three hundred and seventy five under-age boys and men over forty-five.

Although he was addressed by the courtesy title of "Colonel," he was never commissioned as such, and his "brigade" served as a regiment in Clanton's brigade, but it never received an official state or national unit designation. By the end of April of 1864 Thomas' regiment had been assigned to a brigade

A previously unpublished portrait of Bryan Thomas, and his only discovered uniformed portrait, taken during the final eight months of the war. (Alabama Department of Archives and History, Montgomery)

being organized by Brigadier General Gideon J. Pillow. On May 1 Polk ordered Pillow to report to Major General Stephen D. Lee at Tuscaloosa, Alabama, with all his troops. Thomas' regiment was ordered to Selma on May 20. On June 5 Thomas left Montgomery for Oxford, Mississippi, with about three hundred and seventy five men.

On July 22, 1864, when forwarding Withers' choice of commanders for the two brigades proposed for his command General Braxton Bragg, who was then serving as military advisor to President Jefferson Davis, added his personal endorsement of the proposed candidates by stating: "For these he [Withers]...recommends the appointment as brigadier-generals of Majs. B.M. Thomas and J.R.B. Burtwell, both graduates of West Point. I concur, knowing them to be excellent soldiers."

Thomas and his men were transferred to Mobile and assigned to the commander of the defenses at Mobile, Major General Dabney Herndon Maury, who had requested that he be supplied with capable general officers; however, inasmuch as none were available for transfer to him he was still in need of general officers when Thomas arrived in Mobile. Thomas' training at West Point and his experience as a staff officer made of him an attractive candidate for a position on Maury's staff. Maury's recommendation that Thomas be given a brigade to command, coupled with those recommendations made previously by his superiors, won for Thomas a promotion from major to brigadier general on August 4, 1864, to rank immediately. On August 9, 1864, President Jefferson Davis wrote in a communique to Maury: "Some days since Brig. Gen. St. John R. Liddell was ordered to report to you for duty at Mobile, and still earlier B.M. Thomas was appointed brigadier-general for reserves of Alabama. This, I hope will cover your request of yesterday."

By September 3 Thomas commanded a mixed brigade of Alabama infantry, cavalry, and artillery under Major General Franklin Gardner, who commanded the District of the Gulf with headquarters at Mobile. Thomas had 1,370 men effective for duty. By September 30 his effective force numbered 1,250. And by November 1 his "command" consisted of only one regiment of reserves and a battalion composed of Confederate prisoners at Camp of Correction in Mobile. On November 10 Thomas' "division" had only twenty-four officers and two hundred and two enlisted men effective for duty. On November 20 his

"command" had only eighteen officers and one hundred and sixty one enlisted men effective for duty. Although it now contained four units, there were only seventeen and one hundred and sixty officers and men, respectively, on December 1.

On December 7 Maury, who had succeeded Gardner as commandant of the District of the Gulf, ordered Thomas to Meridian, Mississippi, to take charge of the troops guarding the Mobile and Ohio Railroad from Union cavalry moving eastward from the Pearl River. Thomas took up a position at Bucatunna, Mississippi. He was ordered to Citronelle on December 10 and on to Mobile the following morning.

The Mobile commandant's morning report for December 21 showed Thomas' brigade strength as being 1,450 strong. By the end of February of 1865, Thomas' five hundred men "are little to be relied on," as reported by one Confederate staff officer. Units assigned to him in early March raised his troop strength to 1,352.

Thomas was captured when Fort Blakely fell on April 9, 1865, and was released shortly thereafter. On April 16 Brigadier General Randall T. Gibson commended Thomas for his "zealous cooperation and soldierly bearing" during the siege of Mobile. He returned to Georgia after the war where he farmed and served as a deputy United States marshall. He also established a private academy in 1884. After moving to Dalton, Georgia, he became that city's superintendent of schools. He died in Dalton on July 16, 1905, and was buried there.

Benjamin E. Snellgrove

Derry, Joseph T., *Georgia*, Vol. VI in Evans, *Confederate Military History*.

General Edward Thomas post-November 1862. The detail shown on his kepi is particularly outstanding. (Cook Collection, Valentine Museum, Richmond, Va.)

⋆ *Edward Lloyd Thomas* ⋆

Edward Lloyd Thomas was born in Clarke County, Georgia, on March 23, 1825. After graduating with distinction from Emory College in 1846, Thomas volunteered for service in the Mexican War as a 2d lieutenant with the Georgia Mounted Volunteers or Newton County Independent Horse. The Georgians fought with Winfield Scott's army in the campaign against Mexico City. When the war ended, Thomas declined a commission in the Regular Army and returned to his native state, where he became a wealthy planter.

Thomas did not join the state's forces when Georgia seceded in early 1861. Later in the year President Jefferson Davis authorized Thomas to recruit a regiment and, on October 15, Thomas was appointed colonel of the 35th Georgia. They were in Virginia by the spring of 1862, serving in the brigade of James J. Pettigrew.

The Georgians' initial combat came at Seven Pines on May 31–June 1, 1862. Thomas assumed command of the brigade when Pettigrew fell wounded and was captured. During the army's reorganization in June, Thomas' regiment was transferred into the brigade of Joseph R. Anderson in the Light Division of General A.P. Hill.

During the Seven Days' Campaign, Thomas demonstrated skill and bravery as a battlefield commander. At Mechanicsville on June 26, Thomas suffered a slight wound but retained command of the regiment. Anderson cited the Georgian in his report, stating that Thomas "evinced fearlessness and good judgment." Thomas distinguished himself again the next day at Gaines' Mill, leading the Georgians in an attack. On June 30 at Frayser's Farm, the brigade delivered the final assault of Hill's division. Anderson was slightly hurt in the action, and Thomas took command of the brigade. He retained command of the unit until Appomattox, a rare feat in the Army of Northern Virginia.

Thomas' prowess as a hard-hitting officer and capable brigade commander was demonstrated throughout the campaigns during the summer and fall of 1862. At Cedar Mountain, on August 9, his brigade—comprised of the 14th, 35th, 45th, and 49th Georgia—

fought valiantly, suffering 152 casualties. At Second Manassas, his Georgians and Brigadier General Maxcy Gregg's brigades withstood the brunt of Federal assaults against General Thomas J. "Stonewall" Jackson's position behind the unfinished railroad embankment. During the Maryland Campaign in September, Jackson's forces captured Harpers Ferry and when the Light Division raced to Sharpsburg, Thomas and his command remained at Harpers Ferry, paroling the thousands of Federal prisoners.

Confederate authorities rewarded Thomas with promotion to brigadier general to rank from November 1, 1862. Six weeks later, after Fredericksburg, the Georgians again fought with determination. The brigade suffered heavy losses in an assault on Federal works at Chancellorsville on May 3, 1863. After the battle, General Robert E. Lee reorganized the army, creating three corps and breaking up the famed Light Division. Thomas' Georgians were assigned to a new division under William Dorsey Pender.

During the Gettysburg Campaign, Pender suffered a mortal wound. With his record, Thomas deserved consideration for promotion. Lee called him "a highly meritorious officer," but believed that Thomas' assignment to command of the division "might create dissatisfaction" among the two brigades of North Carolinians and the brigade of South Carolinians in the division. Instead, Lee assigned Cadmus Wilcox, a North Carolinian like Pender, to the command. Wilcox was a capable officer and retained the post until war's end.

Thomas' Georgians were transferred during the winter of 1864 to the Shenandoah Valley, where they served under Jubal Early. When active operations resumed in the spring the brigade returned to Wilcox' division, fighting in the battles of the Wilderness and Spotsylvania during the Overland Campaign of May–June. Thomas and the Georgians endured the ten-month siege of Petersburg with the rest of Lee's army and surrendered at Appomattox on April 9, 1865.

For nearly three years, Thomas had commanded a brigade, fought in all the major battles except Sharpsburg, and

A profile taken quite possibly at the same sitting. (National Archives)

fashioned a combat record that made him one of the most reliable and capable brigadiers in the army. Although internal politics perhaps denied him a deserved promotion, Thomas served at brigade level with a skill and devotion matched by few.

Thomas returned to his plantation in Georgia after the war, devoting the next two decades to its operations. In 1885 President Grover Cleveland appointed the Georgia Democrat to a position in the Land Bureau. Later, he transferred to the Indian Bureau, serving as an agent to the Sac and Fox Agency in Indian Territory or Oklahoma. There he died, at South McAlester, on March 8, 1898, and was buried in Kiowa, Oklahoma.

Jeffry D. Wert

Krick, Robert K., *Stonewall Jackson at Cedar Mountain* (Chapel Hill and London, 1990).

Robertson, James I., Jr., *General A.P. Hill: The Story Of A Confederate Warrior* (New York, 1987).

Scheneck, Martin, *Up Came Hill: The Story of the Light Division and Its Leaders* (Harrisburg, 1958).

A variant view taken almost certainly at the same sitting as the profile. (William A. Turner Collection)

✶ *Lloyd Tilghman* ✶

Born at "Rich Neck Manor," near Claiborne, Maryland, on January 18, 1816, Lloyd Tilghman graduated near the bottom of his West Point class of 1836. He briefly served with the 1st Dragoons but resigned his commission on September 30, 1836, to become a railroad engineer. During the Mexican War he served as a volunteer aide to General David Twiggs at the Battles of Palo Alto and Resaca de la Palma. By the end of the war he was a captain in the Maryland and District of Columbia Battalion of volunteers. After resuming his engineering career in the South and Panama Tilghman settled in Paducah, Kentucky, in 1852 and became active in Simon Buckner's Kentucky State Guard.

Given command of the 3d Kentucky Regiment at the beginning of the Civil War, Tilghman was promoted to brigadier general on October 18, 1861, ranking from that date. For a brief time he commanded the Confederate forces at Hopkinsville, Kentucky, but he kept a keen eye on the deplorable defenses of the Tennessee and Cumberland rivers. Tilghman warned General Albert Sidney Johnston of the bad state of affairs on the Tennessee River. He wrote his commander on October 27, "I fear our interests there are well-nigh beyond our control." Thus on November 17 Johnston placed him in charge of overseeing the river defenses at Forts Henry and Donelson.

Tilghman's attempts to organize a viable river defense were hampered by overlapping authority, a lack of men and material, and conflicting orders from Johnston and his immediate commander, Major General Leonidas Polk. Once he became so frustrated in seeking arms that he went over Johnston's head and wrote directly to President Jefferson Davis. Tilghman's abrupt manner and constant complaints of shortages irritated many who dealt with him. He was known as a strict disciplinarian, and one of his colonels resigned because of his style of command.

When the combined Federal forces under Brigadier General U.S. Grant and Flag Officer Andrew Foote approached Fort Henry in February 1862, Tilghman's small force was unsupported by Johnston. With approximately twenty-six hundred men under him Tilghman chose not to contest the Yankees as they moved upstream, but instead to await their attack. On February 6 it came in the form of Union gunboats. Realizing his position was untenable, Tilghman sent all but about one hundred of his men to Fort Donelson for safety. He then personally took charge of the defense of Fort Henry. The Confederate cannons badly shot up Foote's command, and Tilghman once stripped off his coat to help man a gun. After finally raising the white flag, Tilghman went aboard Foote's flagship to discuss surrender. Sources conflict over what happened. One claims Tilghman graciously surrendered to Foote, only to have that officer say that if their positions had been reversed, he would never have given up. Another source portrays Foote as being more gentlemanly. Foote himself described Tilghman as being shell-shocked and claimed he stood around wringing his hands and worrying about his reputation. Foote said he reassured Tilghman by promising to attest to the brave defense of the fort and then generously fed the Confederate officer.

Tilghman was held prisoner, sometimes in solitary confinement, until exchanged in August 1862. He then was given command of all camps of rendezvous and

A little-known portrait of Tilghman taken after October 1861, and specially noteworthy for displaying probably more buttons than any other Confederate brigadier. (*Confederate Veteran*, **IV**)

instruction for exchanged prisoners of war in the Tennessee department. After participating in the Battle of Corinth as commander of Major General W.W. Loring's 1st Brigade, Tilghman was given a division and placed in charge of the rear guard during the retreat from Holly Springs to Grenada. On December 5 he won a small battle at Coffeeville when he attacked and drove back the pursuing Yankees.

In January 1863 Tilghman took over William Baldwin's brigade in Loring's division and fought with it at Champion's Hill on May 16. Placed on the army's right, he once dismounted to direct artillery fire against Union sharpshooters located in some nearby cabins. A Federal shell exploded fifty feet away, and a piece of shrapnel tore completely through his chest. He died soon afterward. Tilghman first was buried in Vicksburg but later was reinterred in Woodlawn Cemetery in New York City.

Terry L. Jones

Cooling, Benjamin Franklin, *Forts Henry and Donelson: The Key to the Confederate Heartland* (Knoxville, 1987).

Johnson, Bradley T., *Maryland*, Vol. II in Evans, *Confederate Military History*.

Tilghman's best-known uniformed portrait, taken when he was colonel of the 3d Kentucky in 1861. (Ernest Haywood Papers, Southern Historical Collection, University of North Carolina, Chapel Hill)

✵ *Robert Augustus Toombs* ✵

No uniformed portrait of Toombs has ever come to light. This is probably a prewar image. (Library of Congress)

Robert Augustus Toombs ranks as one of the Old South's greatest intellectuals and one of the Confederacy's worst political generals. Born in Wilkes County, Georgia, on July 2, 1810, Toombs briefly attended the University of Georgia before completing his education at Union College in New York. Graduating in 1828, he passed the bar and established a lucrative practice near his hometown of Washington. He also had invested heavily in slaves and land in southwest Georgia. With the power that accompanied his position as a planter, Toombs entered politics and served in the Georgia State Legislature (1837–43), the United States House of Representatives (1844–52), and the Senate (1852–61). His appeal largely rested on his oratorical abilities. A neighbor observed: "When you once heard Bob Toombs 'on the stump' you could speak of it in the same tone as that used when one said, I saw Jeb Stuart lead a cavalry charge."

With the election of a Republican administration in 1860, Toombs believed that Southern rights were no longer secure in the Union. After Georgia had cast its lot with the Confederacy, he headed to Montgomery with the hope of becoming president. Toombs was only offered the secretaryship of state, a post he reluctantly accepted. The Georgian resigned five months later, on July 24, 1861, as relations with President Jefferson Davis had quickly soured.

Though he lacked formal military training, Toombs wanted service in the field. Commissioned a brigadier general on July 19, to rank from that same date, he received a Georgia brigade on the Virginia front. Toombs' appearance in the ranks concerned most Southerners. Colonel Thomas R.R. Cobb remarked that "I have sergeants in my legion in whose military capacity I have more confidence" than Toombs. Gilbert Moxley Sorrel shared a similar opinion, writing that Toombs "was for once and all a politician, and in the wrong shop with a sword and uniform on."

Toombs joined the Confederate army near Manassas where General Joseph E. Johnston drilled thousands of ill-trained recruits. Toombs thought Washington should be captured immediately and criticized his superiors for not taking decisive action. He wrote that winter "the army is dying…and set down opposite to it its epitaph, 'died of West Point.'" Toombs' proclivity for carping at people who disagreed with him was widely known. One Confederate official noted: "Bob Toombs disagrees with himself between meals."

When Johnston shifted his forces toward the Peninsula during the spring of 1862, Toombs saw combat as a temporary divisional commander under Major General John B. Magruder. On April 16 the Georgian put up an admirable defense along the Yorktown line near Dam Number One. He was acknowledged for his credible performance, but Toombs' dissatisfaction with the Confederacy's prosecution of the war intensified while Johnston retreated toward Richmond. Toombs asserted at this time: "The truth is Davis has no capacity & his generals but little more than he has & if it be possible to ruin our cause by imbecility they will do it." Cobb believed that Toombs' fondness for alcohol explained these vitriolic outbursts. "Toombs is drinking like a fish," Cobb observed, "and making an ass of himself. His disobedience of orders is notorious."

Toombs' command did not participate in the Battle of Seven Pines (May 31–June 1). When the Seven Days' Campaign opened on June 26, his troops anchored Magruder's left flank and missed any significant fighting. Toombs' men received their call to the front at Malvern Hill on July 1. His brigade had become disorganized during the assault. While Toombs tried to restore order, Major General D.H. Hill rode up to the Georgian and accused him of cowardice. This enraged Toombs; he protested through army channels, but nothing came of the paperwork. Toombs then decided to take matters into his own hands and challenged the North Carolinian to a duel. Hill refused on religious grounds. Considering the prickly honor of both men, it is difficult to determine who was at fault. The incident nevertheless reveals Toombs' divisive influence within the army.

Toombs did not play a major part in the Second Manassas Campaign (August 26–September 1) because he was under arrest for insubordination. On August 17 Toombs had been instructed to post two regiments at a ford on the Rapidan River but inexplicably pulled his units back to camp. When Major General James Longstreet learned of Toombs' unruly

behavior, he sent the officer back to Gordonsville to await formal charges. Longstreet, however, still had a "high opinion" of Toombs. He said that "if Toombs had been educated at West Point, where he could have learned self-control, he would have been as distinguished as a soldier as he was a civilian." Toombs was released on the eve of Second Manassas (August 28-30). There is some question as to whether he reached his command before the battle ended.

Toombs' most noteworthy accomplishment during the war came at Antietam on September 17. His tenacious defense above Burnside's Bridge allowed Confederate reinforcements to restore General Lee's right flank, saving the army from destruction. One Southerner saw Toombs running up and down the line "like one frantic, telling the men to stand firm." The next evening Toombs bumped into some enemy cavalry and was wounded in the hand. He returned to Georgia to convalesce, embittered that his accomplishments at Sharpsburg had not resulted in promotion. Toombs resigned on March 4, 1863. Lee made no objection to his resignation, probably relieved to have the recalcitrant Toombs safely behind the lines.

Back in Georgia, Toombs spent the rest of the war castigating Davis for increasing the powers of the central government. He unsuccessfully ran for a seat in the Confederate Senate in 1863. On August 8 of the same year Toombs reentered military service as a colonel of cavalry in the state guard. He also served as a divisional adjutant and inspector general in the Georgia militia during Major General William T. Sherman's advance toward Atlanta (May 1–September 2, 1864).

With the collapse of the Confederacy Toombs fled the county. He returned in 1867 but never applied for United States Reconstruction and warned Southerners of the coming evils of industrialism. Until his death on December 15, 1885, he "loved the South with all his mind and soul and heart, hating intensely everything and everybody who hated her."

Peter S. Carmichael

Phillips, Ulrich B., ed., *The Correspondence of Robert Toombs, Alexander H. Stephens, and Howell Cobb* (Washington, D.C., 1913).

Phillips, Ulrich B., *The Life of Robert Toombs* (New York, 1913).

Thompson, William Y., *Robert Toombs of Georgia* (Baton Rouge, 1966).

⭐ *Thomas Fentress Toon* ⭐

Thomas F. Toon was born in Columbus County, North Carolina, on June 10, 1840. After receiving a preliminary education, Toon entered Wake Forest College. There on May 20, 1861, during his senior year, he enlisted in the Columbus Guards. After he returned to college and was graduated, Toon was elected 1st lieutenant of Company K, 20th North Carolina on June 17. A month later, when his half-brother, W.H. Toon, was promoted to major, Thomas Toon was elected captain of the company.

The 20th North Carolina remained in its native state until May 1862, when it was transferred to Virginia. Assigned to the brigade of Samuel Garland, the North Carolinians fought at Seven Pines on May 31–June 1. Toon was the second man in the regiment to fall wounded during combat, with the musket ball passing through another man before striking him. At Gaines' Mill, in the Seven Days' Campaign, the regiment charged a Federal battery, capturing it twice and turning the cannon on the enemy. Toon suffered another slight wound but again led his company with gallantry.

The 20th North Carolina suffered heavy losses during the Maryland and Fredericksburg campaigns in the fall of 1862. Garland was killed at South Mountain on September 14 as his brigade defended the right flank on the Confederate position. Three days later, at Sharpsburg, the brigade fought in the slaughter pit of the Bloody Lane. Finally, on December 13, at Fredericksburg, the North Carolinians stabilized the Confederate right.

Toon emerged from these campaigns with the reputation as the finest officer in the regiment. When his half-brother resigned his commission in February 1863, the senior officers in the 20th North Carolina waived their rights to promotion and a board of officers recommended Toon for promotion. He was made colonel and assigned to command of the regiment on February 26.

Toon led the 20th North Carolina throughout the campaigns of 1863. He was hit three times by enemy fire at Chancellorsville on May 3 during a morning assault against Federal works. Not seriously injured, he was with the regiment when its brigade commander, Alfred Iverson, led it into a disastrous attack at Gettysburg on July 1. The brigade lost 455 killed and wounded, with Toon's regiment suffering 122 casualties. Toon, with the 20th North Carolina and five companies of the 12th North Carolina, repulsed a Union cavalry force at Morton's Ford on the Rappahannock River in Virginia on October 11. Division commander Robert E. Rodes described Toon's action as "a very brilliant affair."

In the spring of 1864 Toon and the regiment served under the command of Robert D. Johnston, fighting at the Wilderness and at Spotsylvania. In the latter battle, on May 12, Johnston's brigade counterattacked into the "Mule Shoe" salient. Toon subsequently called the fighting the "hottest conflict we ever engaged in." Although shot in the leg, Toon assumed command of the brigade when Johnston fell wounded. On May 31 he was promoted to brigadier general and four days later was temporarily assigned to command the brigade.

Toon's brigade participated in Jubal Early's raid

Thomas Toon as colonel of the 20th North Carolina during 1863 or early 1864. (North Carolina Division of Archives and History, Raleigh)

Johnston returned to command in August, Toon reverted to the rank of colonel and command of the 20th North Carolina. He led the regiment that fall in the Confederate defeats of Third Winchester, Fishers Hill, and Cedar Creek in the Shenandoah Valley Campaign. By year's end, most of Early's command rejoined General Robert E. Lee's army at Petersburg.

On March 25, 1865, Toon's North Carolinians participated in the assault on Fort Stedman in the Petersburg lines. While standing on the works and rallying his men, Toon suffered his seventh wound. This injury was the worst of all and incapacitated him for the remainder of the war.

Toon returned to his native state after the war and engaged in various pursuits. He was a railroad employee, a state legislator, and a teacher during these years. In 1901 he was elected state superintendent of public instruction and, while serving in this capacity, died in Raleigh on February 19, 1902. The former Confederate brigadier and excellent regimental commander was buried in Oakwood Cemetery in the state's capital.

Jeffry D. Wert

Clark, Walter, *Histories of the Several Regiments and Battalions From North Carolina in the Great War 1861–'65,* Volume II (Raleigh, 1901).

Usually identified as being General Toon, this man shows many similarities, suggesting that if genuine it may be a later wartime image. (Virginia Historical Society, Richmond)

Edward Dorr Tracy ✫

✫

A previously unpublished portrait of Edward Tracy, probably early in 1861 as captain
of a company in the 4th Alabama. (Duke University Library, Durham, N.C.)

Tracy was born on November 5, 1833, in Macon, Georgia. He was educated in private schools and graduated with a law degree from the University of Georgia at age seventeen. After teaching at a school for boys for three years, Tracy began practicing law in Macon. He moved to Huntsville, Alabama, in 1855. In 1860 he campaigned around the northern part of the state for the ticket of John C. Breckinridge after his selection as an alternate elector for the state.

Tracy raised a company in Madison County when the war started and was mustered in as part of the 4th Alabama Infantry Regiment on May 2, 1861. The regiment went to Harpers Ferry, Virginia, and joined the brigade of Barnard E. Bee. When the 12th Alabama Infantry Regiment was organized at Richmond in July, Tracy was appointed its major, but he declined that position. He became major of the 4th Alabama on July 17 and fought with it in the First Battle of Manassas on July 21. The regiment went into quarters at Dumfries after the battle.

On October 12 Tracy was appointed lieutenant colonel of the newly organized 19th Alabama Infantry Regiment, whose colonel was Joseph Wheeler. The regiment was ordered to Mobile as a part of the brigade of Brigadier General Leroy P. Walker. Brigadier General John K. Jackson commanded the brigade when it was ordered to reinforce General Pierre G.T. Beauregard's army at Corinth, Mississippi.

Tracy was with his regiment through the entire Battle of Shiloh, April 6–7, 1862. The brigade fought initially on the army's right flank and saw some action against the left flank of the famous "Hornets' Nest," defended by Brigadier General Benjamin N. Prentiss' division. During the second day's fighting Tracy had his horse killed under him. Wheeler reported that "during the entire two days [Tracy] exhibited marked coolness and noble bearing."

Tracy led a detachment of the 19th Alabama in a skirmish near Farmington on May 9. Wheeler soon assumed brigade command, and Tracy took over the regiment. He commanded it during engagements on the Monterey Road May 28–29 during the Confederate evacuation of Corinth. Wheeler again commended Tracy for "gallant and good conduct" in these actions.

As part of Brigadier General Franklin Gardner's brigade of Brigadier General John P. McCown's division, the 19th Alabama left Tupelo, Mississippi, on June 28 and arrived in Chattanooga, Tennessee, on July 3. There the division joined Major General

Edmund Kirby Smith's Army of East Tennessee. On July 22 Kirby Smith recommended Tracy for promotion to brigadier general: "Upright, intelligent, and accomplished, Colonel Tracy, by his services at Manassas and Shiloh, has attested his soldierly qualities." The 19th Alabama served through the Kentucky Campaign that fall but saw no serious fighting. After Kirby Smith's army returned to eastern Tennessee, Tracy received his promotion to brigadier general, effective August 16. He was given a brigade, in McCown's division, of three Alabama regiments and one from Georgia.

In December the brigade became part of Brigadier General Carter L. Stevenson's division. Tracy's Georgia regiment was traded to Seth M. Barton's brigade for two Alabama regiments. Stevenson's division went to Vicksburg in late December, arriving just after the Battle of Chickasaw Bluffs. On January 2, 1863, Tracy was reported as commanding the left wing of the forces there, consisting of his own and Brigadier General Alexander W. Reynold's brigades. After the threat to Chickasaw Bluffs had ended, Tracy's men moved to a reserve position south of Vicksburg. Several companies of the brigade guarded bridges over the Big Black River east of the city. The brigade remained in the area through the winter and early spring.

In response to Major General Ulysses S. Grant's Union army crossing the Mississippi River below Vicksburg, Tracy was ordered on April 29, 1863, to leave Warrenton and reinforce Major General John S. Bowen's division at Grand Gulf. The men marched that evening and reached their destination the next day. Bowen halted them there to collect stragglers and cook rations. He reported that the fifteen hundred soldiers "were completely jaded and broken down with continuous marching." Nevertheless, Bowen ordered the brigade on to Port Gibson, where Tracy reported to Brigadier General Martin E. Green. The latter sent the brigade out five or six miles on the Bruinsburg Road, where the men slept on their arms. The next morning, May 1, Green detached one of Tracy's regiments to reinforce his left. With three regiments Tracy formed his battle line about sunrise. Federal troops attacked his position about 7 A.M. About an hour later Tracy was shot through the chest with a Minié bullet "and instantly died without uttering a word," according to Colonel Isham W. Garrott, one of his regimental commanders. Colonel Charles M. Shelley and

Customarily identified as James G. Martin, this colonel is almost certainly Edward D. Tracy, taken in 1862. (Virginia Historical Society, Richmond)

one of his company commanders, both of the 30th Alabama, carried Tracy's body from the battlefield. Later the body was taken to a house in Port Gibson, where it was left when the Confederates retreated toward Vicksburg.

Lieutenant General John C. Pemberton called Tracy "a brave and skillful officer, who fell where it is the soldier's pride to fall—at the post of duty and of danger." Bowen wrote that Tracy had given "signal proof of his ability as an officer and bravery as a man." Eventually Tracy's body was taken to Macon, Georgia, for burial.

Arthur W. Bergeron, Jr.

Harwell, J.D., "In and Around Vicksburg," *Confederate Veteran*, XXX (1922), pp. 33–34.

Kelly, William M., "A History of the Thirtieth Alabama Volunteers (Infantry) Confederate States Army," *Alabama Historical Quarterly*, IX (1947), pp. 115–67.

Owen, Thomas M., *History of Alabama and Dictionary of Alabama Biography*, IV vols. (Spartanburg, S.C., 1978).

Wheeler, Joseph, *Alabama*, Vol. VII in Evans, *Confederate Military History*.

⋆ *James Heyward Trapier* ⋆

The only known wartime portrait of General Trapier, taken after October 1861.
(Albert G. Shaw Collection, Virginia Historical Society, Richmond)

James Heyward Trapier was born at "Windsor" on the Black River, near Georgetown, South Carolina, on November 24, 1815. Ranked third in his West Point class of 1838, he graduated with future Confederate generals P.G.T. Beauregard, William Hardee, Edward Johnson, and Carter Stevenson. Because of his high class standing Trapier entered the engineering corps and worked on numerous fortifications, including Fort Pulaski at Charleston. After serving in the Mexican War he was made assistant engineer for the fortifications of New York.

Trapier resigned his commission in 1848 and returned to Georgetown to become a planter and militia officer. With the rank of major he became South Carolina's chief of ordnance, 1851–52, and worked diligently to increase the state's armament. Fifty heavy pieces he acquired from the Tredegar Iron Works were later used to bombard Fort Sumter. During the decade prior to the Civil War Trapier also served as aide-de-camp to the governor with the rank of colonel.

At the beginning of the Fort Sumter crisis Trapier held the rank of captain in the Confederate army and served on Beauregard's staff. Promoted to major, he was made chief engineer of the Morris Island defenses and played an important role in preparing the batteries for the bombardment. One mortar unit on Morris Island became known as Battery Trapier, and his work during the bombardment earned high praise from Beauregard.

Trapier was made commander of the Charleston area after Fort Sumter's surrender and was promoted to brigadier general on October 21, 1861, to rank from that date. He assumed command of the Department of Eastern and Middle Florida and earned the hostility of the people of Florida for not having his headquarters on the front lines. Amelia Island on the Atlantic coast was threatened with invasion, but Trapier rarely went there. Although ordered in February 1862 to evacuate the island, he failed to do so before the Yankees attacked, and he had to abandon fifteen valuable cannons. Afterward the Florida state convention introduced a resolution requesting that the government either force Trapier to remain with his troops "at some threatened and exposed point" or replace him. Trapier wrote President Jefferson Davis, complaining that the convention had "greatly insulted" him, and asked to be relieved of duty in Florida.

Davis granted Trapier's wish and transferred him to General Albert Sidney Johnston's army in March 1862.

He was given a division in Lieutenant General Leonidas Polk's corps and served in the Battles of Corinth and Farmington, Mississippi, under Major General Braxton Bragg. Bragg was less than impressed with Trapier, however, and in August put him on a list of generals unfit for important commands.

In November Trapier left Bragg for Georgetown to take over the 4th Military District in the Department of South Carolina. When Rear Admiral Samuel DuPont attacked Charleston in April 1863, Trapier was put in charge of the defenses on Sullivan's Island. With Trapier's help Charleston's batteries riddled the Union fleet and turned it back. Proud of his contribution, Trapier was understandably upset when ordered back to his administrative post at Georgetown. Complaining that he had not been charged with negligence or incompetence, he branded the demotion as being "in flagrant violation...of every consideration of military courtesy, military etiquette, and military propriety, and in contempt of every principle of common right and common justice." His superior, Brigadier General Roswell S. Ripley, forwarded Trapier's complaint to Beauregard with the note, "In my opinion General Trapier would consult the good of the service...better by obeying his orders...rather than caviling and criticising those orders in language which appears to me to be unmilitary and disrespectful." Told by Beauregard to obey his orders, Trapier served out the rest of the war in Georgetown.

Trapier only briefly survived the war. He died near Georgetown on December 21, 1865, and was buried in the cemetery of the Church of St. George, Winyah.

Terry L. Jones

Capers, Ellison, *South Carolina*, Vol. V in Evans, *Confederate Military History*.

⋆ *Isaac Ridgeway Trimble* ⋆

The uniform in this portrait of General Trimble is heavily retouched suggesting that it is entirely an artist's creation. No other genuine uniformed portrait of the general has surfaced. (Library of Congress)

Isaac Ridgeway Trimble was born May 15, 1802, in Culpeper County, Virginia. His family moved to Kentucky shortly thereafter, and Trimble received appointment to the United States Military Academy from that state. He rose through the scholastic ranks at West Point and graduated seventeenth in a class of forty-two in 1822. He excelled particularly in engineering.

Trimble spent the next ten years as a lieutenant of artillery in the Regular Army but succumbed to the lucrative temptations of civilian life and resigned in May 1832. In the remaining decades before the Civil War Trimble engaged in railroad engineering. Despite his mixed regional background, he soon settled in Maryland and thereafter was always identified with that state.

Isaac Trimble went immediately to Virginia in May 1861, brandishing his engineering skill. He landed a commission as lieutenant colonel of Virginia forces on May 25, 1861, with engineering duties. Trimble subsequently distinguished himself during the war as a fiery leader of combat infantry; his fondness for engineering was set aside by the spring of 1862. Trimble received appointment as brigadier general on August 9, 1861, effective immediately, with responsibilities for battery construction along the Potomac River and for the defenses around Norfolk.

Perhaps because of the paucity of professional officers at brigade level in the Confederate forces under General Joseph E. Johnston, Trimble received an infantry brigade in the early spring of 1862. The brigade contained four regiments from four different states, and Trimble meshed them into a reliable tool for Major General Thomas J. "Stonewall" Jackson during the fabled Shenandoah Valley Campaign of 1862. Trimble behaved most gallantly at Cross Keys on June 8, 1862, blunting a Union assault and then seizing the initiative and counterattacking.

Trimble and his brigade were relatively quiet during the Seven Days' Campaign around Richmond, although they saw action at Gaines' Mill on June 27. The grizzled general—by then sixty years old—and his troops followed Jackson against Major General John Pope in August, and the ensuing battles were certainly the highlights of Trimble's career. His brigade fought at Cedar Mountain and aggressively handled some careless Federals in an obscure action at Hazel River in mid-August. Trimble personally played a leading role in Jackson's capture and destruction of Manassas Junction, August 26–27, 1862. The zealous Marylander apparently volunteered his brigade for a forced march on the junction to culminate with an assault on the Union detachment there. Trimble met with success, and his performance even elicited praise from the subdued Stonewall Jackson, who termed the affair "the most brilliant that has come under my observation during the present war."

For Trimble, however, the euphoria of Manassas Junction was soon snuffed out by a serious wound on August 29. The damage to Trimble's leg was so severe that it provoked speculation that perhaps he had been hit by some type of exploding bullet. The general avoided amputation, but his rehabilitation moved slowly. During the recovery his promotion to major general arrived, to rank from January 17, 1863. No doubt Jackson's fervent recommendation contributed to the promotion.

Trimble's next action proved to be his last. After commanding all Confederate troops in the Shenandoah Valley in June 1863, Trimble hastened to Gettysburg, where the army needed his services to help fill the gaps in command. General R.E. Lee gave him the division of the wounded Major General Dorsey Pender, part of the III Corps, and Trimble led those brigades in the famous assault (Pickett's charge) on July 3, 1863. A conspicuous target on horseback, Trimble rode with the division all the way to the Emmittsburg Road. There another Federal bullet hit him, again in the leg. Despite feeling faint, the sixty-one-year-old general followed his troops *"at a walk"* back to their lines. The injury was so severe that Trimble remained behind when his army retreated, and he fell into the hands of the enemy. The leg wound necessitated amputation, and Trimble convalesced in the Seminary Hospital at Gettysburg until August.

General Trimble found his period of imprisonment quite unpleasant. He spent time at Fort McHenry, Johnson's Island, and Fort Warren. According to Brigadier General James L. Kemper, also wounded at

Gettysburg, Trimble reposed at Fort McHenry under "singularly rigorous and unjust restrictions." Kemper felt the treatment to be in retaliation for Trimble's agitations in the politically charged Baltimore of 1861.

One-legged Isaac Trimble always had a taste for authority, and during his captivity he represented his fellow prisoners in most matters. His official service record is replete with protests to prison commandants and other similar correspondence. After being exchanged in mid-March 1865, Trimble loyally headed for the Army of Northern Virginia, only to be halted by the news of surrender.

General Trimble never achieved substantial fame in the Confederacy, yet his accomplishments as a brigadier general had few equals. He was perhaps, even too aggressive on occasion, but his superiors uniformly praised his battlefield talents. Predictably, only General Jackson could find fault with his subordinate, writing: "I do not regard him as a good disciplinarian...."

The troops under Trimble also displayed a marked fondness for their leader. When a Mississippi regiment transferred from his brigade against their wishes, the entire regiment repaired to the general's tent, where their band serenaded him until he delivered an emotional farewell speech. These qualities, displayed both on the battlefield and in camp, combined to make Isaac R. Trimble one of the better Confederate generals in Virginia.

After the war Trimble resided in his adopted state at Baltimore, where he died on January 2, 1888, at the age of eighty-five. He was buried there at Green Mount Cemetery.

Robert E. L. Krick

Myers, William S., ed., "The Civil War Diary of Isaac Ridgeway Trimble", *Maryland Historical Magazine*, XVII (1922).

✯ *William Feimster Tucker* ✯

The uniform in this portrait of Tucker is very possibly an artist's addition. (U.S. Army Military History Institute, Carlisle, Pa.)

Tucker was born in Iredell County, North Carolina, on May 9, 1827. He attended Emory and Henry College in Virginia and graduated from that institution in 1848, when he was twenty-one years old. During the same year of his graduation, he moved to Houston, Mississippi. It is not known what occupation he was engaged in between 1848 and 1855. Although he was not trained in law, he was elected probate judge of Chickasaw County, Mississippi, in 1855. Subsequent to his being elected judge, he studied law, was admitted to the bar, and became a practicing attorney. He continued to practice law until the advent of the Civil War.

Upon the secession of Mississippi, Tucker raised the Chickasaw Guards and served with his company at Pensacola, Florida, in January of 1861. The company, along with others from Mississippi, were ordered to Lynchburg Virginia, where in May Tucker was mustered into Confederate service as captain of Company K, 11th Mississippi Infantry. He trained at Harpers Ferry and, as part of Brigadier General Barnard E. Bee's brigade in General Joseph E. Johnston's Army of the Shenandoah, maneuvered in the Shenandoah Valley in June and July. Tucker fought in the First Battle of Manassas on July 21, where Bee's brigade suffered the brunt of the Federal assault.

Following the fighting at Manassas, Tucker returned to Mississippi and organized a battalion which was increased to form the 41st Mississippi Infantry. Tucker was commissioned colonel of this regiment on May 8, 1862. Attached to the Army of the Mississippi at Corinth, the regiment soon moved to Tupelo. Although assigned to Brigadier General J. Patton

Anderson's brigade, during the invasion of Kentucky that fall, Brigadier General John C. Brown commanded the brigade after Anderson assumed divisional command. Tucker sustained a wound while leading his regiment in the successful Confederate attack at Perryville on October 8. Returning to Tennessee later that month, the 41st Mississippi was temporarily assigned to Colonel W.S. Dilworth's brigade until December 12, when the regiment was placed in Brigadier General Edward C. Walthall's brigade. Two weeks later, the regiment was transferred to Brigadier General James R. Chalmers' brigade, and it was with that brigade that Tucker and his men participated in the Battle of Murfreesboro.

As senior colonel, Tucker was assigned to command the brigade on February 1, 1863, Chalmers being absent, sick. On March 5, Tucker engaged Union cavalry at Unionville, Tennessee. By April 1, Chalmers had been transferred to Mississippi and Anderson assumed command of the brigade, which was now part of Major General Jones M. Withers' division. Prior to the Battle of Chickamauga, the brigade was assigned to Major General Thomas C. Hindman's division. During the Confederate attack at Chickamauga on September 20, three regiments alone managed to gain the top of the ridge defended by Union Major General Gordon Granger. One of these was Tucker's, and he wanted "to call particular attention to the fact that at this time, so far as I know, the colors of the Forty-first Mississippi alone, of this brigade or any other, reached and passed over the crest of this hill." Tucker then participated in the Siege of Chattanooga and was in command of the brigade during the Battle of Missionary Ridge. On December 14, 1863, following the Confederate retreat into Georgia, Tucker's regiment was reduced to 273 effective soldiers with only 219 rifled muskets among them. The remainder of the brigade, the 7th, 9th, 10th, and 44th Mississippi Infantry Regiments and the 9th Mississippi Battalion of Sharpshooters, had only 710 men with 610 weapons available for duty.

Tucker was appointed a brigadier general on March 7, 1864, to rank from March 1, and permanently assigned to command the brigade. At the opening of the Atlanta Campaign, he led his brigade of Hindman's division of Lieutenant General John Bell Hood's corps in the repulse of the Federals at Rocky Face Ridge, before Dalton, on May 8.

On May 14, three days after his brigadier's commission had been confirmed by the C.S. Congress, Tucker participated in his second, and last, engagement as a brigadier. Lieutenant General John Bell Hood, in his report on that engagement, stated: "...the enemy made repeated assaults on Hindman's left, but not in very heavy lines. Walthall's brigade, occupying the left of Hindman's, suffered severely from an enfilade fire of the enemy's artillery....Brigadier Tucker, commanding brigade in reserve, was severely wounded." In his report of the same battle, Walthall said: "Tucker's...fine brigade which was posted in my rear for support, though it had the shelter of the ridge, sustained considerable loss, mainly from the enemy's artillery. Its commander, Brig. Gen. W.F. Tucker, was severely wounded while observing the enemy's movements from my position during the first day's engagement, and was succeeded in command by Col. Jacob H. Sharp....To both of these efficient officers I am indebted for valuable suggestions and repeated offers of assistance, for which their command was kept in a constant state of readiness."

The wound sustained by Tucker at Resaca was of such severity and of such nature that it rendered him unfit for further duty in the field. Although he never returned to field duty, he did serve as commander of the District of Southern Mississippi and East Louisiana during the closing weeks of the Civil War. While in that position, he attempted to work with Union officers to prevent the lawlessness displayed by marauding bands preying upon innocent citizens. He negotiated an end of hostilities in his district with Union Major General Napoleon T.J. Dana on April 27, 1865. Tucker received his parole at Jackson, Mississippi, on May 15, 1865.

After the war ended, Tucker returned to Chickasaw County, Mississippi, where he resumed his law practice. He also engaged in politics, serving two terms in the state legislature, and was elected to that body first in 1876 and again in 1878. On September 14, 1881, Tucker was assassinated at Okalona, Mississippi. Allegedly, the deed was committed by two men hired by a certain Shaw, against whom Tucker had a case pending for the misappropriation of guardianship funds. He was buried at Okalona.

Benjamin E. Snellgrove

Rowland, Dunbar, comp., *The Official and Statistical Register of the State of Mississippi* (Nashville, 1908).

✶ *David Emanuel Twiggs* ✶

No photo of General Twiggs in Confederate uniform has been found, and quite probably he never had one taken since his service was so short. (Library of Congress)

David Emanuel Twiggs was born in 1790 at "Good Hope," the family plantation in Richmond County just south of Augusta, Georgia. His father, John Twiggs, served in the Georgia militia during the revolutionary war, and his mother, Ruth Emanuel, was the sister to David Emanuel, one-time governor pro tem of Georgia. Twiggs had a distinguished career in the Regular Army and was known as "Old Davy," the "Bengal Tiger," and "The Horse." He fought in the War of 1812 and was appointed captain of the 8th U.S. Infantry when the war began, and major in the 28th Infantry two years later. After the regiment was disbanded in June 1815, he was reinstated as captain of the 7th Infantry in December 1815. He was promoted to major of the 1st Infantry in May 1825, lieutenant colonel of the 4th Infantry in July 1831, and colonel of the 2d Dragoons in June 1836. His service included fighting in the Black Hawk and Seminole wars. During the Mexican War he was promoted to brigadier general on June 30, 1846, and brevet major general on September 23, 1846, for his service at Monterrey. Although Winfield Scott had claimed that Twiggs was unfit to command an army "either in the presence or in the absence of an enemy," his official battle reports gave Twiggs surprisingly high praise. Moreover, Twiggs received the Sword from Congress for his actions in Mexico.

Twiggs was not a West Pointer; he did not conform to the standards set by the West Point ideal, and this may have been one of the reasons he was not popular with the professionals. An officer who knew him in Mexico stated: "He was not a man well beloved by officers or soldiers; he possessed no magnetic power; he was not genial in temper or disposition and yet he enjoyed a joke and at times made a pun." When Jefferson Davis served as secretary of war, Twiggs was angered with changes in the military and blamed them on Davis. Twiggs had a domineering personality as well as a powerful build; he was nearly six feet tall with a bull neck and heavy cherry-red face. In his later life he had bristling white hair, and when army regulations permitted, wore a bushy white beard.

His military career was colored by controversy. In March 1857 he took command of the Department of Texas but in 1858 was court-martialed for a breach of military discipline when he contradicted an opinion of President James Buchanan. Twiggs had appointed a court of inquiry in a matter in which the President had also appointed a court. Twiggs' selection, all members of the 2d U.S. Cavalry Regiment, included such notables as Albert Sidney Johnston, Robert E. Lee, George H. Thomas, and Edmund Kirby Smith. For his action Twiggs was relieved of his command for several weeks but returned to his post in June 1858. In December 1859 he requested a leave of absence for bad health. In fact, the Washington *Evening Star* reported that he was near death. Jefferson Davis, in explaining to a friend why Twiggs was so obdurate, wrote that "the malignity of Twiggs towards you sprung from his hostility to me… As Twiggs is reported to be dying, and many believe it, I think it better for you to press him no further." But Twiggs made a remarkable recovery and was back in charge of the Department of Texas when the secession crisis began. At the beginning of 1861 Twiggs was one of the four general officers of the line in the United States Army, the others being William S. Harney, John E. Wool, and Winfield Scott. Twiggs wrote Scott in December 1860 and again in January 1861, asking what he should do in the event of Texas' secession. Twiggs' sympathies lay with the South; he had written Scott on January 15: "As soon as I know Georgia has separated from the Union I must, of course, follow her." In fact, soon after his home state seceded, Twiggs was offered a command in Georgia, which he declined on the basis of poor health. In late February Confederates at Charleston, South Carolina, also appealed to the governor of Georgia for General Twiggs.

Twiggs made it plain to the Texans and to Washington that "he would not be instrumental in bringing on civil war," and he told the Texans that "he would die before he would permit his men to be disgraced by a surrender of their arms…" To help Twiggs out of this embarrassing position, Winfield Scott directed Colonel C. A. Waite to relieve him, but before this happened, Ben McCulloch, a future Confederate brigadier general, raised a force of five hundred volunteers and marched on the army headquarters at San Antonio. Twiggs, with only 160 troops, surrendered February 18, 1861, without a shot being fired. The Texas Committee of Public Safety explained the necessity for a military takeover. "Believing that General Twiggs would neither do nor consent to anything being done that might possibly place him in a false or an apparently false position, either before the Government whose interests he represented or before any portion of the American people," the Texans were forced to this drastic action. President Buchanan failed to agree, however, and ordered Twiggs "dismissed from the Army of the United States, for his treachery to the flag of his country" on March 1, 1861.

Soon after this occurred, President Davis offered Twiggs a commission as a brigadier general in the Confederate Regular Army, which he declined because of his age. But in late May he agreed to accept a commission in the provisional army and was appointed a major general. On May 27 he was assigned to command Department #1 which included the state of Lousiana as well as southern Mississippi and southern Alabama. Twiggs, over seventy years old, was unable to perform his duties very long. By September the government in Louisiana petitioned for his removal; one letter to Davis pointed out that "in spite of his good intentions the infirmities of General Twiggs, which confine him to his armchair, disqualify him completely for the situation he holds." He was replaced by General Mansfield Lovell in October. Twiggs returned to Georgia, where he died July 15, 1862, and was buried in the Family cemetery at Good Hope. His daughter Marion was the wife of the first Confederate quartermaster general, Colonel Abraham C. Myers. Twiggs, one of the forgotten generals in the Civil War, nevertheless had a distinguished military career that bridged half a century.

Anne Bailey

"An Episode in the Texas Career of General David E. Twiggs." *Southwestern Historical Quarterly* 41 (1937): 167–173.

Brown, Russell K., "An Old Woman with a Broomstick: General David E. Twiggs and the U.S. Surrender in Texas, 1861," *Military Affairs* (April 1984), 57–61.

Brown, Russell K., "David Emanuel Twiggs," *Richmond County History* (Summer 1983), 12–26, (Winter, 1982), 22-31.

☆ *Robert Charles Tyler* ☆

The only known photograph of Robert Tyler. His collar insignia suggests it could have been taken before February 1864, but his brigadier's buttons argue that it was made after his promotion. (Albert G. Shaw Collection, Virginia Historical Society, Richmond)

No general of the Confederacy presents a more frustrating case of mystery and missing information than Robert Charles Tyler. Almost literally nothing is known about him other than a few small snippets of information, and his obscure military career.

He was born in 1832 or 1833, possibly in Baltimore. In 1856 he went to Nicaragua on the filibustering expedition of the "gray-eyed man of destiny," William Walker. Returned from the enterprise, Tyler seems to have traveled to Baltimore, but then moved on to Memphis by 1860. When the war erupted, he raised a company of recruits, perhaps capitalizing on his experience with Walker to persuade others that he knew how to command. On April 18, 1861, he led his men to Jackson, Tennessee, and there enlisted them into the 15th Tennessee Infantry.

Thereafter Tyler must have impressed others, for he was soon promoted from captain to major, then made quartermaster in the command of Tennessean Gideon Pillow. By November he had risen to lieutenant colonel of the 15th Tennessee, and led it at Belmont. He fought at Shiloh, taking a wound, and by June 1862 was colonel in command of his regiment, and also apparently something of a favorite with Braxton Bragg, who later that year made him provost of the army. If he was engaged at Stones' River, no record of it survives, but a year later he did fight at Chickamauga, and then on Missionary Ridge on November 25, 1863, suffered a terrible wound that resulted in the amputation of a leg.

During the winter that followed, Tyler received an appointment as brigadier general on March 5, 1864, to date from February 23. It may or may not be significant that this appointment came after Bragg left the Army of Tennessee to go to Richmond as President Davis' chief military advisor. He was convalescing at the small military hospital at West Point, Georgia, at the time. Perhaps Davis intended that Tyler would resume command of Bate's Brigade, which he had led at Missionary Ridge when Bate rose to division command. However, even though the unit changed its name to "Tyler's Brigade," he would never leave West Point to resume its leadership.

Perhaps because he was too infirm to leave West Point, Tyler received assignment to command the place, though it hardly merited one of his rank. He oversaw the earthworks constructed to guard the post and the West Point Railroad, and was there at the end of the war when Yankee raiders approached. Though he had no command other than a few convalescents and a scattering of militia, barely the equivalent of a few companies, he manned West Point's works on the morning of April 16, 1865, as cavalry approached. The skirmishing had only just begun when Tyler, on his crutches, stepped outside the works briefly to get a better view of the enemy. A sharpshooter brought him down with a fatal bullet. He and the few others who fell in the subsequent doomed defense of West Point and Fort Tyler were buried there.

So little is known of Tyler that it is not even possible to conjecture on his skill as a commander, since Fort Tyler was his only "battle" as a general. Certainly he won the confidence of others on his way up the ladder of command, though there is a hint that he may have been equally adept at ingratiating himself to influential men like Bragg. In the end, he remains as much a mystery today as he was in his own time.

William C. Davis

Slatter, William J., "Last Battle of the War," *Confederate Veteran*, IV, November 1896.

Warner, Ezra J., "Who Was General Tyler?" *Civil War Times Illustrated*, IX, October 1970.

✶ *Robert Brank Vance* ✶

An elder brother of Governor (and Senator) Zebulon Vance, Robert Vance was born in Buncombe County, North Carolina, on April 24, 1828. He attended the common schools of the district and acquired what was considered to be the standard education of the day. After completing his education, he became a farmer and engaged in commerce. He was elected Clerk of the Court of Pleas and Quarter Sessions, and for some years he served his county in that capacity.

When North Carolina seceded from the Union, Vance recruited a company known as the "Buncombe Life Guards." He served as captain of the company until it was incorporated into a newly formed regiment, the 29th North Carolina Infantry. He was commissioned colonel of the regiment in October of 1861 and sent to Raleigh for further training. Posted to East Tennessee in November, Vance and his regiment served primarily as a railroad garrison until early in 1862 when they were transferred to Cumberland Gap, Tennessee. They took part in the

defense of Cumberland Gap until the Confederates abandoned that mountain position in June of 1862.

In August, while serving under Brigadier General Carter L. Stevenson, Vance and his men participated in the assault and defeat of the enemy at Tazewell, Tennessee. Next, while in command of his own as well as some other regiments, he held Baptist Gap until the Union forces retreated. He then joined Major General E. Kirby Smith on his late summer campaign in Kentucky. In September of 1862, after he had reached Frankfort, Kentucky, Vance returned to Tennessee through the Cumberland Gap, marching his men some five hundred miles in forty days.

During the Battle of Stones' River when his immediate commander, Brigadier General James Edward Rains,

The only known genuine uniformed portrait of R.B. Vance is this group photo taken in prison at Fort Delaware sometime in the first half of 1864. Vance sits third from the left, with legs crossed. (Indiana State Library, Indianapolis)

fell on December 31, Vance was elevated to command of the Rains Brigade in Major General John Porter McCown's division, and according to McCown's report of his conduct during the ensuing battle, he "bore himself gallantly." After General Braxton Bragg had fallen back to Shelbyville, Vance was invalided with typhoid fever. During his convalescence the 29th North Carolina Infantry was sent to Jackson, Mississippi, and as a consequence, Vance never commanded his regiment again. In June, while still convalescing, Vance received his commission as brigadier general, to rank from March 4, 1863.

Upon recovering from his illness Vance was assigned to duty in western North Carolina with approximately five hundred men under his command. Of these men, most of whom were raw troops, conscripts, and stragglers from the army, only a few were regular troops. In October of 1863 Vance sent an expeditionary force of one hundred and fifty men, of the 14th North Carolina Cavalry Battalion, under Major John W. Woodfin, to engage the enemy at Warm Springs, North Carolina. The enemy force was reportedly preparing for an invasion of Greenville, South Carolina, since it was the nearest town of importance and contained a state armory.

Later intelligence informed Vance that Warm Springs was occupied by five hundred Federals, while an additional five thousand Union troops occupied the adjacent area to the west. Upon receiving this added intelligence, Vance immediately dispatched a courier to Woodfin, countermanding his earlier order to attack the enemy. The messenger arrived too late, because the Confederates had already attacked at Marshall on October 20 and been repulsed by the enemy force; several Confederates had been killed, including Woodfin.

Vance left Asheville, North Carolina, on January 8, 1864, with a cavalry unit of three hundred men. He went through Waynesville, Quallatown, and eventually arrived at Gatlinburg, Tennessee. Having split his force, he made a raid toward Sevierville, fourteen miles from Gatlinburg, at about 3 P.M. on the afternoon of January 14 and captured a train of eighteen wagons. He then proceeded eastward toward Newport via Schultz's Mill. After traveling some twenty-three miles, he reached Schultz's Mill on Cosby Creek, in Cooke County, shortly after noon on the following day. He stopped to rest his men and to give the animals a chance to feed. Feeling safe from pursuit, he did not mount a rearguard nor did he post pickets. Consequently, the pursuing Union cavalry caught up and got within one hundred yards of

Vance's men before they were detected by the Confederates. Having been taken completely by surprise, Vance surrendered. There were none killed and only two Confederates wounded during the surprise attack. The Union forces recaptured their wagons and all the equipment that the Confederates possessed, as well. Vance was one of the fifty-two prisoners taken by the Federals.

Vance's capture on January 14, 1864, effectively ended his military career because he remained a prisoner until he was released for exchange on March 10, 1865. He experienced prison life in the prison camps at Nashville, Louisville, Camp Chase, and Fort Delaware. While at Fort Delaware, he was permitted to assist paroled Confederate Brigadier General William Nelson Rector Beall, who functioned as a procurement agent, supplying clothing and blankets for the relief of Confederate soldiers held in Northern prison camps.

After the war was over Vance returned to his native state of North Carolina, where he became a prominent citizen and enjoyed a distinguished career as a public servant. After serving one term as a representative in the state legislature he entered national politics. Elected as the representative for the Eighth Congressional District, he served with distinction in the United States House of Representatives. First elected to Congress in 1872, he was re-elected in each successive election up to and including the election of 1882. Although he declined renomination in 1884, he did take an active part that year in the Democratic campaign. In the spring of 1885 President Grover Cleveland appointed him assistant commissioner of patents, and for the next four years he served as such in Washington, D.C. From 1894 to 1896 he served in the state house of representatives.

Vance founded a national temperance organization, served the Methodist church as a delegate to general conferences and the ecumenical conference in London, gained prominence in the masonic order as the grandmaster of masons in his state, and became a noted lecturer and author. He died near Asheville, North Carolina, in Buncombe County, the county of his birth, on November 28, 1899, and was buried in Riverside Cemetery in Asheville.

Benjamin E. Snellgrove

Hill, D.H., Jr., *North Carolina*, Vol. IV in Evans, *Confederate Military History*.

An outstanding portrait of Major General Van Dorn, probably taken in 1862 or later. (Alabama Department of Archives and History, Montgomery)

⋆ *Earl Van Dorn* ⋆

Earl Van Dorn was born on September 17, 1820, at the "Hill," near Port Gibson, Mississippi. His father was Judge Peter Aaron Van Dorn of the Claiborne County Probate Court and his mother, Sophia Donelson (Caffery) Van Dorn, was Mrs. Andrew Jackson's niece. Judge Van Dorn was a 1795 graduate of the College of New Jersey (Princeton) and had moved first to Virginia before settling in Mississippi. Earl was educated in the Claiborne County common schools and on July 1, 1838, he entered the United States Military Academy.

Van Dorn graduated from West Point on July 1, 1842, fifty-second in a class of fifty-six. Commissioned a brevet 2d lieutenant in the 7th U.S. Infantry, he reported to his unit, then stationed at Fort Pike, Louisiana. The next year saw a brief tour of duty at Fort Morgan, Alabama, followed by an eighteen-month assignment at the Mt. Vernon, Alabama, arsenal, where he married Caroline Godbold in 1843. He was promoted to 2d lieutenant on November 30, 1844, while stationed at Fort Barrancas, Florida. He was ordered to Texas with his regiment in the autumn of 1845 and participated in the defense of Fort Texas (May 3–9, 1846) when it was invaded by Mariano Arista's Mexican army. He was with Major General Zachary Taylor's army on its advance from Camargo to Cerralvo and fought in the Battle of Monterrey (September 21–23).

The 7th U.S., along with most of the regulars, was transferred from northern Mexico to join Major General Winfield Scott's army that landed at Veracruz and carried the war into the Valley of Mexico. Van Dorn, having been promoted to 1st lieutenant on March 3, 1847, was named aide-de-camp to Brigadier General P.F. Smith. He was brevetted captain on April 17 for gallantry and meritorious conduct at Cerro Gordo, and major on August 20 for similar actions at Contreras and Churubusco. He was wounded in the September 13 fight for Garita de Belen that led to the capture of Mexico City. Van Dorn returned to the United States in 1848 with the 7th Infantry and was

posted first at Baton Rouge and then Jefferson Barracks, Missouri. It was then to Florida and duty in the Third Seminole War. From 1851–55, Van Dorn was posted at New Orleans, from where he served as secretary of the East Pascagoula Military Asylum.

On March 3, 1855, he was promoted captain and transferred to the recently constituted 2d U.S. Cavalry, one of the two elite mounted regiments organized by Secretary of War, Jefferson Davis, with the mission of bringing peace and order to the frontier. Captain Van Dorn's company was posted to Camp Cooper, Texas. On July 1, 1857, he participated in a skirmish against the Comanches. Two years—1856–58—were spent at Camp Colorado, and on October 1, 1858, he led an attack on a Washita village in Indian Territory, in which he was struck by four arrows. On May 3, 1859, while posted at Camp Colorado, he again engaged the Comanches, this time at Nessentunga. He was promoted major on June 28, 1860, and three weeks after Mississippi's withdrawal from the Union, Van Dorn resigned his commission in the "Old Army" dated January 31, 1861. He was named brigadier general of Mississippi state troops and in early February was made major general and placed in command of the state troops, succeeding Jefferson Davis, who had been elected provisional president of the Confederacy.

On March 16 Van Dorn was commissioned colonel of cavalry in the Confederate army and briefly commanded the garrisons at Forts Jackson and St. Philip, guardians of the Mississippi River approach to New Orleans. Some four weeks later on April 11, he was named to command the Department of Texas. In rapid-fire order he captured *Star of the West* at Galveston (April 20); five days later received the surrender at Saluria of seven companies of United States regulars; and on May 9, near San Antonio, compelled six companies of the 8th U.S. Infantry to lay down their arms. His Texas successes earned him promotion to brigadier general on June 5.

The War Department had high expectations for Van Dorn and on August 14 he was ordered to turn over

Not precisely dated, this portrait of Van Dorn in Federal uniform probably shows him as major of the 2d U.S. Cavalry, but he may have worn the uniform briefly in his early days of Confederate service. (Mississippi Department of Archives and History, Jackson)

A profile variant apparently taken at the same sitting as the first Van Dorn portrait.
(Library of Congress)

Van Dorn's best known portrait in uniform, and probably his last. (National Archives)

his Texas responsibilities to his second in command and to hasten to Richmond. He arrived in the capital city in mid-September. Promoted major general to rank from September 19, Van Dorn reported to General Joseph E. Johnston and on October 4 took charge of the Army of the Potomac's First Division, then camped on Bull Run. He led the division until January 13, 1862, when he was detached and returned to the trans-Mississippi where on his January 29 arrival in Little Rock he assumed command of the recently constituted Trans-Mississippi District.

In late February he headed for the Boston Mountains where on March 3 he took charge of the sixteen-thousand-man Army of the West. The next day he put his columns in motion by forced marches, expecting to overwhelm Samuel Ryan Curtis' army. Alerted to Van Dorn's approach, Curtis regrouped his four scattered divisions and posted his ten thousand, five hundred soldiers on the bluffs overlooking Little Sugar Creek. Van Dorn made a night march and, on March 7–8, the Battle of Pea Ridge raged. By noon on the second day, Van Dorn lost his nerve and the Confederates abandoned the field and retreated south of the Boston Mountains.

Van Dorn led his Army of the West across the Mississippi as reinforcements for the Army of the Mississippi, and dropped his responsibilities as district commander. He reached Corinth on April 23, two weeks after the Confederate defeat at Shiloh, and reported to General P.G.T. Beauregard. During the Siege of Corinth (April 29–May 30), Van Dorn and his troops—posted in the rifle-pits east of the town—three times moved out to assail Major General John Pope's Army of the Mississippi at Farmington. On May 4 and again on the 9th, the Yankees pulled back. Then, on the 22nd, when Van Dorn's army was to trigger an all-out attack by the Confederates, he and his generals got lost and Beauregard scrubbed the attack.

On the night of May 29 the Confederates evacuated Corinth and regrouped. On June 28 Van Dorn was named to command the Department of Southern Mississippi and East Louisiana and rushed to Vicksburg. Flag-Officer David G. Farragut's deep-water fleet had captured New Orleans and ascended the Mississippi and before daybreak on the 28th (the day Van Dorn reached Vicksburg) fought its way upstream past the "Hill City" river batteries. On July 1 the river gunboats arrived from upriver and, except for the three miles of the Mississippi under the

Vicksburg guns, the Federals controlled the great river from source to mouth. Van Dorn rallied the defenders; the ironclad ram *Arkansas* sortied; the river stage fell; and in late July the Union threat was mastered and the fleets recoiled. The ocean-going ships retreated downstream and the river squadrons headed up the Mississippi to Memphis.

Van Dorn's military success was dimmed by a political miscue on July 4, when he declared martial law in a number of Mississippi counties and Louisiana parishes. The resulting howl reached Richmond and though Van Dorn was a native Mississippian, President Davis found it necessary to replace Van Dorn with Lieutenant General John C. Pemberton. Pemberton reached Jackson and assumed command of the department on October 14.

Meanwhile, Van Dorn had marched against Major General William S. Rosecrans' twenty-two-thousand-man army posted in and around Corinth. A savage two-day battle (October 3–4) ended in Confederate defeat. This was the second time that Van Dorn had been bested in a major battle in which the Confederates had the heavier battalions. The Corinth fight and the ensuing retreat caused much bitterness among the Confederates, and Brigadier General John S. Bowen preferred serious charges against Van Dorn at a court of inquiry. The court, as to be expected, held that the evidence "fully disproves every allegation…."

On December 12, General Pemberton named Van Dorn to command his cavalry. This decision by Pemberton demonstrated that he was a keen judge of character. Van Dorn, a mediocre or worse army commander, proved to be a hard-hitting, first-rate cavalry leader. His Holly Springs raid (December 17–28) destroyed a major Union depot with hundreds of thousands of dollars in supplies and in conjunction with Bedford Forrest's West Tennessee raid, derailed U.S. Grant's initial campaign aimed at destruction of Pemberton's army and capture of Vicksburg.

Van Dorn and his mounted corps were transferred from north Mississippi to Middle Tennessee in late January and early February 1863. There he reported to General Braxton Bragg, established headquarters at Columbia, and assumed the task of guarding the Army of Tennessee's left. Van Dorn aggressively carried out his mission, crushing the twenty-eight-hundred-man Union column led by Colonel John Coburn at Thompson's Station on March 5 and capturing more than twelve hundred prisoners. Two weeks later on March 25, Forrest's division, under orders from Van Dorn, attacked the Federals at Brentwood and captured seven hundred and eighty five prisoners and sixteen wagons and teams. On April 10 Van Dorn's forced reconnaissance drove the Federals back into the fortifications covering the Franklin approaches. Meanwhile, Van Dorn had transferred his headquarters to Spring Hill, which was closer to the enemy. There his relations with Forrest soured and there was a confrontation. Both drew their swords before passions cooled.

Van Dorn, short of stature, lithe of figure, sensuous-eyed, was a ladies' man. The general's frequent riding companion while at Spring Hill was Jessie McKissack Peters, the young wife of Dr. James Bodley Peters, a man in his late forties. On May 7, 1863, Dr. Peters called on the general in his quarters in the Martin Cheairs house and shot and killed Van Dorn as he sat at his desk. Peters fled to Union-held Franklin. He justified the killing, testifying that Van Dorn had "violated the sanctity of his home." Van Dorn was first buried at Spring Hill, Alabama, in his wife's family plot, but in 1902 his remains were sent to Port Gibson and interred in Wintergreen Cemetery.

Edwin C. Bearss

Hartje, Robert G., *Van Dorn: The Life and Times of a Confederate General* (Nashville, 1967).

Hooker, Joseph, *Mississippi*, Vol. VII in Evans, *Confederate Military History*.

Miller, Emily Van Dorn, *A Soldier's Honor: With Reminiscences of Major General Earl Van Dorn, by His Comrades* (New York, 1902).

Vaughan as colonel of the 13th Tennessee, probably in early 1863. (Albert G. Shaw Collection, Virginia Historical Society, Richmond)

✷ Alfred Jefferson Vaughan, Jr. ✷

Alfred Jefferson Vaughan, Jr., was born in Dinwiddie County, Virginia, May 10, 1830. He graduated from the Virginia Military Institute July 4, 1851, as the corps' first captain and with a degree in civil engineering. He headed west, first locating in St. Joseph, Missouri, and then California, where he became deputy United States surveyor for the southern district of that state. Next, he became private secretary to Alfred Cumming—an uncle of the future Brigadier General Alfred Cumming, C.S.A.—and traveled to the upper Missouri River country to negotiate treaties with the native Americans to permit construction of a railroad across their lands.

When he returned from the west in 1856 he settled on a Marshall County, Mississippi, farm. Vaughan was against secession, but when first his adopted state of Mississippi and then his native state of Virginia left the Union, he cast his lot with the Confederacy. He raised a company, the Dixie Rifles, but since Mississippi had already raised its quota and was unable to provide needed arms and accoutrements, he and most of the Dixie Rifles crossed into Tennessee. At Jackson, on June 4, Vaughan was mustered into state service as captain of Company F, 13th Tennessee Infantry. When the troops elected their field and staff officers, Vaughan was chosen lieutenant colonel.

The regiment was soon called to Randolph, forty-five miles upstream from Memphis on the Mississippi River, where it was assigned to the River Brigade. On July 26, the 13th Tennessee was transferred by steamboats to New Madrid, Missouri, where on August 13 it was inspected and accepted into Confederate service. Three weeks later, on September 7, Colonel Vaughan and his troops arrived at Columbus, Kentucky, which had been occupied by the Confederates only seventy-two hours before.

Vaughan with his regiment, commanded by Colonel John V. Wright, was assigned to Brigadier General Gideon J. Pillow's division, and participated in his first fight with the enemy at Belmont on November 7. The regiment, on being alerted to the attack on the Belmont encampment, boarded a steamboat and was rushed across the Mississippi to the Missouri side and received the first brunt of the Yankee attack. In the fighting, Vaughan had two horses shot from under him and was cited by Colonel Wright for "most gallantly discharging his duties."

On December 4, 1861, Wright, who had been elected to represent Tennessee in the Confederate Congress, resigned his commission and Vaughan became the regiment's colonel on the same day. With the Confederates' March 3, 1862, evacuation of Columbus, he and his troops moved first to Union City and then Corinth, Mississippi. Vaughan's regiment took up the march for Pittsburg Landing on April 3 as one of the four regiments and one artillery company in Colonel R.M. Russell's brigade, Major General Leonidas Polk's corps. At Shiloh on both the 6th and 7th, Vaughan and his Tennesseans saw bitter fighting. On the first day, they charged units of Major General William T. Sherman's division camped near Shiloh Church, routed the 57th Ohio, and captured the cannon of Captain A.C. Waterhouse's six-gun battery. The next day, they battled fresh troops of the Army of the Ohio southwest of Duncan's field. Vaughan again earned the commendation of his commanding officer, who reported that he exhibited great bravery under fire.

During the Corinth Siege (April 28–May 30), the regiment was reorganized in accordance with the "Bounty and Furlough Law" and the men showed their confidence in Vaughan by reelecting him colonel. On the night of May 29, the Confederate evacuated Corinth and withdrew to Tupelo, where in mid-June, General Braxton Bragg replaced General P.G.T. Beauregard as the Army of the Mississippi's leader. Early in July there was a reorganization that brigaded Vaughan's regiment with the 12th, 47th, and 154th Tennessee under Colonel Preston Smith and assigned the brigade to Major General B. Franklin Cheatham's division.

Following the army's movement by rail from Tupelo to Chattanooga, Smith's brigade was detached

Brigadier General Vaughan late in 1864 or early 1865, following the loss of his leg in action. (Courtesy of Herb Peck, Jr.)

Vaughan's progressing baldness is evident in his war pictures. This image is either an early postwar shot in uniform, or else was taken just as the conflict was closing. (*Confederate Veteran*, V)

to Knoxville on August 10 and assigned to Brigadier General Patrick R. Cleburne's division of Major General Edmund Kirby Smith's army. Vaughan led his regiment into Kentucky and on August 30, helped rout an enemy army at Richmond. During the first phase of the fight, Cleburne was wounded and Smith took charge of his division and Vaughan of the brigade. His conduct that day earned for Vaughan a commendation from his immediate superior. The brigade rejoined Cheatham's division at Harrodsburg just before the Perryville battle. Vaughan and his men were in reserve and, except for receiving some artillery fire, saw no action. The army then retreated back to Tennessee through Cumberland Gap, and late November found Vaughan at Murfreesboro.

An outbreak of smallpox in the regiment caused it to be detached, but it rejoined the army on December 28. Meanwhile, General Smith had been hospitalized at Chattanooga and Vaughan, as senior officer present, commanded the brigade when it advanced and assailed the enemy at Stones River on December 31. Although initially repulsed, Vaughan recoiled, reformed, and pressed ahead, driving the Federals across the Wilkinson Pike, through the cedars, and nearly to the Nashville Pike, earning a commendation from General Cleburne. On January 2, Smith reported for duty, and Vaughan resumed command of his regiment.

In March 1863, following the Confederate withdrawal behind the Duck River line, Vaughan oversaw the consolidation of the 13th and 154th Tennessee. He and his consolidated regiment saw lots of rain but no combat during the Tullahoma Campaign (June 23–July 4). At Chickamauga, although the brigade saw desperate fighting during the early afternoon of September 19, it participated in the evening advance in support of Cleburne's attack. About the time that General Smith was killed, Vaughan and his men captured the colors of the 77th Pennsylvania and three hundred soldiers, who were turned over to General Cheatham. With Smith dead, Vaughan, as senior officer, led the brigade on the 20th, a day in which the unit was "not actively engaged."

On November 10 Vaughan was promoted to brigadier general. Meanwhile, an army reorganization had resulted in the breakup of Cheatham's division and Vaughan's brigade had been assigned to Major General Thomas C. Hindman's division. Vaughan and his Tennesseans were routed from Missionary Ridge, November 25, and retreated, along with the army, to winter quarters at Dalton. On February 20 Cheatham's division was reconstituted. Including Vaughan's brigade, it was now assigned to Lieutenant General William J. Hardee's corps.

Vaughan and his brigade took the field on February 20. They were rushed by rail and boat to western Alabama as reinforcements for Lieutenant General Leonidas Polk's small army. Unable to cope with Major General William T. Sherman's legions, Polk had abandoned Jackson and Meridian, Mississippi, and retreated eastward to Demopolis, Alabama. By the time Vaughan and his men reached Demopolis, Sherman was en route back to Vicksburg, and Vaughan's Tennesseans entrained and returned to Dalton.

The next time Vaughan engaged Sherman there was no respite. On May 7, Sherman's "army group" advanced and engaged the Army of Tennessee, now led by General Joseph E. Johnston. From May 9 until the end of June, Vaughan was never far from the enemy. He skirmished with the foe at Resaca on May 15, at Adairsville on the 17th, and at New Hope Church on May 26–30. On June 8–9 he supported the cavalry covering the Confederate left in front of Lost Mountain; and on June 27 he and his brigade, along with George Maney's, held the Dead Angle on Cheatham Hill when it was assailed by the Army of the Cumberland's best. On July 4, two days after Johnston's army had evacuated its Kennesaw Mountain line, Vaughan was badly wounded in the Smyrna riflepits. Fragments from an incoming artillery shell so mangled his left foot that it had to be amputated at the ankle. This was the general's first life-threatening wound, though he had had eight horses shot from under him.

Incapacitated for further service in the field and, with the end of the war the next year, Vaughan was paroled at Gainesville, Alabama, May 10, 1865. He returned to Mississippi and farmed until 1872, taking the lead in the state's Grange movement. In 1873 he relocated to Memphis and opened a mercantile house. Five years later, Shelby County voters elected him clerk of the criminal court. He was reelected in 1882. In 1897, he was elected commander of the Tennessee Division, United Confederate Veterans, a post he held until his death in Indianapolis, Indiana, October 1, 1899. His body was returned to Mississippi for services and burial.

Edwin C. Bearss

Porter, James D., *Tennessee*, Vol. VIII in Evans, *Confederate Military History.*

⋆ *John Crawford Vaughn* ⋆

John Crawford Vaughn, a Tennessean, served in military departments from the Mississippi River to North Carolina, although he spent most of his career as brigadier general commanding mounted and dismounted cavalry in eastern Tennessee and southwestern Virginia.

Vaughn was born in Roane County, Tennessee, on February 24, 1824. He served as captain in the 5th Tennessee Volunteers during the Mexican War, returning to East Tennessee to become a merchant in the town of Sweetwater. In 1861 he witnessed the fall of Fort Sumter in South Carolina and hurried home to raise a regiment of volunteers for the Confederacy. On July 6, 1861, he became colonel of the 3d Tennessee Volunteers, mustered in at Lynchburg, Virginia, and was assigned to the army of General Joseph E. Johnston at Harpers Ferry and Manassas.

Vaughn experienced perhaps his brightest moments early in the war. He received praise from then-Colonel A.P. Hill for marching soldiers thirty-six miles in sixteen hours to disperse Federal troops and burn a bridge along the Baltimore & Ohio Railroad at New Creek, Virginia, on July 19, 1861. President Jefferson Davis congratulated General Johnston "on the brilliant movement of Vaughn's command" in breaking the line of the B&O. Vaughn's overall efforts during the Manassas Campaign earned him special mention in Johnston's report.

Vaughn subsequently became assigned to Major General E. Kirby Smith in East Tennessee—a difficult job in a countryside that was familiar but hostile, because it harbored Unionists who did not hesitate to ambush the Confederates. Vaughn earned promotion to brigadier general on October 3, to rank from September 22, 1862, and was sent to Lieutenant General John Pemberton's Department of the Mississippi. He arrived a few weeks ahead of the assault by Union Major General William Tecumseh Sherman on Chickasaw Bayou and Bluffs (December 27–29, 1862). Vaughn commanded the Confederate left, where heavy abatis prevented the approach of the enemy. Pemberton cited the 60th, 62d, and 81st Tennesseans under Vaughn, who, although not prominently involved, performed satisfactorily.

Fortunes of the Confederates in general and Vaughn in particular worsened as the Vicksburg Campaign continued. Pemberton ordered Vaughn's brigade to anchor an effort to contest the advance of Major General Ulysses S. Grant's Union army at a railroad bridge over the Big Black River on May 17, 1863. Positioned in the center, the brigade broke. Grant's men soon sealed the entire Confederate army into Vicksburg for an extended siege that lasted until July 3. Vaughn's performance in command of the upper defenses of the city earned the gratitude of Pemberton and eased the sting of earlier criticism for action at the Big Black. When Pemberton surrendered the city Vaughn became a prisoner. He was paroled, shortly exchanged, and allowed to return to service on July 16. He went to East Tennessee in charge of a mounted brigade and, while assigned to Lieutenant General James Longstreet's I Corps during the winter of 1863–64, performed reconnaissance on Union positions. Vaughn's brigade remained in the state when Longstreet's Corps returned to the Army of Northern Virginia.

No uniformed portrait of Vaughn has been found. This is a postwar civilian view. (Evans, *Confederate Military History*)

The effectiveness of the brigade deteriorated as the war continued. Vaughn continually replenished his ranks from East Tennessee but apparently could not mold the recruits into a dependable fighting force. Vaughn's brigade increasingly consisted of undisciplined and poorly supplied men—what even Confederates referred to as "wild" cavalry. During April 1864, Major General Simon Bolivar Buckner reported the condition of Vaughn's brigade as "lamentable" because of supply shortages and noted it had to be sent to North Carolina to find forage. Others blamed Vaughn more than the Confederate supply system for the condition of the men. An inspector general claimed that Vaughn "had no idea of discipline" and that the men should fight dismounted until they received better leadership. The Tennessean did little to dispel his reputation. At the battle of Piedmont, Virginia (June 5, 1864), inaction by him and another officer contributed to the defeat and death of Brigadier General W.E. "Grumble" Jones. When Lieutenant General Jubal A. Early arrived in the Shenandoah Valley to begin his campaign in June 1864, he petitioned Richmond for a cavalry officer other than Vaughn. However, the brigade remained with Early on his march to Washington, D.C., with Vaughn sustaining a wound near Martinsburg. Vaughn's men were sent back to southwestern Virginia in September—most of them, as Early noted, having already left without permission.

If nothing else, Vaughn proved tenacious. After recovering from his wound in Tennessee, he continued to patrol the Cumberland Gap and guard the Confederate salt works at Saltville, Virginia. His men skirmished with Union soldiers on a number of occasions and were often stampeded, although it would be only fair to note that they typically served without food, supplies, or pay. After Brigadier General John Hunt Morgan died in early September 1864, Vaughn succeeded him as commander of the Department of Western Virginia and Eastern Tennessee. Vaughn continued in Confederate service to the bitter end, deciding to take his men to Joseph Johnston in North Carolina after learning of General R.E. Lee's surrender at Appomattox. Vaughn's brigade then joined three others as escort for President Jefferson Davis' unsuccessful attempt to reach the Trans-Mississippi; the brigadier was present at the council of war that the President held at Abbeville, South Carolina. Vaughn finally surrendered and was paroled in Washington, Georgia, on May 9, 1865.

After the war Vaughn returned to Tennessee and served one term in the state senate. He then spent the rest of his life in southern Georgia as a merchant and planter. He died near Thomasville, Georgia, on September 10, 1875.

William Alan Blair

Early, Jubal Anderson, *Autobiographical Sketch and Narrative of the War Between the States,* (Wilmington, 1989).

Porter, James D., *Tennessee*, Vol. VIII in Evans, *Confederate Military History.*

⋆ *John Bordenave Villepigue* ⋆

A South Carolina native of French descent, John Bordenave Villepigue was born at Camden on July 2, 1830. He graduated from West Point in 1854, where he finished twenty-second among the forty-six graduates, and was brevetted a 2d lieutenant in the 2d Dragoons. He served in Missouri and in the territories of Kansas and Nebraska before being promoted to 2d lieutenant on March 3, 1855. Later that year he participated in an expedition against the Sioux, and in 1856 he joined the column destined for Fort Lookout, Dakota Territory. Promoted to 1st lieutenant on May 27, 1857, he participated in the 1857–1858 Utah Expedition. After a brief assignment to the cavalry school at Carlisle, Pennsylvania, Villepigue returned to Utah, where he submitted his resignation on March 31, 1861.

Villepigue entered the Confederate Regular Army as a captain of artillery and was assigned to Pensacola, Florida. By the end of September, he had been promoted to lieutenant colonel in the provisional army and given command of the 1st Georgia Battalion, which included both Georgia and Mississippi troops. The unit garrisoned Fort McRee, which defended the mouth of Pensacola harbor. On November 22, Federal gunners in Fort Pickens and aboard two warships began a two-day bombardment of Fort McRee, Fort Barrancas, and the Pensacola Navy Yard. Both sides suffered considerable damage, and a piece of shrapnel struck Villepigue in the arm. Of Villepigue's performance, Major General Braxton Bragg reported: "An educated soldier, possessing in an eminent degree the love and confidence of his officers and men, he had been specially selected for this important and perilous post. The result fully

vindicates the fortunate choice, and presents for our admiration, blended in perfect harmony, the modest but heroic soldier with the humble but confiding Christian." Now clearly a favorite of Bragg, the latter appointed Villepigue to his staff as chief of engineers and artillery.

On January 31, 1862, Villepigue's battalion was reorganized and became the 36th Georgia Infantry Regiment with Villepigue as its colonel. When Bragg transferred his departmental headquarters to Mobile, Villepigue found himself in command at Pensacola until the town was evacuated and its garrison ordered to Mobile. When Bragg departed for Corinth, Villepigue briefly found himself in charge of the defense of Mobile until he, too, was ordered to join Bragg at Corinth.

Promoted to brigadier general on March 18, 1862, to rank from March 13, Villepigue immediately caught the attention of General Pierre G.T. Beauregard. Deeming Villepigue "the most energetic young officer available," Beauregard assigned him on March 25 to command Fort Pillow, located on the east bank of the Mississippi River about forty-five miles north of Memphis. When word of his transfer arrived, Villepigue was serving on Bragg's staff at Corinth. When he issued his orders of reassignment to Villepigue, Bragg noted: "The regret which is felt at parting with this accomplished and gallant officer is compensated by a knowledge of his transfer to a command where his industry, ability, and professional skill will be eminently useful to our cause." Villepigue

The only known uniformed photo of Villepigue is prewar, dating from the late 1850s and showing him as a lieutenant in the 2d U.S. Dragoons. (Museum of the Confederacy, Richmond, Va.)

conducted a masterful defense of Fort Pillow against monumentally superior Federal forces, both afloat and ashore. When ordered to evacuate the post in June because of Union naval supremacy, Villepigue blew up the fortifications and successfully withdrew the garrison on June 4.

Although Brigadier General Daniel Ruggles ordered him to take command of the land forces at Memphis, Villepigue notified him that "the only effect of keeping an armed force around the city will be to make the enemy bombard it." Besides, Beauregard had already instructed Villepigue to organize a defensive force for the protection of the railroad depot at Genada, Mississippi. To accomplish this task, Villepigue promptly assumed a position where the Mississippi Central Railroad crossed the Tallahatchie River near Abbeville. In late June, when Ruggles left his sub-department for points south, General Bragg replaced him with Villepigue, who was now charged with the defense of the Mississippi Central Railroad between the Tallahatchie River and the thirty-third parallel. On August 12, Bragg wrote Major General Earl Van Dorn: "It is with deep regret I see you lose General Villepigue, as I consider him equal to any officer in our service."

During the first week of September Villepigue's command moved to Holly Springs. Organized into a brigade, his troops were assigned to the division of Major General Mansfield Lovell on September 8. As part of Van Dorn's army, the division participated in the Corinth Campaign in October, Villepigue was praised for his participation in the assault against the Union fortifications about that town and for his coverage of the Confederate withdrawal after Van Dorn's attacks proved unsuccessful.

Villepigue's performance at Fort Pillow and during the Corinth Campaign clearly demonstrated that he was qualified to exercise independent command. Shortly after Lieutenant General John C. Pemberton took charge of the Department of Mississippi and East Louisiana, he ordered on October 24, 1862, that Villepigue assume command of the Third District of that department, with headquarters at Port Hudson, Louisiana.

It has been stated that following Van Dorn's retreat from Corinth, "a long and serious illness" forced Villepigue to give up an active field command and that situation prompted Pemberton to send Villepigue to Port Hudson. Notwithstanding, no evidence has been found that indicates that he was plagued by medical problems when he arrived at Port Hudson in late October, and it is certain that nothing prevented his immediate assumption of command of the district. Within a few days, however, he succumbed to a fever. He lingered for several days before dying on the evening of November 9. The cause of death was variously reported as typhoid, pneumonia, cholera morbus, and simply "fever." Brigadier General William N.R. Beall resumed command of the Third District immediately. On the afternoon of November 10, Beall had Villepigue's body escorted to the railroad depot for shipment to Camden, South Carolina, where he was buried. Beall also ordered all officers to "wear the usual badge of mourning for thirty days." Villepigue's last name is often spelled Villepique.

Lawrence L. Hewitt

Capers, Ellison, *South Carolina*, Vol. V in Evans, *Confederate Military History.*

Hewitt, Lawrence Lee, *Port Hudson, Confederate Bastion on the Mississippi* (Baton Rouge, 1987).

⋆ *Henry Harrison Walker* ⋆

Henry Walker as colonel of the 40th Virginia early in 1863. (Cook Collection, Valentine Museum, Richmond, Va.)

Henry Harrison Walker was born in Sussex County, Virginia, on October 15, 1832, at "Elmwood." In hopes of pursuing a military career, he secured appointment to the United States Military Academy from his native state. Walker's performance at West Point showed little promise; his first year he finished thirty-second out of sixty, and by graduation in 1853 he had dropped to forty-first out of fifty-two. Cadet Walker had the worst marks of any graduate that year in engineering and was fifty-first in artillery. His strong point was infantry tactics, in which he stood thirty-eighth. Walker also scraped through in conduct, for which he was in the bottom ten percent for the whole academy. His 196 demerits left him perilously close to the limit of 200. Among his classmates were John B. Hood and Philip H. Sheridan.

Despite the gruesome West Point statistics, Walker's career moved evenly through the prewar years. He served as a lieutenant of infantry for the entire period but enjoyed some unusual duties. After service in Kentucky and New Mexico Lieutenant Walker acted as an aide to the governor of Kansas, where he saw action in the violence that continuously disrupted that region before the war. He then moved west to San Francisco, where he spent three years as a staff officer away from the traditional frontier. Walker resigned on May 3, 1861, to join his state in the forthcoming conflict. He initially served as a captain of infantry, with rank backdated to March 16. He quickly obtained a staff position, serving as acting assistant adjutant general to Brigadier General Theophilus H. Holmes around Fredericksburg.

On December 2, 1861, Walker received appointment as lieutenant colonel of the 40th Virginia Infantry, a unit with which he had no previous ties. The regiment was from the Northern Neck, and Walker was from Southside Virginia. General Holmes perhaps influenced the selection by effusively praising Walker as "genial, intelligent, and zealous in the cause we have at heart."

Before the regiment ever really saw action, Walker was part of a peculiar juggling of officers. He took temporary command of the 5th Alabama Battalion in April 1862, but that mysterious assignment was of short duration. He returned to the Virginians in time for the Seven Days' Campaign. The unit served at Mechanicsville with gallantry. The following day, June 27, Walker and the 40th Virginia were in the center of the Confederate assault at Gaines' Mill, participating as part of Charles W. Fields' brigade. The entire brigade suffered heavy casualties, and among the injured was Lieutenant Colonel Walker. According to Brigadier General Field, Walker was closer to the enemy than any officer or man in the brigade when he fell twice wounded.

Because his wounds unfitted Walker for active field duty, at least temporarily, he resigned on August 26, 1862, citing the wounds and the depleted condition of his regiment. He particularly desired new duty under his old benefactor, Holmes. Instead Walker languished in Richmond after being promoted to the temporary rank of colonel in the Provisional Army of the Confederate States. He commanded a camp for convalescents and in May 1863 was active in the defense of the capital with a City Guard of seven companies.

The situation in Field's old brigade, meanwhile, induced the Confederate high command to seek an officer to lead the unit permanently. Field had been wounded at Second Manassas, and for the next eleven months the men had been under the leadership of colonel John M. Brockenbrough of the 40th Virginia. He was "much loved & respected," according to his subordinates, but the brigade had posted uninspired showings. Rather than promote Brockenbrough, Walker was returned to take command as he knew the brigade from previous service.

Walker's promotion to brigadier general occurred on and dated from July 1, 1863. There was much ill feeling among the officers of the brigade and especially from Colonel Brockenbrough, who felt himself the victim of a plot. He belittled Walker as "a mere youth"— and accused him of deserting the 40th Virginia in time of danger. More recently the colonel found Walker guilty of engaging in "puerile exertions" to secure command of the brigade.

Brockenbrough resigned, and Walker calmly brought order to the organization under his command. The remnants of James J. Archer's brigade temporarily joined Walker in an unsatisfactory amalgamation.

The post-Gettysburg lull kept Walker from exercising his new authority in earnest until the following May, when he handled his brigade (reduced only to Virginians by then) with skill at the Battle of the Wilderness. As part of Major General Henry Heth's division, Walker's brigade engaged Union troops during an expedition to the Po River on May 10, 1864, as part of the dramatic events around Spotsylvania Court House. Casualties were light, but General Walker had his foot shattered. He was taken to the rear, where Surgeon William R. Weisiger of the 22d Virginia Battalion amputated the foot, and Walker's career on the battlefields ended.

After a period of convalescence Walker again did odd jobs around Richmond. He served on court-martial duty for a time, then on February 18, 1865, was ordered to take command of the defenses of the Richmond & Danville Railroad, numbering about twelve hundred troops. On April 2 he took charge of the post at Danville and apprehensively eyed the approaching armies. On April 10, in the chaos after Appomattox, Walker wired General P.G.T. Beauregard for personal help: "I have what is likely to be a very active command, and only one foot; but will do my best if you cannot come."

General Walker spent the early years after the war "buffeting about," by his own admission, and had difficulty adjusting to the life of a civilian. He felt compelled to escape the "Poor South," as he called it, and had settled on the outskirts of New York City by 1867. Walker took up the career of an investment broker, with apparent success, and remained distant from post-war discussions and memoirs. His only known participation in the commemoration of the war was in 1890, when he journeyed to Richmond to be present for the unveiling of the R.E. Lee statue.

Henry H. Walker died at the age of seventy-nine on March 22, 1912, in Morristown, New Jersey. He was buried there in Evergreen Cemetery.

Robert E. L. Krick

Hotchkiss, Jedediah, *Virginia*, Vol. III in Evans, *Confederate Military History.*

⁎ James Alexander Walker ⁎

James A. Walker was born on August 27, 1832, near Mt. Meridian in Augusta County, Virginia. He attended the Virginia Military Institute for nearly four years and was within a few weeks of graduation in 1852 when he ran afoul of Thomas J. Jackson in an incident that came close to rearranging American history. Professor Jackson sternly disciplined Cadet Walker in an affair that seemed from available evidence to show Jackson in a poor light. Although Walker stood very high in his class and had all but completed his education, he was expelled from the institute; in 1872 someone thought better of the deed and Walker received his diploma. In the aftermath of his ordeal in 1852 Walker attempted to kill Jackson with a brick hurled from a dormitory window in outrage over his mistreatment and then talked of shooting his scrupulously rigid professor.

For a time after his misfortune at V.M.I. James Walker taught school, then he worked on a railroad engineering team in western Virginia and Kentucky. In 1854 Walker studied law at the University of Virginia and—in Jackson's absence—completed his education successfully. For the rest of the decade the young lawyer practiced in Pulaski County. He married Sarah Ann Poage there in 1858. When excitement over John Brown's incursion riveted Virginia's attention, Walker raised a local company known as the "Pulaski Guards" and became its captain. Captain Walker led the guards into state service in April 1861. The company went on to forge a distinguished record as Company C of the 4th Virginia Infantry of the famous Stonewall Brigade, but Captain Walker's career took him up and away from the guards early in the war. He was promoted to lieutenant colonel of the 13th Virginia Infantry—A.P. Hill's original regiment—on May 17, 1861.

Eleven months later Walker became colonel of the 13th and commanded it with marked distinction for more than a year at that rank.

Lieutenant Colonel Walker arrived at Manassas just too late to participate in the first major battle in Virginia, but he missed few others during the next four years. In the 1862 Shenandoah Valley Campaign that made his old adversary, Major General T.J. "Stonewall" Jackson, immortal, Walker fought brilliantly, performing particularly well at Cross Keys. At Malvern Hill during the Seven Days' Campaign an artillery round buried itself right under the colonel, "elevating him a few feet." At Sharpsburg a piece of shell hit Walker, and his horse was killed under him (the Confederate government paid a $350 reimbursement for the animal). At Fredericksburg and Chancellorsville in May 1863, in fact on virtually every field contested by Lee's army, James A. Walker could be seen in the midst of the action.

Subordinates and superiors found much to praise about Colonel Walker. A private in the 13th reported that Walker "was rough in his manner, a very large man with massive head, and fearless in battle" and noted that he endeared himself to some soldiers who serenaded headquarters by treating them to a tot of very fine whisky. The men in the regiment called Walker "Old Bull Dog," and when he left to assume a larger command, they expressed their dismay at losing him in moving fashion. The colonel's peers displayed their favorable impression of Walker when twenty-seven of them signed a letter on November 20, 1862, urging

---

No uniformed portrait of James A. Walker has surfaced. This pose is considerably postwar.(*Confederate Veteran*, X)

his promotion. Long and close service with Walker had convinced them of his worth: "[We] felt it due to the public as well as just to the individual" to support his advancement to rank of brigadier general.

During early 1863 a chorus of endorsements from general officers and others poured into Richmond on Walker's behalf. Seventy members of the Virginia legislature wrote to President Jefferson Davis in January, citing their native son's qualifications and his successful service as acting commander of his own (Early's) brigade and Trimble's too. On January 23 Major General Jubal Early wrote to Major General Richard S. Ewell soliciting support for Walker's advancement, saying: "The whole Division is anxious for Walker's promotion." On the same day Early also addressed a letter directly to the secretary of war that enthused of Walker, "No colonel in the service…has done better or more fighting…." General R.E. Lee's endorsement on the document used a nearly identical sentence and added that Walker "has proved himself worthy of promotion." Major General Arnold Elzey insisted that "Virginia has not a better Colonel in the Army," and Ewell honored Early's prompting by "heartily" concurring in "one of the very few promotions I have recommended."

Perhaps the most interesting recommendation came by way of Major General A.P. Hill, who added to his own kudos this phrase: "He has already been strongly urged by Gen Jackson…." On Hill's letter Lee wrote in his own hand, "I concur." In predictable result, James A. Walker became a brigadier general on May 16, 1863, ranking from the previous day, and took command of the famous old Stonewall Brigade. After a time the soldiers began calling the general "Stonewall Jim." Few knew the irony involved—that Walker was now sharing at second hand the fame and the name of the man he had hoped to kill in 1852. General Walker first led his new brigade in the bitter chaos on the Confederate left at Gettysburg near Culp's Hill. Five months later he commanded it at Mine Run, where a captain saw him galloping through the confused Southern ranks. When the general directed an orderly to take his spare horses to the rear, the man reasonably enough asked, "Where is the rear, General?" "Damned if I know," Walker replied, "but take them out of here."

Randolph Barton of the brigade, who sometimes served close to the general, insisted that "General Walker enjoyed the thrilling excitement of battle." Barton told of Walker's narrow escape from capture or death at the Wilderness. When the brigade briskly repulsed a minor enemy thrust at Spotsylvania on May 11, 1864, Walker exclaimed in delight, "If this is war, may it be eternal." The next day,

however, was his worst of the war. Walker had moved his troops out of a swampy mire near the nose of the Confederate "Mule Shoe" salient, leading to a "sharp altercation" with Ewell. Early the next morning a Federal tidal wave poured over the position. At the first hint of the onset Walker bellowed, "'Fall in!'" in a voice that could have been heard half a mile. " Soon thereafter a bullet hit the general's arm with tremendous force, "producing terrible shock and great pain," according to an artillery captain standing beside him. After the war Walker had to ask the captain whether the wound had knocked him down—"the shock was so great that he did not know himself." The bullet doubtless saved General Walker from the captivity that befell most of his men that morning. Friends hurried him to the rear, where he had his "elbow joint cut out." Although Walker later managed to restore considerable use to the arm, this wound resulted in long convalescence and some impairment for the rest of his life.

General Walker recuperated in Pulaski County for two months. On July 16, 1864, he was ordered to assume command of the defense of the Richmond & Danville Railroad. He remained in that post until February 18, 1865, when Brigadier General H.H. "Mud" Walker, another officer crippled at Spotsylvania, assumed the command. James A. Walker returned to the Army of Northern Virginia and played an important role in its last offensive thrust, at Fort Stedman on March 25. Two weeks later he surrendered with the army at Appomattox.

After the war Walker farmed for a time in Pulaski County, then resumed the practice of law with notable success. He also engaged in the development of mineral interests in southwest Virginia. Walker earned considerable postwar prominence in the political arena. He was elected to the Virginia legislature in 1871; to the office of lieutenant governor in 1877; and to the United States House of Representatives in 1894 and 1896. Walker's election to the national congress came on the Republican ticket; he had switched parties because of strong convictions supporting a conservative money policy. In 1899 General Walker was nearly killed in a politically inspired shooting in a Bristol, Virginia, courtroom. He died on October 20, 1901, in Wytheville and was buried there in the East End Cemetery.

Robert K. Krick

Barton, Randolph, *Recollections* (New York, 1913).

Caldwell, Willie Walker, *Stonewall Jim* (New York, 1990).

Slemp, Bascom, *Addresses of Famous Southwest Virginians* (Ohio 1939).

⋆ John George Walker ⋆

Walker came of distinguished colonial Virginia ancestry. Born in Jefferson City, Cole County, Missouri, on July 22, 1822, the son of Missouri state treasurer John Walker, he was educated at the Jesuit College in St. Louis. On May 27, 1846, at the outbreak of the Mexican War, he was appointed 1st lieutenant of the 1st Mounted Rifles, United States Army, and was brevetted captain on August 1, 1847, for gallant and meritorious conduct in an affair at San Juan de los Llanos, Mexico. He took part in the battles of Contreras and Churubusco and was severely wounded at Molino del Rey. Walker remained in the army after the war, serving in New Mexico, Texas, Oregon, and California. He was promoted to captain on June 30, 1851, and resigned from the army at that rank on July 31, 1861.

On September 13, 1861, Walker was assigned to command as a colonel in an infantry brigade in Virginia, consisting of the 1st Arkansas, 2d Tennessee, and 12th North Carolina. "Colonel Walker is, I doubt not, a very competent officer," General Joseph E. Johnston wrote approvingly. "I knew him as an excellent captain." On December 21, 1861, Walker was nominated as a major of cavalry in the Confederate Regular Army, to rank from March 16, 1861. (He was not the Captain John G. Walker elected lieutenant colonel of the 8th Texas Cavalry, "Terry's Texas Rangers," in January 1862, as some biographical sketches state.)

Promoted to brigadier general in the provisional army on January 9, 1862, to take effect immediately, Walker served under Major General Theophilus H. Holmes in the Aquia District and in the Department of North Carolina. During the Seven Days' battles his brigade of thirty-six hundred effectives and two batteries were temporarily attached to Major General Benjamin Huger's division and was held in reserve before being sent elsewhere, returning to Holmes on the evening of June 29. The brigade was exposed to "exceedingly heavy fire" during the evening of the 30th from Federal batteries on Malvern Hill and gunboats on the James River but suffered only eleven wounded and one dead. Walker met with an incapacitating "painful accident," and Colonel Van H. Manning of the 3d Arkansas took command.

When General R.E. Lee began his campaign against Major General John Pope in northern Virginia, Walker was in command of a division of three brigades—his own, Robert Ransom's and Junius Daniel's—one of four divisions left behind to watch Major General George B. McClellan's Army of the Potomac until it was evacuated from Harrison's Landing. Leaving Daniel's brigade on the James, Walker rejoined the Army of Northern Virginia after Second Manassas with his remaining two brigades. He occupied Loudon Heights during Major General Thomas J. "Stonewall" Jackson's successful investment of the Federal garrison at Harpers Ferry and was the first to open artillery fire upon the enemy's batteries and troops along Bolivar Heights. His small division performed magnificently at Antietam on September 17, 1862; but it was one of his regimental commanders, Colonel John R. Cooke of the 27th North Carolina, who was singled out for praise in the reports of senior officers from Walker upward to Lee himself. Cooke was promoted to brigadier general and given Walker's former brigade.

On November 6, 1862, Lee wrote President Jefferson Davis that he was ordering Walker and Colonel S.D. Lee to report to the Adjutant General in Richmond, noting that "I feel that I am much weakened by the loss of these

John G. Walker in his Old Army uniform. No wartime portrait in Confederate costume has been found. (Tulane University Library, New Orleans, La.)

two officers,…but I hope the general service will be benfited." Although Davis replied that "Walker need not be sent" as was contemplated to the Trans-Mississippi Department and he was held in Richmond, Lee did not exercise the option and appointed Brigadier General Robert Ransom to command Walker's division. Promoted to major general to rank on November 8, 1862, to take rank immediately, Walker on November 11 was ordered to Little Rock, Arkansas, for duty under Major General Theophilus Holmes.

On December 23, 1862, Walker was assigned to command Brigadier General Henry McCulloch's division of Texas infantry; and it was known thereafter as Walker's Texas Division. The three brigades of twelve regiments during most of the war comprised the largest single unit of Texas troops in the conflict. The division made a reputation for long forced marches in good order from one threatened point to another in Arkansas and Louisiana and earned from the Federals the soubriquet of "Walker's Greyhounds." The fighting was often as fierce in the Trans-Mississippi as east of the river, and Walker's division participated in four hard-fought battles: Milliken's Bend, Mansfield (Sabine Cross Roads), and Pleasant Hill, Louisiana; and Jenkins' Ferry, Arkansas. "He [Walker] was beloved by his officers, almost adored by his men," noted the division's historian, Joseph P. Blessington, "a private soldier" in the command. "As a general, Walker is calm and cautious; does everything by rule; leaves nothing to chance…Nothing disturbs or unnerves him." Major General Richard Taylor, in his account of military operations in Louisiana in 1863, wrote of Walker: "Seconded by good brigade and regimental officers, he had thoroughly disciplined his men, and made them in every sense soldiers; and their efficiency in action was soon established."

After fighting in the Red River Campaign and receiving a severe contusion in the groin at Pleasant Hill, Walker was assigned in June 1864 to command the Department of West Louisiana, in place of the hot-tempered Taylor, who was relieved of duty at his own request by the departmental commander, Lieutenant General E. Kirby Smith. In August 1864 Walker was ordered to assume command of the District of Texas, New Mexico, and Arizona. His division was given to Major General John Forney, whose arrival in camp inflamed the Texans, who regarded him as too strict a disciplinarian.

Displaced from his district post by Major General John Bankhead Magruder on April 4, 1865, and given command of the recently slain Major General John

Wharton's cavalry corps, Walker on May 12 was ordered to relieve Forney in command of the Texas division, which had reached Camp Groce near Hempstead, Texas, on April 15. One of Walker's staff, Douglas French Forrest, noted in his diary on May 15: "The Genl. is the most popular General in the Trans Mississippi & has acquired his popularity by gallant service in the field & an equal & regular, but very rigid discipline. Genl. Forney's Division have clamored so loudly for their old General that Forney has been relieved from the command & it has been tendered to Walker to whom they are warmly attached. He is a small spare man, very quiet, courteous in his deportment to all, of great force of character & great capacity."

But not even Walker could hold his troops to their duty after they learned of Lee's surrender at Appomattox. He tried to persuade the officers and men to go to Mexico with him and other senior Confederates but was unsuccessful. He wired Kirby Smith that his infantry had mutinied on May 19, seized all transportation and supplies, and carried off to their homes everything they could lay their hands on. On June 6, without waiting for parole, Walker left Hempstead for San Antonio and from there continued his journey to Mexico with a party of forty men.

From Mexico Walker went to England. While in London he wrote "The War of Secession West of the Mississippi River During the Years 1863–4–&5," which was never published. Returning to the United States in the late 1860s, Walker made his home during the last fifteen years of his life in Winchester, Virginia, where he engaged in mining and railroad operations in the South. On July 20, 1887, during President Grover Cleveland's first administration, he was appointed United States consul general at Bogotá, Colombia, and later served as a special commissioner to invite the South American republics to a Pan-American Conference at Washington, D.C, which met from October 2, 1889, to April 19, 1890. Walker died in Washington on July 20, 1893, and was buried in Winchester.

Norman D. Brown

Blessington, Joseph P., *The Campaigns of Walker's Texas Division* (New York, 1875).

Brown, Norman D., ed., *Journey to Pleasant Hill: The Civil War Letters of Captain Elijah P. Petty, Walker's Texas Division, CSA* (San Antonio, 1982).

✴ *Leroy Pope Walker* ✴

No photograph of Leroy P. Walker in uniform has been found. This civilian view dates from the early postwar years. (National Archives)

"In truth, he was no politician," Leroy Pope Walker's son would say of him in 1906; "Could he have adapted himself in the ways of the true politician he would probably have attained his end." In the same way, it might have been said, he was no general either.

He was born February 7, 1817, in Huntsville, Alabama, the son of Senator John W. Walker. Thus destined for an influential role in whatever profession he chose, young Walker first entered the University of Alabama, and then later studied at Charlottesville's University of Virginia. Studying law, he won admission to the Huntsville bar in 1837 when he was not yet 21 years old, and then waited a mere six years before embarking on a political career by winning a seat in the Alabama legislature. In 1847 he was selected as speaker of the house of representatives, holding that post until 1850. Twice he narrowly missed being selected by the legislature as a United States Senator. He became an outspoken proponent of Southern rights, slavery, and of the resort to session if necessary, serving as a delegate to the 1850 Nashville Convention of Southern states.

From 1850–53 he served as judge of the Fourth Judicial Circuit, then returned to the legislature immediately before leaving it once more in 1855 to tend to his personal fortunes. Five years later in 1860 he was one of the wealthiest lawyers in the state, and the acknowledged legal leader of the northern half of Alabama. In 1860 he was one of the most outspoken adherents to the "Alabama Platform," the decree that if protection of slavery did not become a plank in the Democratic presidential platform that year, then

Alabama should secede. Walker found himself put in charge of the state delegation to the Charleston convention that year, and when Southern rights supporters bolted from the convention, Walker went with them, later participating in the Richmond convention that nominated John C. Breckinridge for the presidency.

With the election of Lincoln, Walker took a leading hand in bringing about Alabama's secession, then went to Tennessee as a state commissioner to promote that state's cooperation with the other seceding states. When the new Confederate government was formed in Montgomery, and Jefferson Davis arrived to assume its presidency, influential Alabamians began campaigning immediately for Walker to receive a cabinet appointment. He joined in the wire-pulling himself, and may have preferred the post of attorney general, but Davis instead offered him the post of secretary of war after another Alabamian, Clement Clay, declined the office. Walker, with no military or administrative background whatsoever, accepted.

No Confederate secretary of war except George Randolph and Breckinridge ever achieved much general popularity. Walker would achieve none. Men found him apparently self-important and disinterested. "Apparently cold and unapproachable," said his son, "he was one of the kindest and most charitable of men. He was often therefore misjudged and misunderstood." Worse, he was no judge of current affairs. As Walker himself admitted years later, he believed there would be no war, or that it would be brief and bloodless, and he opposed early motions to purchase huge quantities of arms from Europe. And he made intemperate speeches in which he predicted after Fort Sumter that Confederates would soon plant their banners over Washington and point further north.

Walker's task was a thankless one even if well performed, for Davis interfered constantly, in part out of natural inclination, and moreso because of Walker's inexperience. Within a few months he found that he had a growing cadre of enemies in Congress and with the press, and was losing whatever confidence he had enjoyed with the president. Finally on September 16, 1861, he resigned, in part over what he later described to his son as "a decided difference of opinion on the policy to be pursued in the conduct of the War Office" growing out of Walker's attempt to stop Leonidas Polk's foolish occupation of Columbus, Kentucky, which led to that state abandoning its neutrality. Worse, Walker's health was bad, and worse yet was

that he found that his position was "fast becoming subordinated to a mere clerkship without latitude or power." Davis accepted the resignation, but attempted to soften the act with an appointment as brigadier general on September 17, effective immediately. Walker accepted his commission the same day, though never intending to hold it for long, for he expected to run for a Senate seat at the next election.

Returning to Huntsville, Walker began organizing a new brigade assigned to him, but was then transferred with his men to Mobile, under the overall command of Braxton Bragg. Bragg loathed Walker, being one of many generals outraged at what he felt had been the incompetence of the War Department. Bragg openly boasted that he would get even by making life unpleasant for Walker, and proceeded to do so for the next five months, repeatedly reassigning him and writing venomous reports of Walker to Richmond. Finally Walker resigned on March 31, 1862, without having seen any action at all. Thereafter he returned to law until appointed a judge in June 1864, presiding over a military court with the rank of colonel.

Following the war Walker obtained a pardon in September 1865, and thereafter returned to the practice of law. Though he never again held office himself, he was prominent in president of the state constitutional convention in Montgomery in September 1875, and in 1884 was a delegate to the Democratic national convention that nominated Grover Cleveland. A month later he fell ill and quickly deteriorated, dying on August 23. He was buried in Huntsville.

William C. Davis

Harris, William C., *Leroy Pope Walker, Confederate Secretary of War* (Tuscaloosa, Ala., 1962).

Woods, Michael L., Papers, Alabama Department of Archives and History, Montgomery.

✱ *Lucius Marshall Walker* ✱

Lucius Marshall Walker was born in Columbia, Tennessee, on October 18, 1829. His mother, Jane Maria Polk, was a sister of former president James K. Polk, and Walker's sister, Maria Polk Walker, married Confederate Brigadier General Frank C. Armstrong. Walker, who graduated from West Point in 1850 a respectable fifteenth out of forty-four, did not choose to make the military his career. He resigned after two years to open a mercantile business in Memphis, and when the Civil War began sided with the South. His health, however, seems to have been delicate. He was sick on November 11, 1861, at the time when he was appointed colonel of an unusual command organized by the Confederate States and composed of companies from Alabama, Arkansas, and Tennessee. Since Walker was from Tennessee, the regiment was given the designation of the 40th Tennessee, but it was listed on the Confederate roster as a provisional regiment not a volunteer regiment, and it was an odd combination of men: part enlisted for the war and part joined for twelve months. The regiment was poorly armed; only around one hundred of the men actually had guns.

Walker took command of the post at Memphis, but in February after learning that New Madrid was in danger, Brigadier General J.P. McCown sent Walker with two of his regiments to occupy "the position on the shore of the mouth of the Bayou Saint John." McCown was pleased with his subordinate and informed Brigadier General Leonidas Polk that Walker was "a good man, but has not rank...I must have reliable men to command and with rank. Colonels do not like to be under their equal in rank." In March Polk assured McCown that Walker would be promoted, and Walker became a brigadier general, on April 11, to rank from March 11, 1862. Six days later McCown turned the command over to Walker and left for Fort Pillow. During the fighting for New Madrid and Island No. 10 McCown reported: "In this long conflict I beg to express my obligations to Brig. Gens. A.P. Steward and L.M. Walker and Colonel [W.E.] Travis, who at different times commanded the force at the mouth of the bayou. I express my thanks for valuable services rendered in that capacity." Walker, who was in command of the portion of New Madrid called the Upper Fort, or Fort Bankhead, failed to make an immediate report of the evacuation. McCown explained to his superiors, however, that he did not attribute Walker's failure to report "to a desire to avoid the matter, but to official duties and illness." In fact, sickness prevented Walker from participating in the Battle of Shiloh. At the time of the battle Walker was recuperating in Saint Francis County, Arkansas, but was well enough by April 9 to pen his official report of the events at New Madrid. "In justice to myself," he pointed out, "I will state that this report would have been regularly forwarded at an earlier date but for ill-health."

Walker soon returned to the army and was there during the siege of Corinth. He fought on May 9, 1862, in the battle of Farmington, Mississippi, where he commanded the 3d Brigade, composed of the 13th Louisiana, 20th Louisiana, and 37th Mississippi. Sometime during the next few months Walker provoked the anger of Major General Braxton Bragg. In

No uniformed portrait of General Walker has come to light. This is a prewar civilian view. (Albert G. Shaw Collection, Virginia Historical Society, Richmond)

November while Walker was again on sick leave, Bragg wrote to Adjutant General Samuel Cooper that Walker and Brigadier General William H. Carroll "were not safe men to intrust with any command, and I much prefer leaving their brigades with such colonels as accidents may place in position." Moreover, Bragg pointed out: "Imputations now rest on this officer, which will cause his case to be placed before the examining board." Carroll did indeed appear before a court of inquiry and resigned in February 1863. But Bragg may have had reservations about doing the same to a fellow West Pointer; Bragg may have even given consideration to Walker's family connections, because he did not take any action. Instead he told Cooper that Walker's "application for transfer to Arkansas [was] approved." In March Walker received orders to proceed to Alexandria, Louisiana, and report to Lieutenant General Edmund Kirby Smith for assignment.

In the Trans-Mississippi Walker took command of a cavalry division consisting of a small Texas brigade, Archibald S. Dobbin's 1st Arkansas Cavalry, and Robert C. Newton's 5th Arkansas Cavalry. Not long after Walker arrived at Little Rock, he took part in Lieutenant General Theophilus H. Holmes' July 4, 1863, attack on Helena, Arkansas, where he led the two Arkansas regiments in an unsuccessful assault upon the Federal line. When the Union army under Major General Frederick Steele began moving toward Little Rock in early August, Walker's Arkansas regiments met the advance. The last week of August Major General Sterling Price, who commanded the District of Arkansas while Holmes was sick, ordered the cavalry divisions of Walker and Brigadier General John Marmaduke to make a stand at Bayou Metoe.

This was the last battle for Walker. When the Union army attacked, the Southerners fell back. As a result of the retreat a dispute developed between Walker and Marmaduke. Soon after the fighting ended, Marmaduke criticized Walker's handling of the affair and promptly applied for a transfer. Marmaduke insisted "he had never accused Walker of cowardice, but that his conduct had been such upon several occasions that he would no longer serve under him" Angered over this insult, Walker demanded an apology and then issued a challenge, and the two men dueled at dawn on September 6, 1863. Both carried fully loaded Colt navy revolvers, and although each missed his first shot, in the second round Walker was hit; he died the next day.

Price placed Marmaduke and both seconds under arrest but had to release them because of the pending battle at Little Rock. Price placed Marmaduke in charge of the cavalry, and Archibald Dobbin, part of Walker's command, refused to obey his commander's assailant. Marmaduke arrested Dobbin, who was later charged with disobeying orders. When Holmes resumed command of the district, he absolved Marmaduke in Walker's death, and both seconds were also released. This event, however, was a striking example of how the Confederates were fighting among themselves when they needed unity.

Walker was buried in Elmwood Cemetery in Memphis.

Anne Bailey

Huff, Leo E., "The Last Duel in Arkansas: The Marmaduke-Walker Duel." *Arkansas Historical Quarterly*, 23 (Spring 1964), 36–49.

Huff, Leo E., "The Union Expedition Against Little Rock." *Arkansas Historical Quarterly*, 22 (Fall 1963), 224–237.

Reuben Walker late in the war as a colonel. (Cook Collection, Valentine Museum, Richmond, Va.)

⭐ Reuben Lindsay Walker ⭐

On May 29, 1827, Reuben Lindsay Walker was born at Logan in Albemarle County, Virginia. He was the son of Captain Meriwether Lewis and Maria (Lindsay) Walker, and his family was connected by blood an affinity with others of wealth, refinement, and prominence in that region of the state. He attended the Virginia Military Institute and graduated from that school in 1845, when he was but eighteen years old. He later established himself in New Kent County, Virginia, where he practiced civil engineering and established himself as a farmer. His projects included work upon the extension of the Chesapeake & Ohio Railroad. He married Maria Eskridge in 1848, and after her death, he married Sally Elam in 1857. Walker and his two wives had a total of eight children. He served as the sergeant-at-arms of the Virginia convention which determined secession in 1861, and immediately following the adoption of the ordinance of secession Walker asked Governor John Letcher for permission to organize an expedition to capture Fortress Monroe.

Although Letcher denied his request regarding an attack on Fortress Monroe, he appointed Walker captain of the Purcell Battery, which was the first artillery company to depart Richmond for active duty. Stationed on the Potomac near Aquia Creek in April, the unit remained in the vicinity of Fredericksburg until July 21, 1861, when Walker and his battery arrived on the battlefield of First Manassas in time to shell the fleeing Union troops. General Joseph E. Johnston commended Walker for the "great skill" he demonstrated in the use of his six cannon. Except for engaging two U.S. vessels at the mouth of Potomac Creek on August 23, Walker remained inactive for the remainder of the year.

On March 31, 1862, Walker was promoted to major and placed in command of the batteries attached to Major General Ambrose P. Hill's division. Although illness compelled Walker to remain in Richmond during the Seven Days' Battles, supposedly his only leave during the war, he was promoted to lieutenant colonel shortly after the close of that campaign on July 1.

Remaining in command of Hill's artillery, Walker's battalion consisted of seven batteries during the engagement at Cedar Mountain in August. During the reduction of Harpers Ferry the following month, Hill praised Walker for his display of "indomitable resolution and energy" while deploying several of his guns during darkness on Loudoun Heights, from which position they commanded the Federal fortifications. After four of his batteries participated in the fighting at Sharpsburg on September 17, Walker returned to Virginia. On October 29 Major General Gustavus W. Smith notified Major General Samuel G. French that he had secured the transfer of Walker "to take charge of the artillery defenses of Petersburg and vicinity. You will find Colonel Walker an energetic and determined officer. He has served with marked distinction in the field...." Smith's statement proved to be premature however, and Walker remained with the Army of Northern Virginia.

On December 13 Walker's performance while directing fourteen guns of his battalion on the Confederate right wing earned considerable praise. General Robert E. Lee reported that Walker's guns opened upon the advancing Union infantry "with such destructive effect as to cause it to waver and soon to retreat in confusion." Lieutenant General Thomas J. "Stonewall" Jackson commented that Walker's gunners made the enemy "at last seek shelter by flight." Hill reported that Walker "directed the fire from his guns with admirable coolness and precision." Jackson's chief of artillery, Colonel Stapleton Crutchfield, also praised Walker, whose position was "peculiarly trying, from his being required to endure for a long time a very heavy fire without replying to it." Walker had been ordered to withhold his fire until the enemy infantry advanced. Partly as a result of his performance at Fredericksburg, Brigadier General William N. Pendleton, Lee's chief of artillery, informed Lee on February 11, 1863, that Walker, "so justly distinguished for long and gallant service, has been recommended for the full rank of colonel. He might justly receive it...." His promotion was made official in late March or

While the uniform shows considerable evidence of retouching, it appears to be genuine making this a late war image. (Cook Collection, Valentine Museum, Richmond, Va.)

early April, and Walker demonstrated that he merited it by his performance during the Chancellorsville Campaign, where his accomplishments earned him the praise of Lee, Hill, and fellow artilleryman, Colonel Edward P. Alexander.

When Lee reorganized his army into three corps following the death of Jackson, Walker was officially designated to command the artillery of the newly created III Corps on June 3. Walker would remain in that position until the end of the war, being promoted to brigadier general on February 18, 1865. Walker headed the retreating column from Petersburg; his command included all of the artillery not needed with the troops. Also, two divisions of infantry were nominally under his control. On April 8, at a point between Appomattox Court House and Station, he encountered Union cavalry under Major General George A. Custer and successfully repulsed repeated attacks until he was outflanked about 9 P.M. Apparently, Walker left the army prior to its surrender the following day, because no record of his surrender or parole has been found.

After the war, Walker returned to his farm in Virginia. In 1872, he moved to Selma, Alabama, and worked for two years as the superintendent of the Marion & Selma Railroad. Returning to Virginia in 1876, he worked as a construction engineer for the Richmond & Danville Railroad, the Richmond street railways, and the Richmond & Allegheny Railroad. After he successfully supervised the construction of an addition for women to the Virginia State Prison, Walker became construction superintendent of the Texas State Capitol. He resided in Austin from 1884 to 1888. After completing this project, he returned to his farm in Fluvanna County, Virginia, at the confluence of the James and Rivanna rivers, where he died on June 7, 1890. He was buried in Hollywood Cemetery, Richmond.

He has been described as being "six feet four inches in height and of massive frame, with long dark hair, sweeping moustache and imperial beard...a superb horseman." Despite his large build and his participation in sixty-three engagements, Walker was never wounded, a fact he was quick to point out after the war "was not my fault."

Benjamin E. Snellgrove

Hotchkiss, Jedediah, *Virginia*, Vol. III in Evans, *Confederate Military History.*

⋆ *William Henry Talbot Walker* ⋆

Walker was born on November 26, 1816, in Augusta, Georgia. He attended Richmond Academy in that town and in 1837 graduated forty-sixth in a class of fifty at West Point. Commissioned in the 6th U.S. Infantry, he fought against the Seminoles in Florida in 1837 and 1838. Walker received three wounds in the Battle of Okeechobee on Christmas Day of 1837 and resigned from the army on October 31, 1838, because of those wounds. He rejoined the army on November 18, 1840, and was promoted to captain five years later. As a result of gallant and meritorious conduct in the Mexican War, he was brevetted major and lieutenant colonel. Walker was seriously wounded at Molina del Rey, and the surgeons feared he would die. After his recovery he filled several posts, including commandant of cadets and instructor in tactics at West Point from 1854 to 1856.

Walker resigned from the army as a major on December 20, 1860. Governor Joe Brown appointed him a major general of Georgia volunteers on April 25, 1861. Walker wrote the Confederate War Department if his division could be activated for field service, saying, "I desire to leave in person for Virginia if I can't take a command there." On May 25 he was commissioned a Confederate brigadier general and ordered to Pensacola, Florida, to serve under Major General Braxton Bragg. The latter requested that Walker be transferred to Richmond in August because of his "feeble and failing" health.

On August 26 Walker was ordered to report to General Joseph E. Johnston at Manassas. There he assumed command of the 8th Brigade, which consisted of four regiments and one battalion of Louisiana troops. He led the brigade on a reconnaissance toward the Potomac River in late September. When the army was reorganized on October 22, Walker took charge of a brigade of four Georgia regiments. Citing poor health, Walker resigned his commission on October 29, but several sources state his action resulted from dissatisfaction over being removed from command of the Louisiana brigade. Governor Brown soon made him a brigadier general in the Georgia militia, but those forces being disbanded due to the Conscript Act of April 1862, Walker was out of service for nearly a year.

He again received an appointment as brigadier in Confederate service on March 2, 1863, to rank from January 9, and assumed command of a brigade of Georgia regiments in the District of Georgia. In addition to duty at Savannah and Charleston, Walker sat on a board of officers convened at Oglethorpe Barracks in Savannah to investigate the state of the city's defenses. On May 5 his brigade was ordered to reinforce General Joseph E. Johnston's army in Mississippi. Reaching Jackson, the brigade was sent toward Raymond but did not reach that town before the Confederates there were defeated by Major General Ulysses S. Grant's army. Walker and his men were only lightly engaged in the Battle of Jackson on May 14, and he "declined to make a report" of their role.

At the request of Major General John C. Pemberton, Walker was promoted to major general on June 27,

No uniformed portrait of General Walker has come to light. This is a prewar civilian view. (Albert G. Shaw Collection, Virginia Historical Society, Richmond)

effective May 23. He assumed command of a division of six brigades. Johnston sent the division to Yazoo City to protect it from possible Union threats. By the time Walker's men had returned to Jackson in early July, his division had been reduced in size to four brigades. The division participated in the Siege of Jackson, July 9–15, but saw little fighting. On August 23 Walker was ordered with three brigades to reinforce General Braxton Bragg's Army of Tennessee at Chattanooga. There the division joined Lieutenant General Daniel H. Hill's Corps. Just prior to the Battle of Chickamauga, however, Bragg placed Walker in command of the Reserve Corps, consisting of his old division and that of Brigadier General St. John R. Liddell. The latter, a West Point classmate of Walker's and ever critical of his superiors, wrote later, "General Walker was well-known to be a crackbrained fire-eater, always captious or cavilling about something whimsical and changeable and hardly reliable." During the first day's fighting, Walker exercised little command, as his troops were detached to support other divisions, and Liddell stated that Walker and Hill argued over this situation. Walker's divisions were reunited the next day, September 20, and played a role in the attack on the Union army's left flank.

The Reserve Corps was broken up after the battle, and Walker's division joined Lieutenant General James Longstreet's Corps. Walker's soldiers participated in the early stages of the operations against Chattanooga. On October 27 the division was ordered west of Chattanooga Creek to replace Brigadier General Micah Jenkins' division, and by early November Walker was commanding all troops west of the creek. The reorganization of the army on November 12 resulted in the breakup of one of Walker's brigades and the transfer of Brigadier General George E. Maney's brigade to the division. Walker went on sick leave that day and did not return to duty until January 1864 when the army was at Dalton, Georgia. By this time his division was in Lieutenant General William J. Hardee's corps. Maney's brigade was exchanged back to Major General Benjamin F. Cheatham's division for that of John K. Jackson about February 20.

Walker's men left their winter camp on May 6 and marched to support soldiers defending Mill Creek Gap. Walker led his division through the opening stages of the campaign against Atlanta. They acted primarily in a supporting role but saw some skirmishing near Kennesaw Mountain. Brigadier General Hugh W. Mercer's brigade had joined the division prior to June 30. Shortly afterward Jackson's brigade was broken up. The division was on Hardee's center during the Battle of Peachtree Creek on July 20. Walker's men hit the enemy works first and were repulsed with heavy losses. On July 22 Walker led his men on a march intended to strike the left flank of the Union army east of Atlanta. During the march a misunderstanding led Hardee to issue a blistering criticism of Walker, and he later apologized for his hasty words. Walker, however, became irate and told a staff officer, "I shall make him remember this insult—if I survive this battle he shall answer me for it." A few minutes later, about noon, as he was looking for the enemy through his binoculars, Walker was killed by a single shot from a Union picket. His body was taken toward the rear, and the Battle of Atlanta erupted almost immediately. Walker was later buried in his family's burial ground in Augusta.

Joseph Wheeler said of Walker that he "never did an act which was not consistent with and which did not emanate from a soul filled with truth, honor, generosity, and courage." Liddell, despite his criticism of Walker, remembered: "Under a rough exterior and brusque mannerism, there was a large heart. A truer man and brave, existed not in the army."

Arthur W. Bergeron, Jr.

Derry, Joseph T., *Georgia*, Vol. VI in Evans, *Confederate Military History*.

Hughes, Nathaniel C., ed., *Liddell's Record* (Dayton, Oh., 1985).

Kurtz, Wilbur G., "The Death of Major General W.H.T. Walker, July 22, 1864," *Civil War History*, VI (1960), pp. 174–79.

McDonald, John C., "Gen. W.H.T. Walker Killed in Battle," *Confederate Veteran*, VI (1899), p. 515.

✴ William Stephen Walker ✴

General William S. Walker, photographed sometime after October 1862. (Albert G. Shaw Collection, Virginia Historical Society, Richmond)

Although Walker was born on April 13, 1822, in Pittsburgh, Pennsylvania, he was reared by his uncle, Senator Robert J. Walker of Mississippi (a native Pennsylvanian as well), who was Secretary of the Treasury under President James K. Polk. Young Walker attended school in Georgetown, D.C.. On February 27, 1847, he was commissioned a 1st lieutenant in the Regiment of Voltigeurs and Foot Riflemen, the elite regiment that was formed in February of 1847 as part of the Regular Army for service during the Mexican War only, for it was disbanded in August of 1848. He later served as a staff officer, and he was brevetted captain on September 13, 1847, for gallant and meritorious conduct at the battle of Chapultepec. On August 1848, he mustered out of the service.

When the regular army expanded in 1855, Walker received his commission as a captain of the 1st Cavalry on March 3, 1855. He served with that unit until May 1, 1861, when he tendered his resignation in order to accept a commission as captain of infantry in the Regular Confederate Army. Prior to his resigning his commission in the United States Army he had been nominated a captain from Florida on March 16, 1861, and his rank was from that date.

On April 22 Confederate Adjutant and Inspector General Samuel Cooper ordered Walker to proceed to Memphis and establish a recruiting rendezvous for the C.S. Army. Because Tennessee was not yet a member of the Confederate States of America, Walker was instructed to "exercise due caution in carrying on [his] duties;" the recruits were to be forwarded to Baton Rouge in squads. On June 11, he was ordered to muster in with Colonel Thomas C. Hindman's

Arkansas regiment at Memphis. On March 19, 1862, Major General John C. Pemberton assumed command of the Department of South Carolina and appointed Walker his acting inspector general. Within three days Walker had been promoted to the rank of colonel and was permanently assigned to Pemberton's staff as his adjutant and inspector general.

On May 6, 1862, Walker was relieved from his administrative duties by Pemberton and assigned to command the Fourth and Fifth Military Districts of South Carolina, which embraced the area between the Ashepoo River and Oketie Creek. Two weeks later his command was redesignated the Third Military District. On July 19 his district was expanded to embrace the region extending from Charleston, in the rear of Ashepoo River to its headwaters, to the rear of Edisto River to Branchville, and along the southern boundary of the Barnwell District to the Savannah River, and back to Charleston along the coast. This boundary would continue in effect until the area was abandoned in 1865.

Walker established his headquarters at Pocotaligo and quickly set about the task of guarding the coast against sudden incursions by the enemy against the Charleston & Savannah Railroad, a major transportation artery. On September 25, 1862, Walker's troops consisted of forty companies of infantry, cavalry, and artillery dispersed at Hardeeville, Grahamville, McPhersonville, and Green Pond. Although several actions were fought in his district during his tenure as its commander, the most significant occurred on October 22, 1862, when he repulsed a Federal force at Pocotaligo that was attempting to seize the railroad. On October 30, 1862, he was promoted brigadier general, to rank immediately. By April of 1863, he had nearly six thousand effective troops, but the following month saw the transfer of an infantry brigade to join General Joseph E. Johnston's campaign to relieve Vicksburg, which cut the effective strength of Walker's command in half. On December 8, 1863, Walker issued a circular to all slave owners in his district to remove all slaves whose age and physical strength make them suitable for service in the Union army.

Pemberton's successor, General P.G.T. Beauregard, chose to retain Walker as commander of the Third District and it appeared that he would remain in the backwater of the war for the duration. However, on April 16, 1864, Brigadier General Nathan G. Evans was seriously injured in an accident while accompanying his brigade as it moved through Beauregard's department and Beauregard asked Walker if he would assume command of brigade, which was in route to Kinston, North Carolina. Walker accepted and on April 19, 1864, Walker was relieved from command of the Third District and placed in temporary command of the brigade. On April 29 Walker assumed command of Kinston Military District of the Department of North Carolina and Southern Virginia, which included Evans' former brigade.

On May 15 Walker was ordered to assist General Beauregard in the defense of Petersburg. When Major General William H.C. Whiting learned of this movement later that evening he wrote Beauregard, "It will be a week before Walker's brigade can get here, if then." Although he arrived too late to participate in the fighting at Second Drewry's Bluff on May 16, Walker had his men in position to attack the newly established Federal fortifications at Bermuda Hundred, twelve miles below Richmond, by May 20. That day, Walker led what Union Major General Benjamin F. Butler described as "a very daring change" against his right wing. In the ensuing melee Walker unknowingly entered the Federal lines. Realizing his mistake, he requested demands to surrender and attempted to flee, but the 67th Ohio Infantry fired a volley at him. His horse was killed and Walker tumbled to the ground. Minié bullets had penetrated his left arm and had shattered his right leg above the ankle. Captured immediately, Walker was transported to a hospital at Fortress Monroe, where he dictated deathbed letters to his wife, Beauregard, and other close friends and relatives. Fortunately for Walker, a skillful surgeon performed the amputation of his foot and he survived.

In October of 1864 he was exchanged and even though he was not fully recovered, he was ordered back to active duty. On October 29 he was assigned to command the post at Weldon, North Carolina. Although he had not arrived there as of January 6, 1865, he apparently took command of the post before the end of the war.

After the war, Walker resided in Georgia. On June 7, 1899, he died in Atlanta and was buried there in Oakland Cemetery.

Benjamin E. Snellgrove

Dickison, J.J., *Florida*, Vol. XI in Evans, *Confederate Military History*.

✯ *William Henry Wallace* ✯

The only known uniformed pose of General Wallace, taken during the last winter of the war. (South Carolina Confederate Relic Room and Museum, Charleston)

William Henry Wallace was born in the Laurens District, South Carolina, on March 24, 1827. Following his graduation from South Carolina College in 1849, Wallace engaged in various pursuits during the 1850s—planter, newspaper publisher, and attorney. Elected to the state legislature, he voted for secession in December 1860. He completed his term in office and then enlisted as a private in Company A, 18th South Carolina.

The 18th South Carolina remained in the state during the conflict's first year, and Wallace was elected lieutenant colonel of the regiment in May 1862. Two months later, the regiment was transferred to Virginia and assigned to the brigade of Nathan Evans, fighting in the Second Manassas and Sharpsburg campaigns of August and September 1862. In the former battle, on August 30, Wallace assumed command of the regiment when its commander was killed in an attack. Although temporarily promoted to colonel, Wallace's rank was not confirmed by the Confederate Senate until June 10, 1864. He retained command of the regiment during the entire period.

Evans' brigade was transferred to the Western Theater after the Sharpsburg Campaign, and served under General Joseph E. Johnston during the Vicksburg Campaign. Returning to South Carolina in August 1863, the brigade participated in the defense of Charleston during the fall and winter of 1864.

In the spring of 1864, Confederate authorities assigned the brigade of five South Carolina regiments—the 17th, 18th, 22d, 23d, and 26th—to the Petersburg defenses. Stephen Elliott, Jr., now commanded the brigade in the division of Bushrod Johnson. On July 30 Elliott's brigade manned a sector of the lines under which the Federals detonated a mine of gunpowder. Four companies of Wallace's regiment were blown up in the explosion and in the ensuing Battle of the Crater Elliott fell wounded. Wallace assumed command of the brigade and was promoted to brigadier general on September 20.

Wallace retained direction of the brigade until war's end. At Five Forks on April 1, 1865, his command held the Confederate left and was wrecked under the Federal assault. He briefly commanded the division in that action. Five days later, the division was decimated at Sayler's Creek. Wallace led the remnants of the command to Appomattox, where they surrendered with the rest of the army on the 9th.

Wallace returned to his plantation in South Carolina and resumed his legal practice. In 1872 he was elected to the state legislature, serving three terms. In 1877 he was appointed a judge of the circuit court, retaining the position until his retirement in 1893. The capable if undistinguished former brigadier died in Union, South Carolina, on March 21, 1901, and was buried there.

Jeffry D. Wert

Capers, Ellison, *South Carolina*, Vol. V in Evans, *Confederate Military History*.

Freeman, Douglas Southall, *Lee's Lieutenants: A Study In Command* (New York, 1942–44).

An outstanding previously unpublished portrait of General Walthall, his only known portrait in uniform, probably taken after his July 1864 promotion to major general. (Alabama Department of Archives and History, Montgomery)

⋆ *Edward Cary Walthall* ⋆

The future Confederate general and United States senator was born in Richmond, Virginia, on April 4, 1831, to Barrett White and Sally Wilkinson Walthall. In 1841 the family moved to Holly Springs, Mississippi, and Edward received his secondary education at St. Thomas Hall. He read law in his brother-in-law's Pontotoc office for eighteen months and then returned to Holly Springs, where he continued his studies while serving as deputy clerk of the Marshall County Circuit Court. He was admitted to the bar in 1852 and opened an office in Coffeeville. He was elected attorney for the state's tenth judicial district in 1856 and was reelected in 1859.

Soon after the January 9, 1861, secession of Mississippi, Walthall resigned his elective office and helped organize the Yalobusha Rifles and was elected 1st lieutenant. The company was mustered into state service at Coffeeville on April 27 and ordered to report to the Corinth camp of instruction on May 21. On June 6 the company was mustered into Confederate service for twelve months as Company H, 15th Mississippi, and the field officers were elected. On July 21 Walthall was promoted lieutenant colonel and the regiment was ordered into the field, first to Union City, West Tennessee, and then on August 13 to Russellville in East Tennessee, where the Mississippians reported to Brigadier General Felix Zollicoffer. In mid-September the regiment marched from Knoxville and took position at Cumberland Gap.

Walthall first saw combat at Camp Wildcat, October 21. He commanded the 15th Mississippi at the Battle of Mill Springs on January 19, 1862, and was commended by hard-drinking Major General George B. Crittenden, who wrote: "For an hour…The Fifteenth Mississippi, under Lieutenant-Colonel Walthall and the Twentieth Tennessee…of my center and right, had been struggling with the superior forces of the enemy…I cannot omit to mention the heroic valor of these two regiments, officers and men."

On the retreat from Mill Springs to Murfreesboro Walthall was detached and ordered to Grenada. There

on April 11, less than a week after the Battle of Shiloh, Walthall was elected colonel of the newly organized 29th Mississippi Infantry Regiment. In May Walthall and his unit were at Corinth, assigned to Brigadier General James R. Chalmers' Mississippi Brigade, and posted in the earthworks. Along with the army, Walthall and his Mississippians evacuated Corinth on the night of May 29 and retreated to Tupelo.

In mid-summer General Braxton Bragg, who on June 20 had been named to command the Army of Mississippi, used the railroads to beat Union Major General Don Carlos Buell's Army of the Ohio into Chattanooga. He then started his columns northward and the race for Louisville was on. Spearheading the Confederate Army, Chalmers attacked Munfordville on September 14, but was repulsed. Describing the advance of his regiment Walthall wrote, "the charge was attempted, but without success, the earthworks being about ten feet high and surrounded by a deep ditch about eight feet wide." In recognition of their bravery in the assault, Walthall and his troops were the first permitted to occupy the Munfordville works when the four thousand defenders surrendered on the 17th. Upon entering the Bluegrass region, Chalmers' brigade was assigned to Major General Edmund Kirby Smith's Army of Kentucky. Walthall and his men were not with General Bragg when he fought the foe at Perryville on October 8.

By mid-November the Confederates had abandoned their Kentucky adventure and returned to Middle Tennessee where, in and around Murfreesboro, Bragg reorganized his army group into the Army of Tennessee. On November 13 Walthall's abilities were recognized and he was named to command a newly organized brigade that soon included the 24th, 27th, 29th, 30th, 34th Mississippi and the 45th Alabama regiments. Walthall was on sick leave and missed the battle of Stones' River. He rejoined the brigade at Shelbyville, January 17, 1863, as a brigadier general, his promotion to that rank dated December 13, 1862.

Walthall and his brigade, one of the units assigned to Leonidas Polk's corps, saw much marching and lots of rain but no fighting during the Tullahoma Campaign (June 23–July 4, 1863). In the fourth week of July Walthall and his troops were sent to Atlanta. When they returned to north Georgia in mid-September it was with St. John R. Liddell's division of W.H.L., "Shot Pouch" Walker's Reserve Corps. Walthall and his Mississippians initiated the Battle of Chickamauga at Alexander's Bridge on September 18. The next morning they savaged Brigadier General John H. King's brigade of U.S. regulars, capturing more than four hundred prisoners and overrunning a six-gun battery before giving way to a Union counterattack. Late on the 20th they pushed across the Lafayette road in pursuit of the Federals toward McFarland's Gap, but were turned back by the "splendid advance" of a Yankee brigade.

November 24, 1863, found Walthall and his fifteen hundred Mississippians posted upon the western slopes of Lookout Mountain. Assailed by Major General Joseph Hooker's ten thousand men, the Mississippians were reinforced but at dark were withdrawn from the mountain. The next morning Walthall posted his six hundred Mississippians on Missionary Ridge. At 4 P.M., Union troops stormed up the ridge and routed the division on Walthall's left. Wheeling his brigade to the left he checked the onrushing bluecoats and under cover of darkness retreated in good order. Although wounded in the foot Walthall remained in his saddle until his troops had crossed Chickamauga Creek and gone into camp.

The Atlanta Campaign opened on May 7 and found Walthall and his brigade assigned to Thomas C. Hindman's division in John Bell Hood's corps. For two days at Resaca Walthall gamely held the bald knob, where the Confederate line formed a right angle. Here, on May 14, he repulsed three Union attacks and on the 15th was hammered by not less than thirty cannon and his "loss in killed was disproportional to the number wounded." At Cassville, on May 19, Walthall and his Mississippians again came under heavy artillery fire. On June 2, while he was on the New Hope Church-Dallas line, Walthall was transferred to Lieutenant General Leonidas Polk's corps and assumed command of a recently constituted three-brigade division led by Brigadier General James Cantey. Walthall and his division held Big Kennesaw against the advance of reinforced skirmish lines on June 27. On July 6 Walthall was promoted major general.

Walthall and his troops, in the corps now led by Lieutenant General A.P. Stewart, were in the forefront of General John B. Hood's July 20 attack at Peachtree Creek on the Army of the Cumberland, and again in the July 28 Battle of Ezra Church against the Army of Tennessee. At the former, Walthall, before being repulsed, "engaged the enemy with great spirit," and at the latter he spearheaded the attack on Union troops posted at Ezra Church, and was repulsed with the loss of more than one-third of his division.

Atlanta was evacuated on the night of September 1 and Walthall and his troops, along with Hood's army, retreated, first to Lovejoy Station and then Palmetto to regroup and rest. On September 30 the army crossed the Chattahoochee River to begin a three-month campaign that was to take them to Nashville. Walthall had an active role in this drama. On October 4 he struck the Western & Atlantic Railroad, Sherman's lifeline at Big Shanty, and spent the next twenty-four hours burning ties and twisting rails. They resumed their railroad-bashing at Tilton on the 13th.

Crossing the Tennessee River on November 20, Walthall led his division into the Franklin holocaust (November 30), in which his troops were savaged and the general had two horses killed and was himself severely bruised. At Nashville on December 15 Walthall gamely defended the redoubts and stone wall paralleling the Hillsboro Pike that anchored Hood's left until he was outflanked and overwhelmed by superior numbers. On the 20th at Columbia General Hood placed Walthall in command of eight shattered infantry brigades and told him to report to Major General Nathan Bedford Forrest. With this force Forrest and Walthall successfully fended off pursuit by Union cavalry at King's Hill on Christmas and at Sugar Creek the next day and enabled Hood's routed columns to recross the Tennessee at Bainbridge, Alabama, on December 27–28 and push on to Corinth and Tupelo to regroup.

Walthall and his division made the roundabout winter's journey from Mississippi to North Carolina and, with other units of the Army of Tennessee, attacked the Federals near Bentonville at 2:45 P.M. on March 19, driving the foe from a line of breastworks and capturing two cannon. The tide then turned and on the 21st the Confederates disengaged. On April 26, 1865, General Joseph E. Johnston surrendered the armies under his command, and on May 2 Walthall was paroled at Greensboro, North Carolina.

While en route home to Holly Springs, he met Lucius Q.C. Lamar in Oxford, Mississippi, and a lifelong friendship ensued. Walthall and Lamar briefly practiced law as partners in Coffeeville. In 1871 Walthall moved to Grenada and soon became a leader in the successful drive to overthrow the state's "carpet-bag" government headed by Adelbert Ames. From 1868 until 1884 Walthall was a delegate to every Democratic national convention except one.

In March 1885 Lamar, then a U.S. senator from Mississippi, was named secretary of the interior by President Grover Cleveland, and Walthall was named to succeed Lamar. By election and reelection, he remained in the Senate from then until his death in 1898, except for the fourteen months between January 1894 and March 1895 when ill health caused his temporary resignation. Before he resigned he had been elected for another six-year term to begin in March 1895. He served as chairman of the committee of military affairs (1893–98), and as a member of the committees on revolutionary claims (1897–98), and public lands and improvement of the Mississippi River.

Walthall's health in later years was not good and he seldom spoke from the floor. However, he had the respect of his colleagues on both sides of the aisle and he commanded much influence. As a leader of the minority party when the "bloody shirt" was brandished, he displayed the same strength and resourcefulness as when wielding the sword against heavy odds on the battlefield. The olive branch thrust forward so dramatically by Lamar in his Charles Sumner eulogy was carried more quietly, but equally effectively, by Walthall.

He died in Washington, D.C., on April 21, 1898. After funeral services in the Senate Chamber, his body was returned to Mississippi and buried at Holly Springs.

Edwin C. Bearss

Hooker, Charles, *Mississippi*, Vol. VII in Evans, *Confederate Military History*.

✷ *Richard Waterhouse* ✷

Richard Waterhouse was born on January 12, 1832, in Rhea County, Tennessee. Barely fourteen years old when the Mexican War began, Waterhouse left home to take part in the fighting. After the war ended, his family moved to Texas, settling at San Augustine in 1849, also when Richard went into the mercantile business with his father (who was also a Mexican War veteran). At the outbreak of the Civil War he took part in the organization of the 19th Texas Infantry and became its colonel on May 13, 1862. By July the 19th Texas was on its way to Arkansas to take part in the defense of Little Rock but arrived after the Union Army of the Southwest had marched across the state, bypassing the capital.

In October 1862 Waterhouse's regiment became part of a brigade organized at Camp Nelson, near Austin, Arkansas, under Brigadier General Henry E. McCulloch. But when Major General John G. Walker arrived at Little Rock in December, he assumed command, and from that time until the end of the war it was known as Walker's Texas Division. This command earned the nickname "Walker's Greyhounds" in recognition of many arduous marches in Arkansas and Louisiana, and the exploits of the division were carefully followed at home because it was the largest unit composed entirely of Texans to fight in the Civil War.

The first important battle for Waterhouse came when Trans-Mississippi Confederates marched from Arkansas to Louisiana in an attempt to relieve Vicksburg in the late spring and summer of 1863. The battle at Milliken's Bend, Louisiana, on June 7, 1863,

was particularly significant because it involved black troops defending a position on a Mississippi River levee which served as a supply depot for Grant's expedition. McCulloch, who commanded the brigade that included the 19th Texas, gave a detailed account of Waterhouse's part of the assault. "The line was formed under a heavy fire from the enemy," he wrote, "and the troops charged the breastworks, carrying it instantly, killing and wounding many of the enemy by their deadly fire, as well as the bayonet. This charge was resisted by the negro portion of the enemy's force with considerable obstinacy...." Moreover, McCulloch observed: "No charge was ever more gallantly made than this and the enemy were not only driven from the levee, but were followed into their camp, where many of them were killed. In the charge Colonel [Richard] Waterhouse with his regiment...distinguished themselves particularly, not only by a gallant and desperate charge over the levee, but they drove the enemy (leaving the camp covered with the dead) to the very bank of the river, and within short and direct range of the gunboats of the enemy. In fact, from the beginning to the end of the engagement, the colonel behaved in the most gallant manner, and his officers and men seemed to catch the enthusiasm of their commander, and did their duty nobly and gallantly upon every portion of the field."

The rumors of blacks murdered in the fighting brought a swift reaction throughout the North, and

No uniformed portrait of Waterhouse has come to light. His youthful appearance here suggests that this is a prewar image. (Evans, *Confederate Military History*)

Major General U.S. Grant warned Major General Richard Taylor: "It may be you propose a different line of policy toward black troops and officers commanding them, to that practiced toward white troops. If so, I can assure you that these colored troops are regularly mustered into the service of the United States." But the Texans considered Milliken's Bend a victory, and a private in the brigade wrote: "Our gallant troops were led by such men as the gallant and brave Colonel Dick Waterhouse…." McCulloch, however, came under serious criticism for his handling of his troops; the following month a member of Waterhouse's regiment wrote, "our Brigade can do as good fighting as any of them. We have got as brave leaders as there is in the Confederacy. Genl. McCulloch is not very prudent. I think he wants to immortalize his name as well as his little Band of Texans and we will follow him any where that he will lead us. And as to Col. Waterhouse he is as dauntless as McCulloch." When McCulloch was relieved of command, Waterhouse's regiment became part of Brigadier General William R. Scurry's brigade.

The Texans remained in Louisiana for the remainder of the year and took part in the Red River Campaign in 1864. Waterhouse fought under Scurry at Mansfield and Pleasant Hill, Louisiana, and General Taylor reported that Scurry "speaks highly of Colonel Waterhouse, commanding one of his regiments." After Scurry was mortally wounded in the battle of Jenkins' Ferry, Arkansas, April 30, 1864, Waterhouse took command of the brigade. General Edmund Kirby Smith appointed him a brigadier general on May 13, to rank from April 30. When this promotion was not confirmed by the Confederate government, Smith wrote Adjutant General Samuel Cooper in late October, asking for a decision in the matter. In his letter Smith pointed out that Waterhouse "is pronounced a good officer." On March 16, 1865, Smith wrote Richmond again, still trying to legitimize the promotion, as Waterhouse was still serving as an acting brigadier general. In December 1864 he was in command of the 1st Texas Infantry Brigade, 1st Texas Infantry Division; a unit composed of the 3d, 16th, 17th, 19th Texas infantries, and the 16th Texas Dismounted Cavalry. Waterhouse was officially promoted on March 16 to take rank from March 17, 1865, and was confirmed by the Senate on the last day it was in session.

After the war he returned to east Texas and lived in San Augustine and Jefferson. On a visit to Waco in March 1876, he fell down a stairway in a hotel, hurting his shoulder. Apparently his injuries were more serious, and they were complicated by pneumonia, as he died two days later on March 20. He was buried in Oakwood Cemetery at Jefferson.

Anne Bailey

Blessington, J.P., *The Campaigns of Walker's Texas Division by a Private Soldier* (Austin, 1968).

Brown, Norman D., ed., *Journey to Pleasant Hill: The Civil War Letters of Captain Elijah P. Petty, Walker's Texas Division C.S.A.* (San Antonio, 1982).

⋆ *Stand Watie* ⋆

No genuine uniformed portrait of Watie has been found. This civilian view is postwar. (Medford Historical Society, Medford, Mass.)

The son of a full-blood Cherokee father and a half-breed mother, Stand Watie became the only Indian to achieve the rank of brigadier general in the Confederate Army. He was born near the site of present-day Rome, Georgia, on December 12, 1806. At the age of twelve he was sent to the Moravian mission school at Brainerd, Georgia, where he learned English, received a basic education, converted to Christianity, and joined the Moravian church. Subsequently, he completed his education at the interdenominational Foreign Mission School in Cornwall, Connecticut, returned to his home in Georgia, and became a planter. Watie became involved in tribal affairs, and during the period when his brother served as editor of the tribal newspaper, the *Cherokee Phoenix*, he assisted him with its publication.

The agitation for Indian removal reached a climax when the state of Georgia undertook to dispossess the Cherokees by instituting the land lottery whereby whites could legitimately acquire individual plots of Indian land. Watie and other progressives decided that protracted resistance to removal would come to naught. Consequently, in 1835 he and three other tribal leaders signed the Treaty of New Echota in which the Eastern Cherokees agreed to surrender their lands and join the Cherokees West, those who had migrated westward some years earlier and settled in a region now included in the state of Oklahoma. Although the conservative majority of the tribe opposed this treaty, the United States Senate ratified it.

The treaty party, representing about one-third of the Cherokee population, voluntarily migrated westward early in 1836, resettled in the Indian Territory, and aligned themselves politically with those who had migrated earlier. During the winter of 1838–39, the remaining Eastern Cherokees were herded along the "Trail of Tears" by the U.S. Army to the Indian Territory.

The Cherokee Nation remained politically divided, and acting in accordance with a 1829 law which made the disposal of Cherokee land a capital offense, a group of conservative Cherokees executed three of the signers of the treaty on the same day in June of 1839. Although marked for death, Watie escaped and became the leader of the minority group.

By 1861 Watie and the other highly acculturated slave owners were living and thinking like the white upper-class Southerners. Anticipating the Civil War, Watie had organized the Knights of the Golden Circle, later known as the Southern Rights party, for the stated purpose of bringing the Cherokees into the Confederate fold.

Watie acted upon his convictions and raised a company of home guards early in June of 1861 and became its captain. Initially, Watie and his men served on the northern border of the Indian Territory, assisting in protecting the territory from raids by the Jayhawkers of Kansas. On August 10, Watie and his men fought as dismounted cavalry at the Battle of Wilson's Creek and acquitted themselves well, because when other Indians were thrown into confusion when subjected to artillery fire, "Watie and his regiment were firm in their adherence."

After the Confederate victory at Wilson's Creek, Watie persuaded John Ross and his majority group to join the pro-Southern minority in forming an alliance with the Confederacy. On September 1 Brigadier General Ben McCulloch notified the Executive Council of the Cherokee Nation that he had "already authorized Col. Stand Watie to raise a force for the protection of your northern border." Later that month, McCulloch wrote to Secretary of War Leroy P. Walker: "Watie belongs to the true Southern Party…I hope our Government will continue this gallant man and true friend of our country in service, and attach him and his men (some 300) to my command…those with Col. Stand Watie…are educated men, and good soldiers anywhere, in or out of the Nation."

In October Watie received from the Confederate government his commission as colonel of the newly formed "Cherokee Mounted Rifles," a regiment of Cherokee volunteers. On December 27, Watie engaged a sizable force of hostile Indians in a running fight for some two hours or more at the Battle of Chustenahlah, killing fifteen of the enemy and suffering no casualties among his own men. While fighting as part of Brigadier General Albert Pike's brigade, at the Battle of Elkhorn Tavern on March 7–8, 1862, Watie's regiment pushed back a Union division, but later lost ground when the enemy counterattacked.

Watie employed hit-and-run tactics and became a genius at guerrilla warfare; he was involved in more than one hundred raids and skirmishes against Union forces and pro-Union Indians in and around the Indian Territory. While in command of the Indian Territory in 1863 Brigadier General William Steele wrote that he found Watie "to be a gallant and daring officer."

One of Watie's more spectacular raids was his capture on June 15, 1864, of the U.S.S. *J.R.Williams* at Pheasant Bluff on the Arkansas River. The vessel was laden with commissary supplies and en route from Fort Smith to Fort Gibson, when Watie fired upon it, forcing it to run aground. Of the vessel's crew and its guard contingent of twenty-six men, four men were killed and five captured. After confiscating as much cargo as he could, while being fired upon by Union troops, Watie set fire to the vessel and abandoned her on June 17, 1864. In his report of the incident, Major General Samuel B. Maxey remarked, "I am glad the colonel [Watie] has so early given evidence of the correctness of my recommendation of him for promotion." Actually, Watie had been appointed a brigadier general on May 10, 1864, to rank from May 6, but it took several weeks for word of his promotion to arrive from Richmond.

Although Watie was included in the Canby-Smith convention of May 26, 1865, he did not surrender until June 23, the last Confederate general to do so. No record of his personal parole has been found. After the war, he resumed his life as a planter and engaged in other enterprises. He died on September 9, 1871, at his home on Honey Creek, in present-day Delaware County, Oklahoma, and was buried there in Old Ridge Cemetery.

Benjamin E. Snellgrove

Anderson, Mabel W., *Life of General Stand Watie* (Pryor, Ok., 1915).

Harrell, John M., *Arkansas*, Vol. X in Evans, *Confederate Military History*.

An outstanding previously unpublished portrait of General Waul taken after September 1863. (Courtesy of Larry Jones)

⋆ *Thomas Neville Waul* ⋆

Thomas Neville Waul was born January 5, 1813, near Statesburg in the Sumter District of South Carolina. He came from a background of soldiers, as both of his grandfathers had participated in the American Revolution. Waul was an only child, and his mother had died when he was an infant. As a teenager he entered South Carolina College but was forced to leave before graduating, partly because of his own poor health and partly as a result of his father's death. Waul moved to Florence, Alabama, and at seventeen years of age was made principal of a school. At the end of the year he relocated in Vicksburg, where he made the acquaintance of S.S. Prentiss and studied in his law office. He was licensed to practice before the supreme court of the state while he was still a minor and was admitted to the bar in 1835. Waul lived at Yazoo City and Grenada before moving to Gonzales County, Texas, where he owned a plantation and opened a law office. He enjoyed politics and ran for the U.S. Congress in 1859 but lost.

When the Civil War began, Waul was elected to the Provisional Congress of the Confederacy and served until the election of the permanent government. He was one of the representatives from Texas to sign the Confederate Constitution, along with future Postmaster General John H. Reagan and the controversial Louis T. Wigfall. He was part of a committee to draw up detailed instructions for the Quartermaster's, Commissary, and Medical Departments for the Confederate government before he declined reelection to go into the field.

Waul returned to Texas, where he raised Waul's Texas Legion and became its colonel, on May 17, 1862. The legion was organized at Brenham, and one source claimed that it originally consisted of twelve companies of infantry, six companies of cavalry, and a battery of light artillery. The legion went briefly to Arkansas, where the cavalry and the battery left it, and Waul was ordered to cross the Mississippi River and proceed to Vicksburg with the infantry in October 1862. Although the cavalry eventually joined Waul, it did not remain under his command but joined J.R. Chalmers' cavalry brigade. At Holly Springs the command was reorganized into two battalions of six companies each but was still known as Waul's Legion and under Waul's personal command. In January 1863 it was part of the 1st Division under Major General W.W. Loring, and in February Waul was commanding at Fort Pemberton on the Yazoo River. Loring wrote that Waul was "judicious in his arrangements, and I would recommend that he be kept in command of this position."

In May Loring reported on the operations on the Yazoo and Tallahatchie rivers and said that he wished "to express my obligations to Col. T.N. Waul, Texas Legion, for his energy, promptness, and good judgment in the discharge of his duty with his Legion in the fortifications during the engagements. I was greatly indebted to him for the assistance he rendered on so many occasions, and which contributed to our frequent success." After one company was detached, eleven of the companies, along with colonel Waul, were captured at Vicksburg. Waul was promoted to brigadier general on September 19 after his exchange, to rank from September 18, 1863. Four days later he was ordered to report to Lieutenant General Edmund Kirby Smith for assignment in the Trans-Mississippi Department.

In the meantime, the paroled members of the legion returned to Texas, assembled, and reorganized at Houston. Waul was ordered to collect men of the 2d Texas Regiment, the battalion of Louisiana Zouaves, and the various members of his legion. In November Major General John B. Magruder, in charge in Texas, complained that these units had become "splendidly drilled infantry," and if Waul attempted to remount them "it will be a failure, as the horses are not to be had…." The Confederate government agreed, and the order for Waul to remount his command was revoked.

Instead Waul was relieved from command in Texas and ordered to Louisiana, where he replaced Brigadier General James M. Hawes in command of the 1st

Waul as a colonel in command of Waul's Texas Legion. (Albert G. Shaw Collection, Virginia Historical Society, Richmond)

Brigade, Walker's Texas Infantry Division in February 1864. Waul led the brigade in the Red River Campaign, and at Pleasant Hill a private recalled that Waul, "utterly regardless of all danger, rushed into the thickest of the fight" and rallied his troops. He took his command to Arkansas to stop the advance of the Union army under Major General Frederick Steele, and had his arm broken at the Battle of Jenkins' Ferry, Arkansas, on April 30, 1864. He was absent in Texas recovering from this wound at the time command of the division changed. When he returned to the army, he took command of an infantry brigade in the division of Major General J.H. Forney (formerly Walker's Texas Infantry Division).

Following the war Waul returned to politics and was elected to the first Texas reconstruction convention. He later moved to Galveston, where he opened a law office. He died on a farm near Greenville, Hunt County, on July 28, 1908. Waul had no family, and was buried in Fort Worth.

Anne Bailey

Blessington, J.P., *The Campaigns of Walker's Texas Division by a Private Soldier* (Austin, 1968).

Brown, Norman D., ed., *Journey to Pleasant Hill: The Civil War Letters of Captain Elijah P. Petty, Walker's Texas Division C.S.A.* (San Antonio, 1982).

"General Thomas N. Waul," *Confederate Veteran*, III (December 1895), 380.

✶ *Henry Constantine Wayne* ✶

No uniformed portrait of Henry Wayne has been found. This one is considerably postwar. (Evans, *Confederate Military History*)

Henry Constantine Wayne, the son of a former Congressman and mayor of Savannah, Georgia, was born in that city on September 18, 1815. After receiving a good education at schools in Northampton and Cambridge, Massachusetts, he enrolled in Harvard University in 1832. After two years, however, Wayne entered West Point and graduated fourteenth in the class of 1838. He first served in the 4th and 1st Artillery but then taught tactics at the academy from 1841 to 1846. During the Mexican War he served as a captain in the quartermaster department and was brevetted major for gallantry at the Battles of Contreras and Churubusco. Following the war he published a text for sword exercises in 1850 and in the mid-1850s was involved in the famous army experiment with camels in the American southwest. For his role in the latter Wayne was awarded a gold medal by the French Zoological Society in 1858.

Wayne resigned his commission on December 31, 1860, and was appointed Georgia's adjutant general and inspector general in early 1861. He served in Governor Joseph E. Brown's staff until promoted to brigadier general in the Confederate army on December 16, 1861, to rank from that date. When ordered to join General Joe Johnston's army at Manassas, Virginia, in January 1862, Wayne immediately resigned his commission. He was then appointed major general and adjutant general of the Georgia state troops, a position he kept for the rest of the war. To train his men, Wayne employed the cadets of the Georgia Military Institute as drill instructors.

At the beginning of the Atlanta Campaign Wayne took command of two brigades of Georgia militia and cadets. His main duty was to guard the crossings along a one-hundred-mile stretch of the Chattahoochiee River between Roswell and West Point. Major General Gustavus Smith relieved him during the summer of 1864, and Wayne resumed his administrative duties at Milledgeville. When Major General William T. Sherman's armies approached the capital in November 1864, Wayne accompanied Governor Brown on the last train out of the city on the night of November 9. With him went a motley force of cadets, artillery, cavalry, militia, prison guards, and prisoners who were offered pardons if they agreed to fight. Wayne's force took up a position to guard the railroad bridge across the Oconee River east of Gordon, Georgia. With seven hundred men he guarded a twenty-mile stretch of river and was engaged with the enemy on November 23 and 24. Withdrawing from the Oconee, Wayne retreated to the Little Ogeechee railroad bridge and assembled four thousand militia to defend it. He engaged in skirmishing with the Yankees on December 4, but then Major General Lafayette McLaws arrived and assumed command. The Confederates retreated to Savannah on December 6, and Wayne's men dug in around the city. On December 7 Wayne relinquished his command to Major General Gustavus Smith and returned to his duties as adjutant general in Milledgeville. The campaign made Wayne especially proud of his young cadets. "I cannot speak too highly of these youths," he wrote, "who go into a fight as cheerfully as they would enter a ball room, and with the silence and steadiness of veterans."

After the war, Wayne returned to Savannah and worked in the lumber industry from 1866 to 1875. He died in Savannah on March 15, 1883, and was buried in the Laurel Grove Cemetery.

Terry L. Jones

Conrad, James Lee, "Training in Treason," *Civil War Times Illustrated*, Sept./Oct. 1991, pp. 22–29.

Derry, Joseph, *Georgia*, Vol. VI in Evans, *Confederate Military History*.

✯ David Addison Weisiger ✯

This portrait of Weisiger has been artistically retouched to provide a uniform that is almost certainly not genuine. No actual uniformed view has been found. (U.S. Army Military History Institute, Carlisle, Pa.)

David Addison Weisiger was born at "The Grove," Chesterfield County, Virginia, on December 23, 1818. A businessman in Petersburg, Weisiger volunteered as a 2d lieutenant and recruited Company E, 1st Virginia Volunteers in November 1846. The regiment was mustered into service on December 15 and soon departed for Mexico, where it served in the army of Zachary Taylor during 1847. Weisiger was promoted to regimental adjutant and with his comrades mustered out in August 1848. Resuming his business career, Weisiger also joined the state's militia and in May 1853 was unanimously elected colonel of the 39th Virginia Militia. He served as officer of the day at the execution of abolitionist John Brown in December 1859. By 1861 he commanded the 4th Virginia Battalion of militia.

On April 20, three days after Virginia's secession, Weisiger led the battalion to Norfolk. During the next two months Weisiger organized his units into a regiment and on July 1, Confederate authorities accepted into service the 12th Virginia, with him as colonel. The regiment formed part of the garrison of the so-called "Intrenched Camp" outside of Norfolk. On May 3, 1862, the regiment reorganized and Weisiger retained the colonelcy. It was assigned to the brigade of William Mahone.

During the spring and summer of 1862, Mahone's brigade participated in the major campaigns in the east. The 12th Virginia's initial combat came at Seven Pines on May 31–June 1, and the Seven Days' Campaign followed during the final week of that month. On July 1 at Malvern Hill, Weisiger's conduct earned Mahone's praise. The brigade commander reported that Weisiger's "exertions and gallantry...merit high commendation." On August 30 at Second Manassas, Weisiger assumed command of the brigade when Mahone fell wounded, leading it in an attack until he himself suffered a serious wound.

The wound disabled Weisiger for nearly a year. He returned to the 12th Virginia after the Gettysburg Campaign in July 1863, and commanded the regiment throughout the fall and winter of 1864. At the Battle of the Wilderness, on May 6, 1865, Weisiger assumed command of the brigade when Mahone took charge of the division. On May 31 Weisiger was temporarily promoted to brigadier general, with permanent rank dated July 30. He retained command of the brigade—comprised of the 6th, 12th, 16th, 41st, and 61st Virginia—until the end of the war.

On July 30, 1864, the Federals exploded a mine of gunpowder under the Confederate works at Petersburg. Mahone's division was positioned behind the so-called "Crater," and counterattacked. Weisiger's Virginians spearheaded the assault with a brigade of Georgians. In the furious combat his men fought valiantly and he suffered a bullet wound in his side. He subsequently would be called the "Hero of the Crater."

Weisiger and the brigade served in the Petersburg trenches for the next eight months. When the Confederate lines collapsed on April 2, 1865, they joined in the retreat to Appomattox and were paroled there. Although Weisiger missed a number of major campaigns of the army, he had been a fine regimental commander and a capable brigadier.

After the war Weisiger returned to Petersburg, where he served as a bank cashier. Later, he was a businessman in Richmond and died there on February 23, 1899. He was buried in Petersburg.

Jeffry D. Wert

Hotchkiss, Jedediah, *Virginia*, Vol. III in Evans, *Confederate Military History*.

⋆ *Gabriel Colvin Wharton* ⋆

The only known wartime uniformed portrait of Wharton was taken when he was colonel of the 51st Virginia during the first half of the war. (Library of Congress)

Many a competent brigadier never felt the thrill of participating in a triumph, much less playing an integral role in a great victory. Gabriel C. Wharton was one of the fortunate ones. Though all of the rest of his war service may be forgotten, he had his moment in one of the most honored and well remembered Confederate victories of the war.

It was said that there was old Viking blood in the Wharton veins, but when he was born July 23, 1824 in Culpeper County, his blood was pure Virginian. A military tradition ran strong in the family, his great-grandfather being British Major General Sir George Wharton. The young Virginian followed in the paths of tradition by entering the Virginia Military Institute and graduating second in his class in 1847. Leaving the Institute he went into mining and engineering, moving to the part of the New Mexico Territory that would one day become Arizona. When the outbreak of war came, he joined a small but intrepid band of Southerners led by Albert Sidney Johnston in a lengthy trek across the Southwest to Texas, and then on to Richmond, to join with the Confederacy.

Wharton's first assignment was as major of the 45th Virginia Infantry, an outfit raised in the mountains of southwest Virginia in Carroll and Grayson Counties. Yet he served only during July 1861 with the 45th, before raising and being elected colonel of the 51st Virginia. That fall Wharton led his regiment in the unremarkable western Virginia campaign of General John B. Floyd, then went west with Floyd to join the command of General Sidney Johnston in west Tennessee. There he escaped from Fort Donelson prior to its surrender, then served briefly on the staff of his

120

friend Johnston. It is probably out of this episode of leaving Donelson that Wharton incurred the rumored enmity of Jefferson Davis, who never forgave Floyd and Gideon Pillow for abandoning their commands, and may have attached the same stigma to Wharton, even though the Virginian was apparently a favorite of Davis' most worshiped friend Johnston.

Wharton was transferred back to southwestern and western Virginia in the spring of 1862, and would serve in that theater for the rest of the war. If unpopular with Davis, he was much loved by his men who affectionately called him "Old Gabe." He was handsome, full-bearded, nearly six feet tall, yet within himself he kept, after the defeat at Shiloh, a fear that the Confederacy would not succeed. Being one of the senior colonels in the department to which he was assigned, he soon commanded an impromptu brigade composed of his own regiment and the 62d Virginia, with occasionally a battery and even a cavalry company attached to it. However, perhaps because of Davis' ill will, Wharton would not receive commensurate promotion until September 25, 1863, when Davis finally appointed him a brigadier to rank from July 8.

The promotion came just in time for Wharton to be assigned to the Department of Western Virginia and East Tennessee, engaged in repelling Yankee raids on Saltville. His brigade numbered fewer than one thousand effectives, serving in a patchwork division commanded by Robert Ransom. By late winter, in March 1864, Wharton was in East Tennessee serving under Longstreet, now in a division commanded by Simon Buckner, but then in late April came Federal General Franz Sigel's invasion of the Shenandoah Valley, and Richmond ordered Buckner to send Wharton and his command to cooperate with John C. Breckinridge in meeting the threat.

In the ensuing campaign Wharton saw his greatest glory of the war, and showed the kind of performance of which he was capable. In the headlong rush to stop Sigel, Wharton pushed his brigade an astounding 187 miles in eight days. twenty three and one half miles per day, almost ten miles a day farther than "Stonewall" Jackson had pushed his men. By the time Breckinridge's small army reached New Market to give battle to Sigel, Wharton's command had evolved to include several extra elements, now consisting of the 30th Virginia Battalion, the 51st Virginia, the 62d Virginia Mounted Infantry, and Company A of the 1st Missouri Cavalry, 1,557 all told. On May 15

the Confederates resoundingly defeated Sigel in spite of superior Yankee numbers. Wharton held the left half of the Confederate line throughout the day, personally reconnoitering in his front on foot, and withstood a final Federal charge that, when dispersed, was followed by the victorious Rebel advance, Wharton's own men taking several field pieces. In the action, his brigade suffered eighteen percent casualties, the highest in the Southern army excepting the V.M.I. cadets.

That summer Wharton led his brigade in the repulse of Hunter from Lynchburg, and then in the Shenandoah actions under Early as part of a small corps commanded by Breckinridge. He saw action in the Raid on Washington, Winchester, Fisher's Hill, and Cedar Creek, and remained under Early during the pitiful final winter in the Valley, seeing his last battle at Waynesborough on March 2, 1865. Wharton's brigade was completely dispersed in that disaster, but he escaped, finding his way with a small remnant to Lynchburg, where he finally surrendered and gave his parole on June 21, 1865.

In 1863 Wharton had married a woman from Radford, Virginia, and settled there after the war. He turned his energies to mining and development, along with serving successive terms in the state assembly. When he died on May 12, 1906, he was buried in a family cemetery in Radford, wrapped in the colors of his old 51st Virginia.

William C. Davis

Davis William C., *The Battle of New Market*, (New York, 1975).

Wharton, J.H.V., "Gen. G.C. Wharton." *Confederate Veteran*, XIV, July 1906.

⋆ *John Austin Wharton* ⋆

This future major general was born Edwin Waller Wharton on July 3, 1828, near Nashville, Tennessee, after his father's friend, Colonel Edwin Waller. His family moved to Texas the next year; his mother was the daughter of Jared E. Groce, one of the wealthiest men in Texas, and after the Texas Revolution his father served as minister of the republic to the United States. According to one authority the child was called Waller Wharton until his uncle's death, when the elder Wharton renamed his son for his deceased brother, John Austin Wharton. The young Wharton was described as a red-haired, freckle-faced boy whose family owned a huge plantation in Brazoria County. As a young man John attended school in South Carolina, and while there met and married Penelope Johnson, daughter of Governor David Johnson. He also read law with South Carolina statesman William Preston. After Wharton returned to Texas, he was elected the Brazoria County attorney, and then sheriff. Wharton was one of the wealthiest men in the state and in 1861 was the law partner of Clint N. Terry, younger brother to Benjamin Franklin Terry.

When the Civil War began, Wharton, along with a group of men that included Benjamin Franklin Terry and Thomas S. Lubbock, headed for Richmond. All of the Texans fought at First Manassas except Wharton, who was ill. Terry and Lubbock distinguished themselves in the battle and were given permission to raise a regiment with Terry as colonel and Lubbock as lieutenant colonel. Returning to Texas, they raised what would become the 8th Texas Cavalry Regiment, better known as Terry's Texas Rangers. Wharton was elected captain of Company B, Archer Grays, from Brazoria

and Matagorda counties. A member of the regiment recalled: "Wharton was a man of ability, of a distinguished family, liberally educated, a lawyer and a captivating public speaker. Enterprising and ambitious, he never forgot during a wakeful moment that the soldier who survived the war would be a voter."

The regiment joined General Albert Sidney Johnston in Kentucky. On December 17, 1861, the men fought in their first battle, in which Terry was killed. He was succeeded by Lubbock, but after Lubbock became ill and died, Wharton was elected colonel. Before the Battle of Shiloh in April 1862 Wharton learned a valuable military lesson. He allowed the men to fire off their wet arms so they could reload but "was immediately called to headquarters" where he was "severely reprimanded." George W. Baylor recalled when Wharton was placed under arrest, "that brave officer put in an earnest appeal to the General, saying he 'would rather be shot than not allowed to go into the fight' and upon being released did gallant service with the Terry Rangers in the battle."

Indeed, Wharton did win the notice of his superiors at Shiloh. Major General William J. Hardee reported that "the gallant Wharton" was wounded leading a charge. In spite of his injury he refused to go to the rear and headed the rangers as they protected the retreating army with other cavalry. But after two days in the saddle the wound became so painful that he had to relinquish command. Wharton was well aware

The only known uniformed photo of General Wharton, showing him in a unique single-breasted jacket with the buttons in pairs of twos. It dates from 1863-65. (Cook Collection, Valentine Museum, Richmond, Va.)

that he had impressed his superiors, and he quickly learned how the military worked. Early in May after the rangers had moved to East Tennessee, Wharton was unhappy at being placed under Captain John Adams and wrote: "My conduct at Shiloh and elsewhere would not, I think, justify a junior officer being placed over me." As a result of the dispute Adams complained that Wharton "manifested an unwillingness to serve under my command" and allowed him to pull his regiment out of the brigade.

In the summer of 1862 Wharton served in Nathan Bedford Forrest's brigade. At Murfreesboro on July 13, 1862, Forrest had high praise for Wharton, saying that when ordered to charge, "he moved forward in gallant style at the head of his men," and was severely wounded. He participated in Major General Braxton Bragg's invasion of Kentucky, and in a skirmish at Bardstown, when his horse was shot, he again received the notice of his superiors. At Perryville he led a charge that a ranger claimed "was one of three made by Terry's Rangers that surpassed any other made by any troops during the war." He was promoted to brigadier general on November 18, 1862, and in January 1863 commanded a brigade in the Army of Mississippi of over two thousand men.

He took part in Major General Joseph Wheeler's raid in October 1863, and Wheeler wrote that Wharton and his men "behaved throughout with their accustomed gallantry." Wharton was promoted to major general on November 10, 1863, and fought under Wheeler in the Chattanooga Campaign. But there was trouble brewing between Wharton and Wheeler, as many believed Wharton was the superior officer. Wheeler certainly heard these rumors and felt compelled to write General Joseph E. Johnston to explain the difficulties he had experienced with Wharton. Wheeler was angry with Wharton's antics and in December 1863 complained: "The truth is, General Wharton allowed his ambition to completely turn his head, as his friend in Congress [Louis T. Wigfall] had assured him that he should command the cavalry of this army, he being one of those politicians (not statesmen) who looked upon things we would consider dishonorable as legitimate tricks, and he forgot that he was an officer instead of a frontier political trickster." Moreover, Wheeler protested: "This state of things has been going on for some time, the object appearing to be to convince his command that he was their friend, while I was not, and also that he was superior as an officer, &c."

Johnston recognized that his cavalry was not very efficient because of lack of "harmony among superior officer," and he planned "to improve it during the winter." When Johnston learned that Wharton had applied to Davis for a transfer to the Trans-Mississippi, he wrote Adjutant General Samuel Cooper, "I cordially approve the application " and probably felt relieved that at least one of his problems was solved.

In February 1864 Wharton received instruction to report to Lieutenant General Edmund Kirby Smith, and arrived in Texas early in April. He was immediately ordered to Louisiana, where he assumed command of Lieutenant General Richard Taylor's cavalry after the death of Tom Green, and headed the troops who pursued Union Major General Nathaniel Banks back down the Red River. He again received high praise from his superiors, and Taylor said that Wharton would "lead the gallant sons of Texas to victory." Following the successful conclusion of the Red River Campaign Wharton remained in the Trans-Mississippi and headed a cavalry corps. He wanted, however, to return east. In a letter to his friend Wigfall in July he related that he "was urging acceptance of Wigfall's idea to unite Texas troops with Johnston in Georgia."

Wharton, however, did not live to see the war's end. On April 6, 1865, Wharton was visiting Major General John B. Magruder's headquarters in the Fannin Hotel in Houston when he had an argument in the street with Colonel George W. Baylor. Wharton and Baylor had disagreed before, but this time Wharton came into Magruder's quarters, and as Baylor later claimed, "called me a liar." In an angry moment Baylor shot the unarmed Wharton, who died instantly. Perhaps Richard Taylor best assessed Wharton's career when he said that he came "to us with crown adorned with the laurels of many a hard-fought field," and would take his "place at once in the front rank of Texas leaders."

Anne Bailey

Blackburn, James Knox Polk, *Reminiscences of the Terry Rangers* (Austin, 1919).

Giles, Leonidas B., *Terry's Texas Rangers* (Austin, 1911).

Jeffries, C.C., *Terry's Rangers* (New York, 1961).

"Statistics About Gen. Wharton," *Confederate Veteran*, V, 530.

"Terry's Texas Rangers," *Confederate Veteran*, V, 151–254.

⭐ *Joseph Wheeler* ⭐

A previously unpublished portrait of General Wheeler although retouched, appears to be a genuine uniformed view. (Museum of the Confederacy, Richmond, Va.)

It is quite possible that most or all of the known photos of Wheeler were taken at the same sitting, like this unpublished bust view. (William A. Turner Collection)

Joseph Wheeler, soldier and politician, was born September 10, 1836, near Augusta, Georgia. His parents were Joseph and Julia Hull Wheeler, of New England ancestry. Joseph received his primary education in the Connecticut and New York common schools as his family moved about. He was appointed to the United States Military Academy from New York, reported as a cadet on July 1, 1854, and graduated nineteenth in the class of 1859. Among his classmates were William E. Merrill (first), Samuel H. Lockett (second), Robert F. Beckham (sixth), Norman J. Hall (thirteenth), and Edwin H. Stoughton (seventeenth).

Commissioned a brevet 2d lieutenant in the 1st U.S. Dragoons, Wheeler reported for duty at the Carlisle Barracks cavalry school. He transferred to the Mounted Rifles, then posted at Fort Craig, New Mexico Territory, on June 26, 1860, and was promoted 2d lieutenant on September 1 of that year. On March 14, 1861, he was commissioned a 1st lieutenant in the Confederate artillery and ordered on April 16 to Pensacola, where he reported to Major General Braxton Bragg. It was one week later, on April 22, that the War Department in Washington accepted his resignation from the U.S. Army. On September 4 Wheeler was promoted colonel and named to command the 19th Alabama Infantry Regiment, then encamped near Huntsville, Alabama. Wheeler and his regiment were sent to Mobile on November 11 and assigned to Brigadier General Jones M. Withers' command. Following the mid-February 1862 disaster at Fort Donelson and the evacuation of Nashville, General Bragg stripped the defenses of Mobile, Pensacola, and New Orleans and concentrated his six-brigade corps at Corinth.

On April 6 Wheeler and his 19th Alabama, one of four infantry regiments and an artillery company constituting the brigade led by Brigadier General John K. Jackson, attacked the Union army at Shiloh. By late afternoon Wheeler and his people had been in three distinct engagements when they closed on the foe in the thickets west of Wicker field. Those Yanks who had been hiding the Hornets' Nest since mid-morning had finally been isolated, and Wheeler and his Alabamans were there when Brigadier General B.M. Prentiss and his twenty-two hundred men grounded arms and raised white flags. Wheeler was told by General Bragg to take charge of the prisoners and escort them to the rear. He, however, was relieved of

this responsibility by the 18th Alabama. On Monday the 7th, Wheeler first supported Brigadier General James R. Chalmers' Mississippians and late in the day screened the Confederate retreat.

Wheeler was an activist during the siege of Corinth (April 28–May 30). For four days—May 6–10—Wheeler and his pickets north of the state line clashed repeatedly with Union patrols; then, on May 28–29, while he was an acting brigade commander, there was bitter skirmishing along the picket line east of Bridge Creek, as soldiers of the Army of the Ohio inched their way nearer to the Rebel rifle-pits. On the night of the 29th, Wheeler helped cover the evacuation of Corinth and the march south to Tupelo by destroying the Tuscumbia River bridges.

General Bragg, now commander of the Army of the Mississippi, named Wheeler his chief of cavalry on July 13. Before the end of the month, Wheeler led his first raid from Holly Springs and struck deep into West Tennessee, destroying several railroad bridges and besting Yankee horse soldiers on eight occasions.

He and his brigade crossed the Tennessee River at Chattanooga on August 27 to become active participants in the Kentucky Campaign. Beginning at Altamont three days later and continuing until he reached London, Kentucky, on October 22, Wheeler and his cavalry were never far from the enemy. During these fifty-seven days, Wheeler was involved in forty-five skirmishes, two actions, two affairs, and the Battle of Perryville. His abilities as a leader of mounted men were recognized on October 30 when he was made brigadier general. Two weeks before he had been named to the command of all the cavalry in Bragg's army. When he returned to Middle Tennessee, "Little Joe" had become a force to reckon with. However, he had inadvertently aroused the ire of another Rebel cavalry leader—Nathan Bedford Forrest—when Bragg assigned most of Forrest's command to Wheeler in mid-September and sent "Old Bedford" back to Murfreesboro to raise a new brigade.

Little Joe added to his laurels during the Stones' River Campaign (December 26, 1862–January 5, 1863). He and his horse soldiers, in passing around the Union Army of the Cumberland, raised havoc with enemy trains, destroying hundreds of wagons loaded with supplies and capturing more than seven hundred prisoners. Following the army's retreat to the Duck River line, Wheeler struck at the Yankees' Cumberland River lifeline, and at Harpeth Shoals on

January 12–13, captured and burned three steamboats and took more than four hundred prisoners. General Bragg, in calling attention to the raid, asked that Wheeler be promoted as a "just reward." Wheeler, with his command reinforced by Forrest's, next attacked Dover (Fort Donelson), where on February 23 they were repulsed by the small Union garrison. This led to hot words between Wheeler and Forrest, in which the latter stated "...there is one thing I want you to put in that report to General Bragg. Tell him that I will be in my coffin before I will fight again under your command." Wheeler was now a major general, having been promoted to that rank effective January 20.

Bragg confronted the bitterness between Wheeler and Forrest by assigning the former to guard the army's right and the latter the left. The Army of the Cumberland moved out on June 23 to begin the Tullahoma Campaign. At Shelbyville on the 27th onrushing Union cavalry overpowered Wheeler and trapped him and fifty of his men on the north side of the Duck River. Wheeler broke through the encirclement, plunged his horse over a fifteen-foot embankment, and escaped across the rain-swollen river.

At Chickamauga on September 18–20, Wheeler and his corps watched Bragg's left. Victorious, the Confederates closed in on Chattanooga and besieged the Army of the Cumberland. Wheeler and three small divisions crossed the Tennessee River on September 30 to interdict the sixty-mile route over which the Union supplied the forty thousand soldiers holed up in Chattanooga. On October 2 he scored the expedition's only major success, at Anderson's Cross Roads in the Sequatchie Valley, when he intercepted and destroyed more than seven hundred wagons and sabered or shot hundreds of mules. Hotly pursued by Union cavalry, Wheeler pressed on and captured McMinnville with its six-hundred-man garrison. The chase continued with a fight near Murfreesboro on the 5th and at Farmington two days later. Wheeler beat the Yankees to Muscle Shoals, where on October 9 he recrossed the Tennessee with an exhausted and badly used-up command.

In mid-November Wheeler with two divisions marched into East Tennessee with Lieutenant General James Longstreet's columns against Major General Ambrose E. Burnside's army. Wheeler took the lead when the Confederates left Sweetwater on November 13,

striking first at Marysville and then at Kingston as Burnside's troops fell back into the Knoxville fortifications. Wheeler on the 24th left Brigadier General Will Martin in charge of his two divisions and accompanied by his escort headed back to Chattanooga. He was too late.

On the 25th, Bragg's army had been routed from Missionary Ridge. In the fight at Ringgold Gap on the 27th, Wheeler was wounded in the foot as his cavalry and Patrick Cleburne's infantry checked the Union pursuit, saved Bragg's trains, and enabled the army to reach Dalton, Georgia, where it regrouped and General Joseph E. Johnston replaced Bragg.

Wheeler used the winter of 1863–64 to reorganize, rest, beef up, and re-equip his cavalry corps as much as possible. On May 7, the day Major General William T. Sherman put his "army group" in motion to begin the four-month Atlanta Campaign, Wheeler's corps numbered seventy-three hundred, organized into three divisions. By June 10—with the addition of Brigadier General William H. Jackson's division which had arrived from Mississippi in mid-May—his corps had increased to twelve thousand, three hundred. Wheeler and his horse soldiers screened the army's flanks, seeing action daily as Sherman employed his superior numbers to maneuver Johnston out of eight successive positions between Rocky Face and the Chattahoochee.

On July 18, with the Yanks at the gates of Atlanta, General John Bell Hood replaced Johnston and the Confederate strategy changed, with the Army of Tennessee coming out from behind its works to carry the fight to Sherman's "army group" on July 20, 22, and 28. Sherman now became cautious, had his troops entrench, and sent two formidable cavalry columns— George Stoneman's to the southeast and Edward McCook's to the southwest—to wreck the railroads over which Hood supplied the defenders of Atlanta. Wheeler had less than five thousand horsemen. Between July 27 and 31, Wheeler checkmated the enemy, turning back and hammering McCook and beating and capturing Stoneman, causing Sherman to comment, "...the cavalry raid was not deemed a success."

Wheeler's next major encounter with the foe was a Confederate disaster. On August 10, Wheeler and most of his corps crossed the Chattahoochee. His mission was to wreck the single-track railroad over which Sherman supplied his "army group." Several minor breaks in the railroad were made between Marietta and Calhoun before Wheeler struck Dalton on the 14th. Although he captured the town, most of the garrison holed up and held out in a nearby fort until relieved by a column that advanced from Chattanooga. Wheeler then broke off his attacks on the Western & Atlanta and rode into East Tennessee, crossing the Tennessee River above Knoxville. He then headed west, making minor breaks in the Nashville & Chattanooga Railroad near the former city, then heading south and fighting off pursuit at Franklin, Lynnville, and Campbellsville, and recrossed the Tennessee at Tuscumbia, Alabama, on September 2. Wheeler's raid had cost him two generals and the services of one-half his command. But, far more important, his absence from the army had so blinded and deluded General Hood that Sherman outmaneuvered the Rebel leader, beat him at Jonesboro, and compelled the Army of Tennessee to evacuate Atlanta. Wheeler returned to north Georgia in early October and on the 2d, after threatening Dalton for the second time in six weeks, destroyed the railroad bridge at Resaca and on the 8th rendezvoused with Hood's army at Cedartown.

Hood soon thereafter took his army into northwest Alabama preparatory to his march into Middle Tennessee. Wheeler with most of his cavalry remained in Georgia and beginning on November 15 found himself confronted with a "mission impossible"— opposing Sherman's March to the Sea. Initially, Wheeler sought to slow the progress of Sherman's right wing as it feinted toward Macon. Then, as Union columns converged on Milledgeville, he passed in front of them and took position to cover the approaches to Augusta. Here, near Waynesboro, and along Brier Creek (November 27–28), he clashed with Sherman's cavalry, led by Brigadier General Judson Kilpatrick, whom he had known at West Point. The two generals were bitter rivals, fighting as savagely with words as with their swords.

Lax discipline on the part of Wheeler and his principal subordinates caused bitter words on the part of many Confederates, Robert Toombs noting: "…I hope to God he will never get back to Georgia." Another less prominent Georgian wrote to President Davis, calling the cavalry "Wheeler's robbers" and stating that "the people of our state had reached the point where they did not care which army won, as Sherman was not making war any harder on them than our cavalry." Major General D.H. Hill wrote that "the whole of Georgia is full of bitter complaints of Wheeler's cavalry."

Wheeler, in early February 1865, vainly sought to slow Sherman's march into the heart of South Carolina. On the 11th he and his two thousand men beat Kilpatrick at Aiken. But this did not redeem Wheeler's waning reputation and he was replaced as General P.G.T. Beauregard's cavalry chief by Wade Hampton. Fighting under Hampton, Wheeler saw action on the approaches to Columbia and embarrassed Kilpatrick at Monroe's Cross Roads on March 10, compelling him to abandon his mistress and flee in his nightshirt. Kilpatrick, however, rallied his command and counterattacking compelled Wheeler to withdraw. Wheeler was at Averasboro (March 17) and under Hampton at Bentonville (March 19–21). He was in his last fight at Chapel Hill on April 15. In the days following the April 26 surrender by General Joseph E. Johnston of his forces, Wheeler took a small command south hoping to join President Jefferson Davis and the presidential party at Cokesbury, South Carolina. The rendezvous occurred, but not as planned. On May 9, Wheeler and his party were intercepted at Conyer's Station, Georgia, and were taken prisoner.

Escorted to Athens, Georgia, he was confined briefly with Davis and his party, who had been captured near Irwinville. The prisoners were taken to Fort Monroe, where they were separated and Wheeler was sent to Fort Delaware. He was held there in solitary confinement until June 8 when he was paroled and released.

Wheeler located in New Orleans and became a commission merchant. On February 8, 1866, he married Daniella Jones Sherrod. Two sons and five daughters were born to the couple. In 1868 the Wheelers moved to the Tennessee Valley of Alabama, settling in a community that was subsequently named Wheeler in his honor. Here he planted cotton and was admitted to the bar. Upon the rise of the Bourbons and the collapse of the reconstruction governments as a result of the 1876 election, Wheeler entered politics. In 1880 he was elected to the 47th Congress to represent the Eighth Alabama District. He served from March 4, 1882, until June 3, 1882, when he was unseated by William M. Lowe, who successfully contested the election. Upon the death of Lowe soon thereafter, he was elected to the same Congress to fill the vacancy and sat from January 15 to March 3, 1883. Elected to the 49th and the seven succeeding Congresses, Wheeler served from March 4, 1885, until April 20, 1900, when he resigned.

In Congress, he was active in military and fiscal affairs. Longevity made him the ranking Democrat on

Wheeler affected an unusual blouse button arrangement seen on only a few other generals. Most wore their buttons in directly vertical and parallel rows. (U.S. Army Military History Institute, Carlisle, Pa.)

the Ways and Means Committee, and he battled the high-tariff Republican majority. He championed raids on the Treasury by Union veterans seeking increased pensions. He took Fitz-John Porter's side in the latter's successful fight to vindicate his name.

In April 1898 the United States declared war against Spain and Wheeler volunteered his services to President William McKinley. On May 4 he was commissioned major general of volunteers. McKinley's action was applauded as a great step to use the crisis to enhance the spirit of reconciliation, of which Wheeler had been a prominent advocate. Wheeler commanded the cavalry division that landed at Daiquiri, thirteen miles east of Santiago-de-Cuba; participated in the fight at Los Guasimas on June 24 despite sickness; was present at San Juan Hill on July 1; and was the ranking member of the commission that negotiated the surrender of Santiago. Upon returning to the States he commanded the Montauk Point, New York, convalescent and mustering-out camp.

Wheeler then rushed across the Pacific and in the fight against the Philippine Insurrectos (July 8, 1899–January 24, 1900), led a brigade in the Tarlac campaign and other operations in central Luzon. After his return to the United States he was commissioned a brigadier general in the U.S. Regular Army on June 16 and retired at age sixty-four on September 14 of that year.

He resided in Brooklyn, New York, until his death on January 25, 1906. He was buried in Arlington National Cemetery. His continuing reputation in the early 20th century was underscored by his selection as one of Alabama's two heroes to have their statues in the nation's capitol.

Edwin C. Bearss

DeLeon, T.C., *Joseph Wheeler: The Man, The Statesman, The Soldier* (Atlanta, 1899).

Dodson, W.C., *Campaigns of Wheeler and His Cavalry* (Atlanta, 1899).

Dyer, John P., *"Fighting Joe" Wheeler* (Baton Rouge, 1941).

Dubose, John W., *General Joseph Wheeler and the Army of Tennessee* (New York, 1912).

Wheeler's slight frame is evident in a uniform that looks rather too big for him. (U.S. Army Military History Institute, Carlisle, Pa.)

⭐ John Wilkins Whitfield ⭐

John Wilkins Whitfield was born in Williamson County, Tennessee, near the town of Franklin on March 11, 1818. When the Mexican War began, he served as a captain in the 1st Tennessee Infantry, and then lieutenant colonel in the 2d Tennessee Infantry. In the early 1850s Whitfield moved to Independence, Missouri, and became an Indian agent in Missouri and Arkansas from 1853 until 1856. When he relocated in the newly created Kansas Territory, Whitfield became the proslavery delegate to the U.S. Congress. From 1857 until 1861 he lived in Doniphan, Kansas, where he was the register of the land office.

When it became clear that Kansas would not become a slave state, Whitfield, impoverished, moved to south Texas. In 1861 he organized cavalry in Lavaca County, which he took to join Brigadier General Ben McCulloch in Arkansas. When he arrived, he took command of the 4th Texas Cavalry Battalion. He led this command in the Battle of Pea Ridge, or Elkhorn Tavern, Arkansas, in March 1862. Whitfield's Legion, or the 1st Texas Legion, was created at the reorganization in April 1862; it was originally composed of thirteen companies with Whitfield as colonel. After the loss of one company the Legion was officially known as the 27th Texas Cavalry. On April 15, 1862, Whitfield was ordered to dismount his command, take it to Memphis, and report to Major General Sterling Price.

Whitfield participated in the Battle of Iuka, Mississippi, September 19, 1862, in a brigade commanded by Brigadier General Louis Hébert; the legion lost 106 officers and men. Price reported: "Whitfield's Legion not only took a battery with the aid of the Third Texas, but fully established on this occasion its right to stand side by side with the veteran regiments already named, and won under their gallant leader a reputation for dashing boldness and steady courage which places them side by side with the bravest and the best." Unfortunately Whitfield was wounded in the shoulder, although not seriously, and the legion was under the command of the lieutenant colonel at the Battle of Corinth and the fight at Hatchie Bridge.

At Grenada, Mississippi, in November 1862 a brigade was organized that consisted of Whitfield's Legion, and the 3d, 6th, and 9th Texas cavalry regiments (this later gained fame as Ross' Texas Cavalry Brigade). Horses arrived from Texas about this time that allowed the men to remount, and this command was attached to Major General Earl Van Dorn's cavalry. In December the cavalry took part in the raid on Holly Springs, Mississippi, and throughout the winter the cavalry hit locations in Tennessee and Mississippi. In an attack on a Federal force at Thompson's Station on March 5, 1863, the Texas brigade attacked dismounted, and Whitfield headed the charge, his men armed only with revolvers. Whitfield was promoted to brigadier general on May 9, 1863, two days after Van Dorn's death, to rank immediately, and on May 19 was assigned to the 2d Brigade under Brigadier General William H. Jackson. As the threat to Vicksburg intensified, Whitfield was ordered to transfer his brigade to Mississippi. When he arrived near Canton,

No genuine uniformed portrait of Whitfield has been found. This image is postwar. (Barker Texas History Center, University of Texas, Austin)

Mississippi, on June 5, 1863, there developed some sort of misunderstanding, and "having no written orders to report to these headquarters, [Whitfield] is hereby relieved from duty, and will report to General Joseph E. Johnston." Johnston asked Secretary of War James A. Seddon on the same day: "What is your intention in regard to him? I am informed that it will be very unfortunate for him to command the brigade to which he has belonged." Whatever rumors Johnston had heard about Whitfield made no difference to Richmond, as Seddon replied: "General Whitfield was believed to be peculiarly acceptable to his brigade. What is the objection?" When Johnston apparently could not produce one, he had to restore Whitfield to command (Colonel L.S. Ross had temporarily replaced him). But Whitfield continued to displease his superiors, as Jackson complained that along his line at the Big Black River "Whitfield was not carrying out my orders strictly in regard to flags of truce." Nevertheless, he was popular with his men; a Texan recalled that "the boys knew that 'Old Whit'…'was with them' in anything short of desertion."

Whitfield may not have satisfied his commanding officer, but during and after the siege of Vicksburg he earned high praise from the Federals facing him. Major General James B. McPherson wrote Grant in October 1863: "There is no disguising the fact the cavalry of [George B.] Cosby's and Whitfield's brigades is far superior to ours under [Edward] Winslow." Moreover, in September 1863, Major General William T. Sherman wrote Major General Henry Halleck that the Confederate cavalrymen harassing his army were tough. "War suits them," noted Sherman, "and the rascals are brave; fine riders, bold to rashness, and dangerous subjects in every sense…They are splendid riders, shots, and utterly reckless…This class of men must all be killed or employed by us before we can hope for peace…I have two brigades of these fellows to my front, commanded by Cosby, of the old army, and Whitfield, of Texas, Stephen D. Lee in command of the whole…. They are the best cavalry in the world…." High praise indeed for the Texans.

But Whitfield's health was failing. On October 2, 1863, General Lee told the secretary of war that Whitfield was "so feeble as to incapacitate him from active duty in the field," and asked for Colonel L.S. Ross to replace him in command of the Texas brigade. Whitfield was granted a leave of absence; in December Ross was promoted to brigadier general,

took command of the brigade, and from then until the war it would bear his name. But a member of the brigade recalled its first commander: "In personal appearance, General Whitfield was marked, being over six feet in height, and straight as an arrow—he looked every inch a soldier."

Whitfield returned to the Trans-Mississippi and was paroled at Columbus, Texas, on June 29, 1865. After the war he lived near the village of Vienna in Lavaca County. He served as a delegate to the state constitutional conventions of 1866 and 1875. Whitfield died near Hallettsville on October 27, 1879, and was buried in the Hallettsville Cemetery.

Anne Bailey

Barron, Samuel B., *Lone Star Defenders: A Chronicle of the Third Texas Cavalry, Ross' Brigade* (New York, 1908).

Kerr, Homer L, ed., *Fighting with Ross' Texas Cavalry Brigade, C.S.A.: The Diary of George L. Griscom, Adjutant, 9th Texas Cavalry Regiment* (Hillsboro, Tx., 1976).

Rose, Victor M., *Ross' Texas Cavalry Brigade* (1881; reprint 1960).

✳ *William Henry Chase Whiting* ✳

William Henry Chase Whiting was born in Biloxi, Mississippi, on March 22, 1824. He graduated from Boston High School in Massachusetts and finished first in the 1840 Class of Georgetown College, D.C. Possibly because his father was a lieutenant colonel Whiting received an at-large appointment to West Point in 1841. At his graduation in 1845, he set the record for the highest grades ever made by a cadet, a record that stood until Douglas MacArthur graduated in 1903.

Commissioned a 2d lieutenant of engineers, Whiting supervised river and harbor improvements and construction of coastal fortifications in California, Florida, Georgia, and North Carolina from 1845 until 1856. Promoted to 1st lieutenant on March 16, 1853, and to captain on December 13, 1858, he worked on improvements on the Savannah River until he resigned on February 20, 1861.

Whiting offered his services to the State of Georgia and was appointed a major of engineers. He soon attained that same rank in the Regular Confederate Army and received orders to inspect the fortifications at Charleston harbor. On March 6 he became an engineer officer on Brigadier General Pierre G.T. Beauregard's staff. Whiting laid out and supervised construction of several works around the harbor and on Morris Island. On April 12, he became assistant adjutant and inspector general on Beauregard's staff and took charge of the deployment of troops on Morris Island. Two days later, Whiting was appointed Chief Engineer of the Provisional Army. On April 16, he was appointed assistant adjutant general and acting engineer for Morris Island.

In May Whiting was appointed an inspector general and placed in charge of the defenses of North

Carolina. After he turned the coastal defenses over to state officials in June, he joined General Joseph E. Johnston at Harpers Ferry to become his adjutant and inspector general. In July Johnston appointed Whiting his chief engineer and praised him for his efficient destruction of the arsenal at Harpers Ferry. As chief engineer, it was Whiting who arranged for the movement of Johnston's troops to Manassas Junction on July 21 that culminated in a Confederate victory. That evening, President Jefferson Davis rewarded Whiting with a battlefield promotion to brigadier general. Whiting's official appointment came on August 28, to rank from July 21.

Whiting soon offended Davis by describing his plan for reorganizing Johnston's army into brigades consisting entirely of troops from a single state as "a policy as suicidal as foolish...inconceivable folly...solely for the advancement of log-rolling, humbugging politicians." Whiting concluded: "I will not do it." Although Johnston managed to retain Whiting in his army, Davis denied Johnston's request in May of 1862 that Whiting be promoted.

Whiting's performance as commander of his own and Brigadier General John B. Hood's brigades at Yorktown had been noteworthy. While temporarily in command of a full division at Seven Pines, Whiting was largely responsible for preventing a juncture of two Federal forces which might have led to a Confederate defeat. Immediately following that

The only known uniformed view of Whiting, this cannot be accurately dated. (Museum of the Confederacy, Richmond, Va.)

engagement, Whiting even prevented Davis from riding into Federal lines. Moreover, it has been claimed that Whiting recommended the strategy to General Robert E. Lee of reinforcing Major General Thomas J. Jackson in the Shenandoah Valley in order to prevent Union troops in that area from reinforcing those on the Peninsula and then having Jackson hurry to Richmond to fall upon the right flank of the Union army. Lee accepted Whiting's offer to take his two brigades to reinforce Jackson, and this strategy ultimately saved Richmond. During the Seven Days' Battles, it was Whiting's troops that drove the Federals from their defensive positions at Gaines' Mill. Yet, Davis, who had heard rumors about Whiting, including his desire to install Johnston as dictator, remained adamant.

In November when Lee wished to give Hood a division, he secured Whiting's transfer to command the Military District of Cape Fear, where his engineering abilities could be fully utilized. Until his transfer in 1864, Whiting supervised the evolvement of Fort Fisher, which guarded the mouth of the Cape Fear River, into the strongest bastion in the Confederacy. Even Davis finally acknowledged Whiting's talents and promoted him to major general on April 22, 1863, to rank from February 28. Early in 1864 Johnston wrote to Whiting that he had unsuccessfully requested his promotion to lieutenant general in order to assign him as second-in-command of his army. Johnston added: "The reason for putting aside the recommendation was an odd one to me. It was that you were too valuable in your present place."

In May of 1864, Whiting assumed command of Petersburg, Virginia. When he failed to engage the enemy at Port Walthall Junction during General Beauregard's attempt to bottle up the Federals between the James and Appomattox Rivers, Whiting was accused of being drunk or under the influence of narcotics. Apparently his poor performance was actually due to his abstinence from his usual indulgences. He was returned to North Carolina at his own request.

Although he had spent much of the war constructing the Cape Fear defenses, when they appeared threatened in 1864 Davis sent General Braxton Bragg to command the district. Although Bragg ordered Whiting to Fort Fisher, Whiting refused to relieve Colonel William Lamb or actual command of the garrison. Instead, Whiting counseled Lamb and fought as a volunteer during the December attack. When Whiting returned without orders on January 13, he informed Lamb, "I have come to share your fate, my boy. You are to be sacrificed." Whiting remained, despite Bragg ordering him to return to Wilmington. On the afternoon of January 15, after repelling an assault by Union naval troops on the beach, Whiting rallied his men to counter Union infantry that were advancing southward along the peninsula toward the fort. Whiting engaged in hand-to-hand combat and sustained two wounds while in the act of tearing down a Federal flag before the garrison capitulated.

Despite the severity of his wounds, Whiting was transferred to Fort Columbus, Governors Island, in New York Harbor as a prisoner of war. His wounds proved fatal and he died at the fort on March 10, 1865. He was buried in Oakdale Cemetery, Wilmington, North Carolina.

Lawrence L. Hewitt

Gragg, Rod, *Confederate Goliath: The Battle of Fort Fisher* (New York, 1991).

Hill, D.H., Jr., *North Carolina*, Vol. IV in Evans, *Confederate Military History.*

✶ *Williams Carter Wickham* ✶

The only known photo in uniform of Wickham, probably taken in 1864. (Museum of the Confederacy, Richmond, Va.)

Born in Richmond, Virginia, on September 21, 1820, he moved with his family to Hanover County in 1827. He attended the University of Virginia, where he studied law. Admitted to the bar in 1842, he practiced law and later farmed his father's estate in Hanover County. In 1849, he was elected to the House of Burgesses, where he became an influential leader among the Whigs. During the late 1850s, he also served as presiding justice of the Hanover County court. Elected to the state senate to represent Hanover and Henrico Counties in 1859, he was serving in that body at the time of Virginia's secession. Wickham served as the representative of Henrico at the Virginia secession convention, where he vehemently spoke against secession and voted against the Ordinance of Secession. But when the vote went against him, he immediately mobilized his militia company, the Hanover Dragoons, and he and his unit entered Confederate service.

Captain Wickham led his company at First Manassas on July 21, 1861. In September, he was elected lieutenant colonel of the 4th Virginia Cavalry Regiment. On May 5, 1862, he sustained a saber wound during a cavalry charge at Williamsburg. While recovering at his home, Wickham was captured the following month. Almost immediately, however, he was exchanged by special cartel for Union Lieutenant Colonel Thomas L. Kane of Pennsylvania, who was related to Wickham's wife. Promoted to colonel in August, Wickham rejoined his command in time to participate in the Battles of Second Manassas, Boonsboro, and Sharpsburg, and in Major General J.E.B. Stuart's raid through Maryland. After Sharpsburg, he was temporarily placed in command of Brigadier General Fitzhugh Lee's brigade and, during the latter stages of the Maryland Campaign, Wickham was struck in the neck by a shell fragment at Upperville. Recovering quickly, Wickham returned to duty prior to the Battle of Fredericksburg in December. During the winter, Wickham's men picketed the Rappahannock River from Fredericksburg to a point just above the Rappahannock's junction with the Rapidan River. While performing this duty, they skirmished with the Federals during Union Major General Ambrose E. Burnside's abortive attempts to cross the Rappahannock in January of 1863.

Later in 1863, Wickham led his regiment at Chancellorsville and in Stuart's ride around the Union army during the Confederate invasion of Pennsylvania. At Gettysburg, Wickham was posted on the extreme left flank of the Confederate army, and during the Confederate withdrawal into Virginia he helped cover the retreat. On September 2, he was promoted to brigadier general to rank from the previous day. Wickham commanded a brigade under Major General Fitzhugh Lee during the Mine Run Campaign, at Brandy Station, and at Buckland Mills. In February of 1864, his brigade helped repulse Union Brigadier General George A. Custer's attack on Charlottesville. During the Overland Campaign of May and June, Wickham fought at the Wilderness, Spotsylvania Court House, Yellow Tavern, Totopotomoy, Second Cold Harbor, Trevilian Station, and Reams' Station. On August 10, he and his brigade were transferred from the south side of the James River to the Shenandoah Valley, where they served under Lieutenant General Jubal A. Early. Wickham's brigade covered Early's retreat following the Third Battle of Winchester. When Early was routed at Fisher's Hill, Wickham, temporarily in command of Fitzhugh Lee's division, saved Early's army by preventing a Union corps from advancing through the Luray Valley to block Early's retreat. Wickham also fought at New Market and Waynesboro.

In the early spring of 1863, Wickham had announced his candidacy for Congress. Without campaigning, he won the election in mid-May. As already noted, despite having been elected to the Second Regular Confederate Congress from Virginia's Third Congressional District, Wickham remained with his command. Finally, on October 5, he turned it over to Brigadier General Thomas L. Rosser and resigned his commission. On November 9, he took his long-neglected seat in Congress, where he remained until the end of the war. He advocated a negotiated peace and participated in the unsuccessful Hampton Roads Peace Conference. He handled his congressional responsibilities well, and as a member of the Military Affairs Committee, Wickham was especially sensitive to securing promotions for deserving military leaders. Generally, he opposed the administration of President Jefferson Davis.

After General Robert E. Lee's surrender on April 9, 1865, Wickham returned to his plantation. Anxious to restore friendly relations between the two sections and recognizing the need for the South to accept its defeat and to reorganize its labor force, Wickham wasted no time. On April 23, only two weeks after Lee's surrender, Wickham joined the Republican party. Although much criticized for this action, unlike other former Confederate leaders who made a similar political alignment, Wickham's political affiliation apparently had little effect on his business career. From 1871 until his death, he served as chairman of the board of supervisors of Hanover County. Simultaneously, he was a successful businessman. Beginning in November of 1865, he served as president of the Virginia Central Railroad and, in November of 1868, as president to the Chesapeake & Ohio railroad. He continued with the latter company in various positions until his death. Also in 1868, he campaigned for the Republican presidential candidate, Ulysses S. Grant. In 1872, he was a member of the electoral college of Virginia, and cast his vote for Grant. In 1880, President Rutherford B. Hayes offered him the secretaryship of the navy, but Wickham declined. The following year, he also refused to accept the Republican nomination for governor. In 1883, he returned to the state senate, where he fought the legislation proposed by former Confederate Major General William Mahone's Readjusters. He remained in the senate until he died of heart failure in his office in Richmond on July 23, 1888. He was buried in Hanover County, Virginia. Fitzhugh Lee dedicated a statue of Wickham on the grounds of the state capitol on October 29, 1891.

Benjamin E. Snellgrove

Hotchkiss, Jedediah, *Virginia*, Vol. III of Evans, *Confederate Military History*.

✯ *Louis Trezevant Wigfall* ✯

No photo of Wigfall in uniform has been found. This one showing him holding a military kepi is as close as we can get. It was probably taken in Charleston at the time of the firing on Fort Sumter. (William A. Turner Collection)

Louis Trezevant Wigfall achieved the rank of brigadier in the Confederate army but made his reputation as an instigator of secession and as both a United States and Confederate senator from Texas.

Wigfall was born on April 21, 1861, in the Edgefield District of South Carolina, the center of nullification and secession. A son of a well-to-do merchant, he attended the University of Virginia in Charlottesville in 1835 and was graduated from South Carolina College in 1837. He established a law practice in Edgefield, demonstrating more talent for debt and dueling than business. Within a five-month span around 1840, Wigfall was involved in a fistfight, three near-duels, two duels, and one shooting in which one man was killed and two wounded, involving Wigfall and future U.S. Senator Preston Brooks. Wigfall tamed these practices after marrying his second cousin, Charlotte Maria Cross of Rhode Island in 1841, but he never curbed his passion for Southern rights. By 1844 he became a staunch advocate of disunion during the political disputes over the annexation of Texas.

Plagued by debt and a public that refused to forgive his dueling, Wigfall moved to Texas in 1846. He again attempted a law career but proved more successful as a fire-eating orator preaching the gospel of Southern rights. He joined the Texas legislature in 1849 to fill an unexpired term and was elected state senator from Harrison County in 1857. Wigfall advocated protection of slavery, states rights, and lowering the tariff. He also favored a revival of the international slave trade (forbidden since 1808) and filibustering in Latin America.

John Brown's raid on Harpers Ferry in 1859 swayed moderates into choosing Wigfall for the U.S. Senate. He served in the 36th Congress—the final session before the Civil War—and did nothing to cool tempers during those inflammatory times. One Southerner reported that Wigfall "likes to be where he can be as rude as he pleases, and he is indulging himself now to the fullest extent." The senator from Texas, along with five other Southerners, helped scuttle the Crittenden Compromise, a last-ditch effort to save the Union. He also helped write the "Southern Manifesto" of December 1860, in which cotton-state congressmen expressed the need for a Southern confederacy. When Texas went out on March 2, he crowed: "We have dissolved the Union; mend it if you can; cement it with blood." He remained in the Senate until March 21 (he was officially expelled in July), even though he already had been named a delegate to the Confederate Congress.

His looks apparently matched his defiance. A London newspaper correspondent described Wigfall in 1861 as a powerful-looking man with muscular neck, "wild masses of black hair tinged with grey" and a face with a straight, broad brow "from which the hair rose up like the vegetation on a riverbank, beetling black eyebrows—a mouth coarse and grim, yet full of power, a square jaw—a thick argumentative nose—a new growth of scrubby beard and moustache—these were relieved by eyes of wonderful depth and light, such as I never saw before but in the head of a wild beast."

On his way to the Provisional Congress in Montgomery, Alabama, Wigfall became sidetracked by the momentous events in South Carolina. On April 10 he secured a position as a volunteer on General P.G.T. Beauregard's staff. If some had second thoughts about firing on Fort Sumter, Wigfall was not among them. Mary Chesnut, who nicknamed him "Stormy Petrel," remarked that Wigfall was "in his glory. The only thoroughly happy person I see." After the bombardment had gone on for many hours, Wigfall commandeered a rowboat and deposited himself at Fort Sumter to enter into unauthorized negotiations over the surrender of Union forces.

After the fall of Sumter, Wigfall completed his journey to Montgomery, Alabama, but until the early part of 1862 he continued to hold both civil and military positions. When the provisional government moved to Richmond, Virginia, President Jefferson Davis welcomed Wigfall to serve on his staff. On July 8, 1861, Wigfall held a concurrent position as lieutenant colonel of the 1st Texas Battalion, which missed the battle of First Manassas because of a train accident. He was promoted to colonel of the regiment on August 28, 1861, but saw little action beyond the chores of organizing

and training a regiment. Wigfall soon had to choose between military and political leadership. Davis nominated him brigadier general on, and to rank from October 21, 1861, and the Texas legislature elected him senator to the Permanent Congress of the Confederacy. Although he resigned his commission when congress convened in February 1862, Wigfall followed his military inclinations one more time. He briefly joined Major General James Longstreet's staff as an aide, helping care for the wounded during both the second day of the Battle of Seven Pines (June 1, 1862) and in the Seven Days' battles around Richmond (June 25–July 1, 1862).

Wigfall's congressional activity centered on the military. Many officers—including R.E. Lee—looked upon Wigfall as a friend of the army. One particular friend was General Joseph E. Johnston, whom Wigfall passionately supported throughout the war at the expense of the senator's relationship with Davis. As long as the topic concerned the military, Wigfall championed legislation that consolidated national military authority, including conscription, suspension of *habeas corpus*, impressment, and the power of the government to control railroads. Yet his states rights philosophy showed when he opposed legislation allowing a supreme court (which was never established) to overrule state courts. Wigfall's support of national independence also had limits. He refused to support legislation arming slaves as soldiers. Becoming increasingly disenchanted with Davis, Wigfall also threw his efforts into curbing the powers of the president. Mary Chesnut in 1864 proclaimed, "Wigfall…from whom we hoped so much, has only been destructive." As a friend of Davis, her assessment was too severe, yet Wigfall's contentiousness has often been cited as the kind of leadership that contributed to Confederate defeat.

After the war Wigfall made his way to Texas where he remained in hiding until leaving the country in 1866. He lived in England—associating with other Confederate expatriates and mounting his habitual debts—until returning to Baltimore in 1872. Two years later, Wigfall returned to Texas and died in Galveston on February 18, 1874.

William Alan Blair

King, Alvy L, *Louis T. Wigfall: Southern Fire-eater* (Baton Rouge, 1970).

Russell, William Howard, *My Diary North and South*, ed. Fletcher Pratt (New York, 1954).

Woodward, C. Vann, ed., *Mary Chesnut's Civil War* (New Haven, 1981).

An 1861-63 portrait of Wilcox as a brigadier. (Museum of the Confederacy)

⋆ *Cadmus Marcellus Wilcox* ⋆

Cadmus Marcellus Wilcox was born in Wayne County, North Carolina, but grew up in Tennessee from a very early age. Despite having some preliminary college education in Nashville, young Wilcox earned dreary grades after matriculating at the U.S. Military Academy in 1842. He languished in the bottom quarter of his class through all four years at West Point, finally ranking fifty-fourth among fifty-nine graduates in 1846. George E. Pickett held up that class from the fifty-ninth position. Wilcox's classmates destined to become famous included George B. McClellan, Darius Nash Couch, Dabney H. Maury, D.R. Jones, Jesse Lee Reno, and Thomas Jonathan Jackson. Cadet Wilcox apparently behaved about as well as he learned, since his standing in conduct, based on total demerits, was 186th among 213 cadets in all classes at the academy in 1846.

Most of the class of 1846 headed directly to Mexico, where hostilities had just broken out. Brevet 2d lieutenant Wilcox went to war as an officer in the 4th U.S. Infantry. In February 1847 he was promoted to regular rank of 2d lieutenant in the 7th U.S. Infantry, and for bravery in storming Chapultepec near Mexico City later that year Wilcox won a brevet promotion. Cadmus Wilcox never wrote a Civil War book, but his Mexican War experience prompted him to prepare a mammoth and well-written *History of the Mexican War* (Washington, 1892). Belying his weak academic record, Wilcox also wrote a thoughtful and important treatise, *Rifles and Rifle Practice* (New York, 1859), and translated a French military manual. His other experiences before the Civil War included a year's furlough in Europe and postings at West Point, and in Florida, and New Mexico. Wilcox's last antebellum promotion was to captain, on December 20, 1860. He was serving in the southeast at that rank when his home state of Tennessee seceded.

Wilcox began his Confederate career as colonel of the 9th Alabama with a commission dated July 9, 1861. Ten days later Colonel Wilcox stood ready and eager near Manassas, but he played a minor role in that Southern victory. It was about the last time than Cadmus Wilcox missed the heat of any action in the war's Eastern theater. Bearing a brigadier general's commission dated October 21, 1861, ranking from the same day, Wilcox led five Alabama regiments (including the 9th) for two years and made them into one of the most reliable brigades in the Army of Northern Virginia. A pious young artillerist associated with the brigade commented with a mixture of respect and distaste for discipline that Wilcox was "a very wicked and unpopular but skillfull officer." Major General James Longstreet commended Wilcox as "distinguished" at Williamsburg and Seven Pines, then during the Seven Days' Campaign the brigade fought with a zeal that resulted in casualties of more than fifty percent.

At Second Manassas General Wilcox commanded a small division that included his own brigade and two others led maladroitly by W.S. Featherston and R.A. Pryor. At Sharpsburg, Fredericksburg, and Chancellorsville his brigade served in the division commanded by Major General Richard H. Anderson. Wilcox probably did not win promotion to major general as part of the army reorganization during the fall of 1862 because he hated Longstreet, who doubtless reciprocated the feeling. Wilcox sought transfer away from General R.E. Lee's army, but the commanding general soothed him with a warm note. Soon after the war Wilcox expressed his contempt for Longstreet in letters to a fellow I Corps general: "I never had any respect for Longstreet's ability for I always knew he had but a small amount. I always regarded him as selfish & cold harted [sic], caring for little save his own self." Longstreet by then was "spoken of as the hard & stubborn fighter, his troops did fight well, but not from any inspiration drawn from him...."

With such strong feelings about the corps commander, the disgruntled brigadier must have welcomed the opportunity to fight at Chancellorsville (May 1–4, 1863) in Longstreet's absence. The result was Wilcox's greatest single contribution to Lee's army and to the

A variant pose from the same sitting. (Museum of the Confederacy, Richmond, Va.)

Major General Wilcox taken during the last two years of the war. (Courtesy of Lee A. Wallace, Jr.)

Confederate cause. The Alabama brigade had spent much of the winter upstream from Fredericksburg near Banks' Ford. When Federals crossed even farther upriver and concentrated at Chancellorsville, Wilcox and his men became an outpost watching the ford in lonely isolation. By careful observation the general discerned the departure of enemy troops opposite him early on May 3, 1863, and he took the calculated risk of hurrying toward the sound of guns nearer town. Northern troops under Major General John Sedgwick erupted across Marye's Heights just as the Alabamans drew near, and surged westward toward Lee's rear at Chancellorsville. Calmly and skillfully General Wilcox interposed his units between Sedgwick and his goal, crafting a classic delaying action from ridge to ridge and from woodline to woodline. At Salem Church Wilcox turned and hurled back his pursuers. Reinforcements from Lee built a line upon Wilcox' hard-pressed fragments and saved the day.

Despite his shining success at Salem Church, no promotion was forthcoming for Wilcox in the post-Jackson reorganization three weeks later. He remained a brigadier at Gettysburg, where an observer described him as picturesquely outfitted in "a short round jacket and a battered straw hat." In the further reorganization of the army necessitated by its losses in Pennsylvania, Cadmus Wilcox finally won promotion to the rank of major general, to date from August 13. In December 1862 nine officers associated with Wilcox had written to the secretary of war urging his promotion. In February 1863 fifteen members of the Confederate Congress (where his brother held a seat) did likewise. In August Lee's recommendation joined the rest, and that finally carried all of the necessary weight. The army commander called Wilcox "a highly capable officer" who "deserves promotion." Now that the army had three corps, he could be given a division away from Longstreet.

Through the last twenty months of the war in Virginia, Major General Wilcox led a II Corps division solidly and competently but without any dazzling success; the Confederacy's opportunities for that kind of result had dwindled dramatically by the fall of 1863. Wilcox's personal views survive in the form of letters he wrote to his sister-in-law and her children, who called the general "Uncle Cad." The letters reveal discouragement about the cause ("I frequently grow weary & tired of this war") as well as a strong commitment to meeting life's transactions with dignity

and honor: "We must live out our troubles successfully and with a manner in the world that we may be proud of." General Wilcox displayed deep-seated disgust with Northern behavior toward Southern civilians. Because he had always gotten on well with prewar Yankees, he had been surprised to find them revealed during the war as "cowardly, brutal & the most unthinkable of liars." The enemy seemed "maddened with hate and malice and…bent on our total destruction." In a nicely turned summation Wilcox wrote: "Our enemies are Satan's pets." With that mind-set the general faced the challenges of a deteriorating military situation.

At the Wilderness and Spotsylvania Cadmus Wilcox fought steadily and well. He had a horse shot under him that summer as he led his division at Reams' Station, August 25, 1864. A distinguished Irish visitor who saw the general a few months later astride an unprepossessing "old white charger" came to know Wilcox as a "thoroughly competent" officer "of excellent sense & European manner." By Appomattox, the manner was about all that remained. A West Point classmate who had become a Federal general saw Wilcox after the surrender "on a sorry looking old grey horse, whose thin ribs bespoke…scant forage." The rider of the sorry horse sported "a long thick overcoat," which he was wearing, it developed, because his uniform had worn out and "a shirt was the only garment underneath."

After the bitter end at Appomattox Cadmus Wilcox lived in Washington, D.C., with the widowed sister-in-law who had been his wartime correspondent. He turned down foreign commissions in Egypt and Korea and for the last four years of his life held a federal government patronage post bestowed by President Grover Cleveland. Wilcox died in Washington on December 2, 1890, and was buried there in Oak Hill Cemetery.

Robert K. Krick

Porter, James, *Tennessee*, Vol. VIII in Evans, *Confederate Military History*.

✶ *John Stuart Williams* ✶

The only known uniformed portrait of Williams, taken after April 1862. (Cook Collection, Valentine Museum, Richmond, Va.)

Born near Mount Sterling, Kentucky, on July 10, 1818, John Stuart Williams graduated from Ohio's Miami University in 1839. After passing the bar he opened a law practice in Paris, Kentucky, in 1840. During the Mexican War Williams entered the service as a captain in the 4th Kentucky Volunteers and was attached to the 6th U.S. Infantry as commander of a volunteer scout company. Elected colonel of the 4th Kentucky, he led his regiment in storming the heights of Cerro Gordo. Williams' heroics at this battle earned him the nickname "Cerro Gordo."

After the war Williams resumed his law practice in Kentucky and began raising cattle. An active Whig, he was elected to the state legislature in 1851 and 1853. Williams first was against secession and advocated compromise and Kentucky's neutrality when the crisis deepened. His attitude eventually became more pro-Confederate, however, because he believed the North was trying to maintain the Union through coercion. Deciding to join the Confederacy, he traveled to southwest Virginia with Brigadier General Humphrey Marshall to raise a command for himself. Having little success, Williams returned to his native state in October 1861 and raised a regiment from the mountaineers of eastern Kentucky. On November 8 he fought a small battle with Union Brigadier General William Nelson when the latter attacked Williams' camp at Ivy Mountain. Williams then crossed back into Virginia and was commissioned colonel of the 5th Kentucky Infantry on November 16. Given some additional Virginia regiments, Williams skirmished with Nelson along the Virginia–Kentucky border until early 1862.

On April 8, 1862, Williams was promoted to brigadier general, to rank from April 16, and was given command of a Virginia brigade. Although his brigade was racked with mumps and measles, Williams scouted and skirmished with the enemy in the Cumberland Gap region that summer. During this time his superior, Major General W.W. Loring, described him as being an "energetic and valuable officer." After participating in the Kentucky invasion of 1862 Williams commanded a brigade of Kentucky, Georgia, Tennessee, and Virginia cavalry in southwest Virginia until September 1863. He then was placed over all the Confederate forces east of Knoxville, Tennessee, and opposed Major General Ambrose Burnside's advance on that city.

In October Williams fought a sharp battle with Burnside at Blue Springs, Tennessee. Williams' superiors believed Burnside had left Knoxville for Chattanooga and that Williams' cavalry brigade was sufficient to operate around Knoxville. However, Burnside was still in the area. On October 10 Williams took up a defensive position at Blue Springs and was attacked by the Yankees. He was badly outnumbered; nevertheless, as one of Williams' men wrote, "at the first picket shot it became apparent that [he] meant to fight...." Known to swear and storm in battle, Williams put up a stubborn fight and beat off three Federal attacks. He also bluffed the enemy by skillfully using three locomotives to pretend to bring up reinforcements. In a harrowing retreat to Virginia Williams often cursed and used the flat of his sword against his men to hold his rear guard in place. Although Williams showed great bravery and skill during his withdrawal, his superiors still saw it as a defeat. Williams in turn was incensed at having been left alone to contend with Burnside's large force. As a result Williams was relieved from duty in East Tennessee at his own request and was sent to southwest Virginia.

During the Atlanta Campaign Williams commanded a brigade in Major General Joseph Wheeler's cavalry corps. After fighting at Resaca, Georgia, May 17–18, 1864, his brigade sometimes was detached to serve directly under Major General Benjamin Cheatham. Williams rejoined Wheeler for his raid into Tennessee in August and September and convinced Wheeler to let him take two brigades and half the artillery to raid the Union post at Strawberry Plains. Wheeler initially objected to the plan on the grounds it would slow his march. When Williams promised to rejoin Wheeler quickly, Wheeler reluctantly acquiesced. Williams failed to reach his objective, however, and Wheeler fumed. In his report Wheeler censured Williams for his failure to reach Strawberry Plains and for not immediately rejoining the main column.

Williams served in southwestern Virginia for the rest of the war and then returned to Winchester, Kentucky, to become a farmer. He was elected to the state legislature in 1873 and 1875 but lost a bid for the governor's office in 1875. He also was elected to the United States Senate in 1878 but was defeated for reelection in 1883. Williams returned to his farm and died at Mount Sterling, Kentucky, on July 17, 1898. He was buried in Winchester.

Terry L. Jones

Johnston, J. Stoddard, *Kentucky*, Vol. IX in Evans, *Confederate Military History*.

Morris, Roy, Jr., "Old 'Cerro Gordo' and the Battle of Blue Springs," *Civil War Times Illustrated* March 1987, pp. 46–53.

☆ *Claudius Charles Wilson* ☆

Wilson was born on October 1, 1831, in Effingham County, Georgia. He entered Emory College at Oxford, Georgia, in 1848 and graduated with honors in 1851. He studied law and was admitted to the bar in Savannah in 1852. One writer noted that Wilson was respected in his profession because he was "a man of strong analytical powers combined with eloquence in speech." He was elected solicitor general of Georgia's eastern circuit in 1859 but resigned the next year to resume his legal practice.

Wilson did not enter Confederate service when the Civil War started but later raised the Bryan Guards in Chatham County. Commissioned captain of this company on August 9, 1861, he helped organize the 25th Georgia Infantry and was elected its colonel on September 2. The regiment reported for duty with the Department of South Carolina, Georgia, and Florida. Wilson and his men were eventually assigned to the brigade of Brigadier General Hugh W. Mercer in the District of Georgia and were stationed near Savannah. The regiment saw only picket and guard duty for the next year.

In June and July 1862 Wilson was reported as commanding all troops at Carston's Bluff. On October 22 he took his regiment from Savannah to reinforce units defending Coosawhatchie, South Carolina. The men arrived there the next day, but the Federal forces had already retreated. As senior officer, Wilson assumed command of the area. He returned to Carston's Bluff on October 24 with all of the Georgia regiments that had gone to Coosawhatchie.

Major General John G. Foster led a Union force on an expedition from New Berne toward Goldsborough, North Carolina, on December 11. In response, Wilson was given command of the 1st Georgia Brigade (three regiments) and ordered to Wilmington to reinforce Major General William H.C. Whiting's forces. The brigade left Savannah by train on the evening of December 14 and arrived at Wilmington on the morning of December 19. Foster's expedition had started back for New Berne by that time. Whiting, however, retained Wilson's men for a time in the District of Cape Fear. Wilson was sent to Masonborough, eight miles from Wilmington, to garrison that place and watch the coast. His duties there also included apprehending and bringing in deserters.

The U.S.S. *Columbia* ran aground on the bar at Masonborough Inlet on the evening of January 14, 1863. When he learned what had happened, Wilson took his brigade and two artillery batteries to the inlet to prevent the ship's escape. The artillery opened on her on the morning of the sixteenth and soon forced the *Columbia's* commander to raise the white flag. After spiking their guns, the Federal crew went ashore, where their commander surrendered them and the ship to Wilson.

On February 4 the brigade was ordered back to Savannah, and it reached that city four days later. There Wilson reverted to regimental command.

No photo of General Wilson in uniform has surfaced, nor is it likely, considering his early death. The uniform on this has been painted on. (Albert G. Shaw Collection, Virginia Historical Society, Richmond)

Brigadier General William H.T. Walker then took charge of the brigade. On May 5 the brigade was ordered to reinforce General Joseph E. Johnston's army in Mississippi. Reaching Jackson, the brigade was sent toward Raymond but did not reach that town before the Confederates there were defeated by Major General Ulysses S. Grant's army. Wilson and his regiment were only lightly engaged in the battle at Jackson on May 14. Walker's promotion to major general on May 23 and assumption of division command resulted in Wilson again being placed in command of the brigade. One of his soldiers wrote that Wilson was popular with the men and was "always willing to show as much levity as in his power." In early June the division marched to Yazoo City to protect it from possible Union threats. The men had returned to the area of Jackson by the latter part of the month. On July 2 they were within twenty-five miles of Vicksburg but had to retreat to Jackson when they learned of Vicksburg's fall. Walker's division participated in the Siege of Jackson, July 9–15. Wilson's brigade did some skirmishing but suffered most of its casualties from Union artillery shelling.

Shortly after the siege Wilson asked the War Department to recognize him as brigade commander. Walker endorsed the letter with these words: "He has been under my command since I have been in miss and I believe him to be entitled to the command of the Brigade as having been so long with it, having the confidence of the men & duly capable & efficient. I take pleasure in making this statement whilst I do not feel at liberty to recommend any one for office." Wilson and his men accompanied the division to Chattanooga in August as part of the reinforcements for the Army of Tennessee.

Just prior to the Battle of Chickamauga the brigade was assigned to guard the wagon train of Walker's Reserve Corps. Wilson distinguished himself in the first day's fighting on September 19. His and Brigadier General Matthew D. Ector's brigades supported Major General Nathan Bedford Forrest's cavalry in its actions near Reed's Bridge. Just as it appeared that the Federals were going to drive the cavalrymen from the field, the Georgians counterattacked, forced the enemy to retreat, and captured a battery. Forrest himself then led the brigade forward, driving back a second Union line. Federal reinforcements came up and threatened to turn Wilson's left flank. He had to order his men to fall back to avoid being surrounded.

Forrest reported that the brigade's actions "excited my admiration." On September 20 Wilson's troops helped support units on the army's right flank but were not heavily engaged. He had taken about 1,200 men onto the field, and their losses during the two days were 605 men killed, wounded, and missing. Walker, too, praised Wilson, saying he "acted with great distinction" and "is entitled, from long service with the brigade and from gallant conduct, to the command of the Georgia brigade he now commands in the capacity of brigadier-general." On November 1 Walker repeated his recommendation for promotion and called Wilson "active, efficient, intelligent, enterprising & patriotic."

Shortly after the battle Wilson became ill with what is called in some sources "camp fever" but which probably was dysentery. He went to Ringgold, Georgia, to recuperate but died there on November 27, 1863. His commission as brigadier general, dated November 16, reached the army after Wilson's death. The Confederate Senate confirmed the promotion on February 17, 1864. Wilson's body was buried in Bonaventure Cemetery in Savannah.

Arthur W. Bergeron, Jr.

Derry, Joseph T., *Georgia*, Vol. VI in Evans, *Confederate Military History*.

Northen, William J., ed., *Men of Mark in Georgia*, Vol III (Spartanburg, SC, 1974).

Wiley, Bell I., ed., "The Confederate Letters of John W. Hagan," *Georgia Historical Quarterly*, XXXVIII (1954), pp. 170–200.

Wyeth, John A., *That Devil Forrest: Life of General Nathan Bedford Forrest* (New York, 1959).

✷ *Charles Sidney Winder* ✷

Charles Sidney Winder was born near Easton, Talbot County, Maryland, on October 18, 1829, the fifth of eight children of Edward S. Winder and Elizabeth Taylor Lloyd. Winder could trace his ancestry to the colonial founders of Maryland, and both his paternal and maternal grandfathers served as governors of that state. Other relatives included revolutionary war patriot John Eager Howard and "Star Spangled Banner" author Francis Scott Key. His mother's sister was the wife of Franklin Buchanan, U.S. naval officer turned Confederate admiral, and Confederate Brigadier General John Winder was a distant cousin.

In 1840 Charles' father, a captain in the 2d U.S. Dragoons, died from disease contracted in Florida's Seminole War. The boy's education was overseen by his uncle, Colonel Edward Lloyd VI, master of the Talbot County estate "Wye House" and owner of plantations in Mississippi, Arkansas, and Louisiana. In 1846, after four years at St. John's College in Annapolis, Winder received an appointment to the U.S. Military Academy at West Point. A diligent but generally undistinguished scholar, in his final year at the academy Winder ranked first in his class in infantry tactics, which with his paucity of demerits won him promotion to captain in the Corps of Cadets. Graduating in 1850, he stood twenty-second in a class of forty-five members, ten of whom would attain general's rank in the Civil War.

As 2d lieutenant in the 3d U.S. Artillery, Winder served at a succession of military posts on the East Coast before embarking for California with his regiment aboard the steamer *San Francisco*. On December 24, 1853, the ship was disabled by a hurricane that washed more than 120 passengers from its decks, and it was thirteen days before all the survivors were rescued from the derelict and sinking vessel. Winder's superiors credited his "noble exertions" and "tireless zeal" in keeping the *San Francisco* afloat until help could arrive, and rewarded the young Marylander with a brevet captaincy and promotion to 1st lieutenant and adjutant.

In 1855 Winder was appointed captain in the newly organized 9th U.S. Infantry, reportedly the youngest officer of that rank in the army. He took advantage of a brief tour of duty in the east to marry his cousin and childhood sweetheart, Alicia Lloyd, before joining his regiment on the western frontier. Captain Winder performed creditably in a series of campaigns against hostile Indians in Washington Territory, most notably in the battle of Snake River, May 17–18, 1858, and the engagement at Four Lakes on September 1. Winder's reputation in the Old Army could be summed up in the words of a fellow officer who characterized him as "an accomplished gentleman and most excellent soldier."

In the four years that preceded the outbreak of civil war Winder was plagued by a baffling but debilitating illness, characterized by a multitude of symptoms including gastric pain, sore throat, frequent headache, and insomnia. It seems likely that his chronic sickness was traceable to earlier bouts with malaria and "Panama fever." Despite two and a half years on medical leave of absence, Winder was still far from well when on April 1, 1861, he resigned from the Regular Army to cast his lot with the fledgling Confederacy. It was a painful decision for the young officer. "The sad thoughts that filled my brain made me feel miserable," he confided to his diary; "the horrors of a Civil War were in bold relief ever before me."

Winder took part in the siege and bombardment of Fort Sumter, and after a last visit to his wife and three little children in Maryland returned to Charleston as acting ordnance officer at the arsenal there. In July 1861 he was appointed colonel of the 6th South Carolina Infantry of

---

Charles Winder as a captain in the Old Army. No Confederate uniformed portrait has come to light and this is an engraving based on a now lost original. (Evans, *Confederate Military History*)

D.R. Jones' brigade. Arriving too late to participate in the First Battle of Bull Run, he served with General Joseph Johnston's forces during the eight months of inactivity that preceded the Confederate withdrawal from Manassas. Johnston judged Winder "fully competent" for higher command, and on March 7, 1862, he was promoted to the rank of brigadier general, to rank from March 1.

Originally intended to command a brigade in Major General D.H. Hill's division, Winder was instead dispatched to Major General Thomas J. "Stonewall" Jackson's force in the Shenandoah Valley to take charge of the Stonewall Brigade in the wake of Brigadier General Richard Garnett's arrest for alleged misconduct at the First Battle of Kernstown. The circumstances of Winder's appointment, coupled with his strict notions of military discipline and department, made him less than popular with the rank and file of the Stonewall Brigade. Jackson's aide, Henry Kyd Douglas, recalled that "General Winder was received in sulky and resentful silence." John Casler of the 33d Virginia characterized the aristocratic Marylander as "a kind of fancy General," who "put on a good many airs," noting, "the boys all took a dislike to him from the start, and never did like him afterwards."

Though Winder may have failed to win the affections of the private soldiers, in the course of Jackson's Shenandoah Valley Campaign he nonetheless earned the respect of his fellow officers. The Stonewall Brigade arrived on the field too late to participate in the victory at McDowell on May 8, but Jackson praised the "handsome style" of Winder's assault at Winchester on May 25. Brigadier General Richard Taylor thought Winder performed "splendidly" as he fended off Federal pursuers during the grueling march up the Valley—"cool as a professor playing the new German game." Winder was in the thick of action in the hard-won Battle of Port Republic on June 9, his horse shot three times as he rallied his men in the face of a Federal counterattack.

Despite Winder's commendable service in the Valley Campaign, his relations with Jackson were strained at best. Winder confided to his diary that his commander's insistence on "rapid marches" was "insane." At the conclusion of the campaign Winder came near resigning from Jackson's command. Though the dapper and faultlessly uniformed Marylander presented a striking contrast to the rumpled and eccentric Virginian, both were deeply religious men possessed of almost Spartan concepts of discipline and duty. Kyd Douglas was of the opinion that "in determination and wilfulness" the two generals "were too much alike to fit exactly."

Throughout his service with Jackson, Winder battled

sleeplessness, chronic fatigue, and the effects of his lingering illness. Moreover, his wartime diaries poignantly reveal the mental agony he endured over the fate of his family— his "darling pets," as he called them—behind Union lines in occupied Maryland. "Oh that my state were free from her despotic rulers," he wrote, and I c'd know of my dear ones…so long subjected to such dangers and vandalism."

Following the transfer of Jackson's forces from the Valley to the Peninsula, Winder further distinguished himself in the Seven Days' battles. In the latter stages of the engagement at Gaines' Mill on June 27, his brigade helped to carry a formidable position at McGehee's House on the Federal right flank, staunchly defended by troops of the Regular Army. The Stonewall Brigade suffered still heavier losses in the failed Confederate attack at Malvern Hill on July 1, an assault Winder characterized as "very badly managed."

In the two weeks that preceded Jackson's advance from Gordonsville and Orange Court House to strike at Major General John Pope's Federal forces in Culpeper County, Winder was all but prostrated by illness. But as Jackson later noted, his subordinate's "ardent patriotism and military pride could bear no such restraint" and Winder left his sickbed to join his command in the August 9, 1862, battle with Major General Nathaniel Banks' Union corps at Cedar Mountain. At Jackson's behest, Winder assumed command of the division. The fighting had yet to be joined in earnest when Winder, afoot and supervising the fire of two guns of the Rockbridge Artillery, was cut down by an enemy shell. Winder was borne from the field and died at sundown; his last intelligible words were, "My poor, poor wife…My little pets."

Initially buried at Orange Court House, on August 18 the fallen officer received a state funeral in the Congress Hall of the Confederate capitol building. In the fall of 1865 Winder's relative and wartime aide McHenry Howard had the general's remains removed from Richmond's Hollywood Cemetery and brought to the Lloyd family burial ground at Wye House, Talbot County, Maryland.

Brian C. Pohanka

Douglas, Henry Kyd, *I Rode With Stonewall* (Chapel Hill, 1940).

Howard, McHenry, *Recollections of a Maryland Confederate Soldier and Staff Officer Under Johnston, Jackson and Lee* (Baltimore, 1914).

Krick, Robert K., *Stonewall Jackson At Cedar Mountain* (Chapel Hill, 1990).

Winder, Charles S., Papers The Maryland Historical Society, Baltimore.

☆ *John Henry Winder* ☆

Winder was the son of Brigadier General William Henry Winder, who was defeated by the British at the Battle of Bladensburg in the War of 1812. John was born on February 21, 1800, on his father's estate, "Rewston," in Somerset County, Maryland. He was educated by tutors and at several private academies in Baltimore, where the family moved in 1802. Winder entered West Point in 1814 and graduated eleventh out of thirty in the class of 1820. Commissioned a 2d lieutenant of artillery, he received orders to report to Fort McHenry. Later that year he transferred to the United States Rifles and was stationed on the Georgia border. Winder returned to the artillery in June 1821. He resigned his commission on August 31, 1823, to marry and become a planter. After the death of his wife, he reentered the army on April 2, 1827, as a 2d lieutenant in the 1st United States Artillery. He became an instructor of infantry tactics at the United States Military Academy the following September. In November 1828 he was assigned as assistant commissary of subsistence at Fort Johnston, North Carolina. Promoted to 1st lieutenant on November 30, 1833, Winder served in the Seminole War; saw duty in Arkansas, Maine, and Florida; and took his company to Vera Cruz in April 1847 to participate in the Mexican War. There he received brevets as major and lieutenant colonel for gallant and meritorious conduct. Following the conflict Winder commanded posts in New York, Florida, and South Carolina before being placed in charge of Fort Pickens at Pensacola. He went home on sick leave in May 1860 and resigned his commission as major of the 3d U.S. Artillery on April 27, 1861.

Winder's most recent biographer has written that he "was impulsive, stubborn, short-tempered, profane, and aloof, but until he resigned from the United States Army in 1861, he was widely regarded as an honest, efficient, courageous, and distinguished officer." He offered his services to the governor of North Carolina on May 2, 1861, but was commissioned a brigadier general on June 21. President Jefferson Davis appointed him as inspector general of military camps near Richmond. In that capacity he supervised the equipping of soldiers for duty in the field. Winder shortly afterward was placed in charge of soldiers arrested by civilian authorities and awaiting trial. Additional responsibilities soon came his way; charge over Union prisoners in Richmond, some supervision of prison camps in other states, and investigations of suspected incidents of subversion and espionage.

The Department of Henrico was created on October 21, and Winder was appointed its commander. Initially embracing on Henrico County, the department was extended on March 26, 1862, down to Petersburg. On February 27, 1862, Winder became provost marshal of Richmond. Davis had declared martial law, and Winder was to enforce it throughout Henrico County. His duties included looking for and returning deserters and issuing discharges to ill and disabled soldiers in the city's hospitals. In April he imposed price controls on foodstuffs sold in the capital. Exchanged Confederate soldiers at Richmond came under Winder's charge beginning with

Brigadier General John H. Winder, his only known uniformed portrait from the days of the Confederacy. It cannot be dated even approximately. (Courtesy of Dave Mark)

the first exchange in August 1862. He came under considerable criticism by soldiers and citizens alike for the tactics used by some of his detectives and assistants, who were often referred to as "rowdies." Much more criticism flowed from the Northern press and citizens for what they perceived to be mistreatment of Union prisoners not only in Richmond but in other prisons as well. From March until September 1863 he was also in charge of all military and civilian hospitals in Richmond. In addition to all of the duties already outlined, Winder handled the funeral arrangements for high-ranking Confederates such as Thomas J. "Stonewall" Jackson, James E.B. Stuart, and Charles S. Winder.

Senators Benjamin J. Hill and Herschel V. Johnson of Georgia recommended Winder for promotion to major general in April 1863. Later, twelve other senators endorsed the proposal, but neither Secretary of War James A. Seddon nor the Congress as a whole ever acted on the recommendation. Finally, on May 5, 1864, the Departments of Henrico and Richmond were combined under Major General Robert Ransom. Winder was relieved of all previous responsibilities and ordered to report to Ransom for duty. Winder's most recent biographer has provided the following analysis of this phase of his career: "He had done his best to perform his duty, and on the whole, he had succeeded. His actions were not always popular, but they were usually effective."

On May 25 Winder was sent to Goldsboro, North Carolina, to assume command of the 2d Military District of the Department of North Carolina and Southern Virginia. He never had a chance to enter this new office, because on June 3 he was ordered to Andersonville, Georgia, to take over supervision of the prison there. Then on July 26 he was assigned to command all prisons in Alabama and Georgia. After some months Winder moved his headquarters to Camp Lawton, near Millen, Georgia, where a new prison was being constructed. That facility was abandoned after six weeks. Davis created the office of commissary general of prisons on November 21 and appointed Winder to it. He then moved to Columbia, South Carolina. As commissary general he was in charge of all prisons east of the Mississippi River. He inspected some prisons, tried to establish new ones, and received twice-monthly reports on conditions in them all. However, it was too late by this time for him to effect any real improvements in the horrible conditions existing in the system.

Winder died on February 8, 1865, at Florence, South Carolina, of a massive heart attack. Buried at first in Columbia, his body was moved in 1878 to Green Mount Cemetery in Baltimore. Had Winder lived, he, rather than Major Henry Wirz, likely would have been tried and executed for the alleged mistreatment of prisoners, particularly those at Andersonville. As his biographer points out, "In the acrimonious decades following the conflict, Winder was repeatedly vilified by northern historians, politicians, and newspapers." Not until the 1960s did historians provide somewhat balanced assessments of his wartime service. It seems unlikely that anyone else could have performed the job any better unless the circumstances had been different.

Arthur W. Bergeron, Jr.

Blakey, Arch Fredric, *General John H. Winder, C.S.A.* (Gainesville, 1990).

Duffy, Sarah Annette, "*Military Administrator: The Controversial Life of Brigadier General John Henry Winder, C.S.A.*" (Master's thesis, Creighton University, 1961).

Futch, Ovid L., *History of Andersonville Prison* (Gainesville, 1968).

✶ *Henry Alexander Wise* ✶

The only known genuine uniformed portrait of Henry Wise, and never before published. (Museum of the Confederacy, Richmond, Va.)

Henry Alexander Wise never achieved the level of success on the battlefield that had characterized his political career before the war. Born on December 3, 1806, near Accomac Court House, Virginia, Wise graduated from Washington College in Pennsylvania in 1825. After studying law for two years under Judge Henry St. George Tucker, Wise became an ardent supporter of states rights. While maintaining a practice in his home county, he entered the political arena as a Jacksonian Democrat. An electrifying stump speaker, he was a member of the House of Representatives from 1833 to 1844 and received the Virginia governorship for the term 1856–60. Wise earned lasting fame for an active role in quelling John Brown's raid on Harpers Ferry in 1859. He also lobbied tirelessly for the Old Dominion's entrance into the Confederacy during the state's secession convention in 1861.

Without formal military training and past middle age, Wise still offered to serve his new country. His political clout and immense popularity in the western part of the state made it impossible for Richmond authorities to refuse his offer. Wise immediately raised an outfit, called "Wise's Legion," which plodded into the Kanawha Valley that spring. He received an appropriate rank of brigadier general on June 5, 1861, taking rank immediately. The Confederate defeat at Rich Mountain on July 11 forced Wise to retire to White Sulphur Springs. While Wise's command lacked supplies and fell into shambles, he engaged in a verbal battle with his ranking superior, Brigadier General John Buchanan Floyd. Harmony quickly eroded between the two officers, as Wise refused to reinforce Floyd on September 10 at Carnifix Ferry. Wise possessed a petulant temper that quickly erupted, especially when he believed that his honor had been offended. He proved to be an unruly subordinate throughout the war. One of General Robert E. Lee's staff officers thought that Wise had an "inflexible will" and knew "little of subordination." Wise had appealed to President Jefferson Davis to be transferred for some time. A few days after Carnifix Ferry he received orders to return to Richmond without his troops. He remained there for the rest of the year, spending most of the time on sick leave.

Wise returned to duty on January 7, 1862, and took charge of the military district of northeastern North Carolina. He immediately feuded with Major General Benjamin Huger because reinforcements had not arrived at Roanoke Island. Huger seemed oblivious to Wise's predicament, as the Virginian faced a formidable Union force under Brigadier General Ambrose E. Burnside. A noted Richmond diarist believed the situation was "a man-trap of the 'Redtapers'" to get rid of Wise. On February 8 the Confederate defenses on the island crumbled while Wise lay incapacitated behind the lines with an illness. Though exonerated of responsibility for the disaster, Wise returned to Richmond frustrated and bitter.

Lee helped him obtain a new command that spring. While Major General George B. McClellan drove toward the city, Wise's units occupied the extreme right of the Confederate line, far from any danger. General Joseph E. Johnston stated flatly that he had no desire to use Wise's brigade. When Lee took over the army, however, Wise's men were brought closer to the front. On July 1 Wise disregarded orders and tried to enter the fray at Malvern Hill, an act that earned him the condemnation of his fellow officers. For the next sixteen months after the Seven Days' Campaign picket duty at Chaffin's Bluff and forage expeditions occupied the general's attention. Wise's desire for active service grew stronger when he learned that some people called his unit "the Life Insurance Company."

In September 1863 Wise and his brigade headed to South Carolina, where he took command of the military district below Charleston. Although he managed to get along with General Pierre G.T. Beauregard, the Louisianan gave his subordinate little flexibility in handling his troops. The war had taken a physical and emotional toll on Wise. Of his nineteen relatives who served in the army, ten were wounded and two killed, including his own son. He looked sickly, with his emaciated body, sunken eyes, and sloppy dress. The war's tragedies had brought Wise closer to God. He told Brigadier General William Nelson Pendleton that he "'would not give up his faith in Jesus.' Yet [Wise] says the devil makes him kuss sometimes."

Accompanying Beauregard's force from South Carolina, Wise and two of his regiments arrived at Petersburg in the spring of 1864. His other two units had been sent to Florida. On May 16 under the direction of Major General William H.C. Whiting, Wise's men participated in a failed attack near Port Walthall Junction. Wise did not escape blame for this fiasco and made matters worse by criticizing the Confederate high command for its decision to emphasize the defense of Richmond over Petersburg. On June 1 he was detached from most of his brigade and took over

While this is quite probably a view of Wise in uniform, the greatcoat and cape so covers everything that no insignia or elements of a uniform can be seen. (William A. Turner Collection)

at Petersburg as command of the 1st Military District, Department of North Carolina and Southern Virginia. This assignment covered the area south of the Appomattox River to the Virginia line.

Though Confederate officials probably thought that they had exiled Wise to a peaceful sector, the Army of the Potomac assaulted the lightly defended city June 15–18. He stubbornly resisted the enemy's advances and actively sought acknowledgment of his brigade's performance in the Richmond papers. In his efforts to gain recognition Wise offended Major General Bushrod R. Johnson. Without his command he returned to his post as administrator of the 1st Military District for the rest of the summer and fall.

Not until January of 1865 did Wise resume control of his brigade. During the retreat to Appomattox he cut his way through Federal troops at Sayler's Creek on April 7. Lee commended the ex-governor and gave him temporary control of Bushrod Johnson's division. At Appomattox Wise scolded his veterans for not dressing their lines. His soldiers tauntingly replied: "Look at him! he is brave enough now, but he never was so near the Yankees before in his life."

After the war Wise resided in Richmond and practiced law. Though he never applied for amnesty, he admonished younger Virginians to accommodate themselves to the new situation as best they could. In 1872 he wrote *Seven Decades of the Union*, which focused on the life of President John Tyler. Wise died from consumption on September 12, 1876.

Peter S. Carmichael

Simpson, Craig M., *A Good Southerner: The Life of Henry A. Wise of Virginia* (Chapel Hill, 1985).

Wise, Barton H., *The Life History of Henry A. Wise, 1806–1876* (New York, 1899).

✴ *Jones Mitchell Withers* ✴

The only known uniformed portrait of Withers has never before been published, and almost certainly dates from after April 1862, as suggested by the major general's button arrangement. (Alabama Departmemt of Archives and History, Montgomery)

Jones Mitchell Withers was born in Madison County, Alabama, on January 12, 1814. After attending Greene Academy in Huntsville he entered West Point at the age of seventeen. Graduating forty-fourth in the class of 1835, Withers only served briefly at Fort Leavenworth before resigning his commission on December 5, 1835. He began studying law in Alabama and became the governor's private secretary, but volunteered for service during the Creek Indian war of 1836. Withers joined the staff of General Benjamin Patterson and helped train troops at Tuskegee.

After the war Withers resumed his law studies in Tuscaloosa and passed the bar. By the outbreak of the Mexican War he was a successful lawyer and cotton broker in Mobile. Withers volunteered as a private but was then elected colonel of his regiment. The government, however, did not need all of the volunteer regiments that were raised. Therefore Withers had to forego his colonel's commission, but he finally did enter the service on March 3, 1847, as lieutenant colonel of the 13th U.S. Infantry. In September he was promoted to colonel of the 9th U.S. Infantry and served with it until his resignation on May 23, 1848. For the next decade Withers continued his career as a successful cotton broker and became involved in politics. He was elected to the Alabama legislature in 1855 and became mayor of Mobile in 1858.

In 1861 Withers left the mayor's office to become colonel of the 3d Alabama Infantry. Ordered to Virginia, he was given a brigade and command of the eastern district of Brigadier General Benjamin Huger's Department of Norfolk. Withers was promoted to brigadier general on July 10, effective immediately, and in January 1862 took charge of the coastal defenses around Mobile. When General Albert Sidney Johnston began his buildup for the Shiloh Campaign, Withers' brigade was sent to join him at Corinth, Mississippi. At Shiloh Withers commanded the 2d Division in Major General Braxton Bragg's corps and was in the thick of the fighting. Placed on the army's right, he was not engaged until mid-morning on April 6, when Johnston personally led the division into battle. Withers' division was stymied for three hours by a lone Union brigade that stubbornly held its position. When the Yankees finally retreated, Johnston left Withers without giving him any specific orders. Withers could have possibly pushed on and cut off Major General U.S. Grant from the Tennessee River but failed to do so because of his uncertainty as to what Johnston wanted him to do. In any case the irascible Bragg highly praised Withers and wrote that the 2d Division "was gallantly led by [Withers] from the first gun to the close of the action…."

Withers' gallantry at Shiloh earned him promotion to major general on August 16, effective from April 6, 1862, and command of Lieutenant General Leonidas Polk's reserve division. In the Kentucky invasion his division missed the major battle at Perryville when Bragg dispatched it to support Major General Edmund Kirby Smith just prior to the fight. Stones' River, however, proved to be a bloodbath when Withers' division served as the pivot for Bragg's great sweep to the right. Charging into Brigadier General Philip Sheridan's Yankees, Withers lost almost one-third of his division in three bloody assaults. When the enemy failed to retreat, Withers joined Major General Benjamin Cheatham in writing a memorandum on January 3, 1863, urging Bragg to break off the battle and retreat. Although endorsed and forwarded by Polk, Bragg chided the advice, and it became one of the many points of contention that developed between Bragg and his generals.

During the Tullahoma Campaign in the summer of 1863 Withers left the Army of Tennessee because of poor health. In February 1864 he was given command of the District of North Alabama and established his headquarters at Montgomery. That July he was placed in charge of the state's reserve forces with orders to organize for service all males who were either too old or too young for the draft. Withers continued in this duty until the surrender.

Withers returned to his cotton brokerage business after the war and also was editor of the Mobile *Tribune*

for a time. In 1867 he was reelected Mobile's mayor and served as its treasurer, 1878–79. He died in Mobile on March 13, 1890, and was buried in Magnolia Cemetery.

Terry L. Jones

Connelly, Thomas Lawrence, *Army of the Heartland: The Army of Tennessee, 1861–1862* (Baton Rouge, 1967).

Connelly, Thomas Lawrence, *Autumn of Glory: The Army of Tennessee, 1862–1865* (Baton Rouge, 1971).

Wheeler, Joseph, *Alabama*, Vol. VII in Evans, *Confederate Military History*.

✵ *William Tatum Wofford* ✵

Wofford's only known wartime photo dates from after January 1863. (Museum of the Confederacy, Richmond, Va.)

William Tatum Wofford was born in Habersham County, Georgia, on June 28, 1824. After attending local schools, he studied law and entered the bar first in Athens and later in Cassville. During the Mexican War he raised in August 1847 a small body of cavalry, designated Company E of James S. Calhoun's Mounted Battalion. Captain Wofford's subsequent service in the campaign from Vera Cruz to Mexico City elicited a commendation from the Georgia legislature. He mustered out in Mobile on July 12, 1848.

The young Mexican War hero entered public service in 1849, serving as a legislator and clerk in the state house of representatives. Wofford spent the balance of his prewar career in Cassville, practicing law, farming, and editing the *Cass Standard*. He also began a family, marrying Julia Adelaide Dwight (1830–78) on August 16, 1859. By 1860 he owned five slaves and $10,000 in personal property and real estate.

As a delegate to the Georgia state convention in 1861, Wofford at first opposed secession but in the end cast his ballot in favor of the ordinance. Offering his services to the state, Wofford received a commission on April 25, 1861, as colonel of the 1st Georgia State Troops. This unit, redesignated the 18th Georgia Volunteers, departed for Virginia in August.

Wofford's men spent their first winter in the Old Dominion guarding a stretch of the Potomac River near Dumfries. Throughout the spring and summer of 1862 the regiment, assigned to Hood's Texas Brigade, fought in the Peninsula and Seven Days' campaigns. The Georgians subsequently distinguished themselves at Second Manassas and Antietam. During the latter battle Wofford commanded the entire brigade.

The 18th Georgia left the Texans in October 1862, transferring to the brigade of T.R.R. Cobb. Following Cobb's death at Fredericksburg, his command devolved on Wofford. Wofford also received a promotion to brigadier general on April 23, 1863, to rank from January 17 of the same year. The new general was very different from the arrogant Cobb, according to Private E.H. Sutton, and Wofford "soon gained the love of the men."

During the Chancellorsville Campaign the nascent general earned the further approbation of his brigade. Wofford was "constantly all over the field" and "seemed to bear a charmed life." During a charge on May 4, the general rode far in advance of his line, bellowing orders that "could have been heard about two miles."

At Gettysburg on July 2 Wofford garnered additional plaudits. While he was riding past admiring artillerists, the general's bare pate elicited the cry, "Hurrah for you of the bald head!" When ordered to retire later in the day, the Georgian grew angry. Wofford, wrote one superior, was "very ambitious of military fame...and was apprehensive that his coming back might be misconstrued." This brash behavior appeared again on July 22 in an engagement at Chester's Gap when the general, "with his hat off in front," led a successful charge.

Illness forced Wofford to leave his brigade in November 1863. Returning two months later, he assumed temporary division command through late March 1864. The Battle of the Wilderness that spring marked the apogee of Wofford's military career. On May 6 the Georgian proposed and participated in a devastating attack against the Union army's left flank.

Outstanding conduct in the Overland Campaign of 1864 earned Wofford recommendations for promotion to major general. He "constantly exhibited superior zeal, courage, and ability," according the Major General Richard H. Anderson. General R.E. Lee, who had early referred to Wofford as "one of Georgia's best soldiers," wanted him promoted to division command. The War Department concurred with Lee but proved unable to find a suitable opening.

Denied a promotion, Wofford remained with his brigade throughout the summer and fall of 1864. The command spent much of this time in the Shenandoah Valley, participating in a number of engagements. Wofford, as usual, was in the thick of each fight, and at Cedarville on August 16 lost a bay mare valued at $2,600.

Wofford received thirty days sick leave on October 18. After overstaying this furlough at least sixty days, he appeared in Richmond sometime in late December. There Wofford petitioned the Confederate President for an independent command in northern Georgia. The effort succeeded, and on January 25, 1865, the Georgian received orders to proceed to his native region and collect "stragglers and deserters and to dissolve such illegal organizations as may be found in that section." Wofford directed these efforts throughout the spring of 1865, finally surrendering his command on May 12.

North Georgians sent Wofford to Congress immediately following the war, but Radical Republicans denied the ex-Confederate admittance. In 1872 and 1876 he served as a presidential elector and in 1877 participated in Georgia's constitutional convention. Wofford died in Cassville on May 22, 1884, and was buried there in the city cemetery.

Keith P. Bohannon

Atlanta *Constitution*, May 24, 1884.

Cunys, Lucy J., *History of Bartow County, Georgia* (Cartersville, Ga., 1933).

Northen, William J., *Men of Mark in Georgia*, Vol. II (Spartanburg, S.C., 1974).

Sterling Alexander Martin Wood

Sterling Alexander Martin Wood, destined to sign his military correspondence with simply the letters S.A.M., was born March 17, 1823, at Florence, Lauderdale County, Alabama. He attended common schools in Florence and traveled to Bardstown, Kentucky, to attend the Jesuit College of St. Joseph's, graduating in 1841. He read law in Columbia, Tennessee, and in 1845, after being admitted to the bar, opened an office in nearby Murfreesboro.

He then returned to Florence, where he formed a law partnership with his brother. He was solicitor of Alabama's fourth judicial circuit from 1851 to 1857. In the latter year, he was elected to represent Lauderdale County in the state legislature. The year 1860 was an election year, and Wood, as editor of the Florence *Gazette*, championed the candidacy of John C. Breckinridge for the presidency.

In the days following the January 11, 1861, secession of Alabama from the Union, Wood organized and elected captain of the Florence Guards. He and his company were ordered to Fort Morgan, Alabama, where he reported to Brigadier General Braxton Bragg. On May 18 Bragg organized ten independent companies, then posted at Pensacola, into the 7th Alabama Infantry Regiment, and Wood was elected its colonel. During the late summer, Wood assumed command of one of the four brigades into which Bragg had organized his troops posted in and around Pensacola. In mid-November, Wood and his regiment were shuttled by railroad to Chattanooga, where he reported to Colonel Danville Leadbetter. Wood's regiment was broken up into detachments and assigned to guard railroad bridges between Chattanooga and Knoxville. In early December, Wood and his regiment entrained at

Chattanooga and rode the rails to Bowling Green, Kentucky, where they joined Major General William J. Hardee's Army of Central Kentucky. Wood was made a brigadier general on January 7, 1862, and placed in command of a brigade that included the 7th Alabama, the 5th, 7th, 8th, and 9th Arkansas Infantry Regiments, the 3d Mississippi Infantry Battalion, and the 44th Tennessee Infantry Regiment. Wood had not been one of Bragg's favorites. Upon learning of Wood's promotion, Bragg fired off a letter to the War Department, noting that his promotion over Colonel Patton Anderson, his senior, and "much his superior as a soldier," was "very mortifying to the latter."

Union victories at Forts Henry and Donelson compelled the Confederates to evacuate Bowling Green and Nashville and abandon much of Middle Tennessee. The last week of March found Wood and his brigade, assigned to Major General Thomas C. Hindman's division of Hardee's corps, camped near Corinth, Mississippi. On April 6, troops from Wood's brigade (as reorganized, the 16th Alabama, 8th and 9th Arkansas, the 27th, 47th, and 55th Tennessee Infantry Regiments, the 3d Mississippi Infantry Battalion, and the Jefferson Mississippi Artillery) opened the Battle of Shiloh. Their slashing attacks were instrumental in crushing and then routing Everett Peabody's brigade from its camps. Subsequent to the battle and the army's retreat to Corinth, General Hardee reported that General Wood, "though suffering from a fall from his horse, which compelled him to withdraw temporarily, returned to the field and bravely led his men."

General Wood's only known uniformed portrait, taken after January 1862. (Cook Collection, Valentine Museum, Richmond, Va.)

Wood's immediate superior, General Hindman, was not as impressed with Wood's command decisions at Shiloh. Following the Confederates' May 29 evacuation of Corinth and retrograde to Tupelo, a court of inquiry was held which cleared Wood "from any imputation against him in connection with his conduct during the battle...."

While at Tupelo, Wood, as senior officer, assumed command of the division and in this role accompanied the Army of the Mississippi. Now led by General Braxton Bragg, it was moved by rail from northeast Mississippi to Chattanooga. On August 19, Wood was superseded as division commander by Major General Simon B. Buckner, who had been captured at Fort Donelson and had just been exchanged. Wood and his brigade then crossed the Tennessee River on a march that carried the Confederates deep into Kentucky. He was an active participant in the October 8 Battle of Perryville and, along with Major General Benjamin Franklin Cheatham's command, crossed Doctor's Fork, savaged Brigadier General James Jackson's division and participated in the capture of Parsons' battery. In this fighting, Wood was wounded by a shell fragment.

Following the army's retreat through Cumberland Gap and return to Middle Tennessee, Buckner was detached and ordered to Mobile as commander of the District of the Gulf. In an ensuing reorganization, Wood and his brigade were assigned to Major General Patrick R. Cleburne's newly constituted division. Wood and his troops were in the forefront of Cleburne's December 31 Stones' River onslaught and three-mile advance that saw the Confederates of Lieutenant General William J. Hardee's corps crush two of Major General Alexander McD. McCook's three divisions. in the three-day battle, Wood saw five hundred and four of his eleven hundred officers and men become casualties and was commended by Cleburne for his "great exertions."

In mid-January 1863, following the army's retreat to Tullahoma and Shelbyville, where it went into winter quarters, Wood and his brigade were detached and sent to north Alabama. There Wood assumed command of the District of Northern Alabama. On March 25 there was an engagement with Union gunboats at Florence, and in early April upon being relieved by Colonel Philip D. Roddey, Wood and his brigade returned to Middle Tennessee and rejoined Cleburne's division, then posted near Wartrace. Wood saw action at Liberty Gap (June 25–26) in the Tullahoma Campaign.

Wood's brigade, one of three belonging to Cleburne's division, participated in the marches and countermarches associated with Bragg's failed efforts to isolate and crush part of Major General George H. Thomas' corps in McLemore's Cove (September 9–10). At dusk on September 19, Wood crossed the West Fork of the Chickamauga and for the last time led his troops into battle. He engaged the foe, and drove him across Winfrey's field and into the dense woods beyond. Wood's left wing and Brigadier General James Deshler's right flank units became intermixed in the darkness, resulting in considerable confusion. By the time the situation was rectified, Cleburne halted his division, threw out skirmishers, and bivouacked. The advance was renewed at 10 A.M. on the 20th, and Cleburne's division advanced against Thomas' troops, who were posted behind log breastworks several hundred yards east of the Lafayette road.

Wood lost control of his unit and his brigade separated. The 32d Mississippi on the right, along with Lucius Polk's brigade, closed to within 175 yards of the Yanks before being checked, and Wood, with the remainder of his brigade, found themselves coming into line on the right of A.P. Stewart's division. Wood and his men surged into Poe's field only to have their ranks shattered by small arms and artillery fire. More than five hundred men fell within a few minutes, and Wood, as ordered by Cleburne, pulled back and reformed his lines.

Cleburne did not forgive Wood. When he filed his "after action report" for Chickamauga, Cleburne failed to mention Wood, but commended his other brigade commanders. As a result, Wood resigned his commission on October 17, 1863, and saw no more Civil War service. He traveled to Tuscaloosa, where his family had sought refuge, and resumed his law practice.

In the years after Alabama was redeemed, Wood reentered politics and served in the legislature in 1882–83. He joined the faculty of the University of Alabama in 1889 and was attorney for the Alabama Great Southern Railway until his death at Tuscaloosa on January 26, 1891. The general was buried in Tuscaloosa.

Edwin C. Bearss

Brewer, Willis, *Alabama: Her History, Her Resources, War Record and Public Men* (Montgomery, 1872).

Owen, Thomas M., *History of Alabama and Dictionary of Alabama Biography* (Chicago, 1921).

Wheeler, Joseph, *Alabama*, Vol. VII in Evans, *Confederate Military History*.

General Wright as a brigadier between June 1862 and November 1864. (Valentine Museum, Richmond, Va.)

✷ *Ambrose Ransom Wright* ✷

Ambrose Ransom Wright was born in Louisville, Georgia, on April 26, 1826. "Ranse," as he was known, attended local schools but left at the age of fifteen to commence the study of law. Following his admittance to the bar the young attorney struggled for several years in southwest Georgia before returning to Louisville. There he established a successful practice and entered the political arena.

As a member of the Whig party, Wright campaigned vigorously but unsuccessfully for state and national offices. He moved to Augusta in 1859 "to seek a wider and more inviting field" for his political pursuits. Wright ardently supported Georgia's withdrawal from the Union, and following secession received an appointment as the state's commissioner to Maryland. Efforts to induce secession in Maryland proved futile, and Wright returned to Augusta.

On April 26, 1861, he enlisted as a private in the "Confederate Light Guards." Only days after forming, the guards joined other companies in Portsmouth, Virginia, to organize the 3d Georgia Infantry. On May 8 the regiment elected Wright colonel. A soldier in the 3d described the new officer as "tall, finely formed, (and) of commanding appearance." Other men found the colonel to be "reserved and formal" and a "strict" disciplinarian."

The 3d Georgia saw its first action in the fall of 1861 along the North Carolina coast. In a skirmish October 9 "on the Chickamacomico banks" the regiment's colonel singlehandledly captured five Federals. The following spring, on April 19, 1862, a small force of Southerners under Wright defeated Union troops in the battle of South Mills, North Carolina.

The Confederate victory at South Mills elicited praise from Wright's superiors. On June 3 he received a promotion to brigadier general, to rank from that date, and shortly thereafter command of a brigade. Later that month the brigade participated in the Seven Days' Campaign. At Malvern Hill on July 1 one soldier remembered seeing Wright "on all parts of the field, in his blue woolen suit…with his felt hat turned up at the side and his long curly hair and still longer beard waving in the breeze."

The unshorn general subsequently led his brigade at Second Manassas and Antietam. In the latter battle Wright received severe wounds in the breast and leg after having horse shot from under him. Despite his injuries the general remained on the field "and desired himself to be carried forward to give the command on a litter."

Wright remained in Georgia on wounded furlough for seven months following Antietam. Throughout this period he chafed at his inability to serve. "There is no place I like so much as an active fighting campaign," he wrote. In contrast, some of Wright's men apparently enjoyed his absence. On March 25, 1863, thirty-two officers in the 3d Georgia requested the regiment's transfer to another brigade, citing their general's "harsh discourteous temperament" and "interference with internal arrangements" in the regiment. Other officers in the 3d struck down the petition.

Wright returned to the army just prior to Chancellorsville. During that battle on May 4 Wright's horse was struck twice by fragments and the general himself slightly wounded in the right knee. At Gettysburg Wright's brigade stormed up Cemetery Ridge on July 2, temporarily breaching the Union lines. Wright remained in the rear, "sick and at the hospital," during the attack.

Soon after Gettysburg Wright penned a dramatic letter to his wife describing the action and criticizing the other brigades in his division. When the missive appeared in print, Wright's division commander, Major General Richard H. Anderson, placed the Georgian under arrest. The ensuing court-martial tried Wright for "disobedience towards superior officers and for matters connected with publications which appeared in the *Augusta Constitutionalist*." Wright handled his own defense and was acquitted in late August.

The Gettysburg controversy elucidates a major facet of "Ranse" Wright's character. "At times," wrote a

Major General Wright, photographed during the last six months of the war. (Museum of the Confederacy, Richmond, Va.)

contemporary, Wright was "too self-willed and combative. He could not temporize enough, often raising unnecessary antagonisms." An Atlanta newspaper editor praised Wright's gallantry and patriotism, but admitted that the general was "considered vain, and ambitious of acquiring popularity." General Richard H. Anderson, whom Wright despised, believed his subordinate had "too much dash" and needed "a little more coolness."

Ever the politician, Wright ran for and won a seat in the Georgia legislature in the fall of 1863. During his tenure as a senator he emerged as a strong supporter of the central government. When the legislature adjourned, Wright returned to the army and apparently exercised brief division command in February of 1864.

Illness kept Wright from his command throughout most of 1864. On November 30 while in Augusta, Wright was promoted to major general, to rank from November 26. He subsequently participated in the Siege of Savannah, ultimately surrendering with General Joseph E. Johnston in North Carolina.

After the war Wright practiced law, edited the Augusta *Chronicle & Sentinel*, and engaged in politics. He won a congressional seat in the fall of 1872 but contracted a serious illness shortly after the election. He died in Augusta on December 21, 1872, and was buried there in Magnolia Cemetery.

This appears to be a very slight variant of the previous image. (Cook Collection, Valentine Museum, Richmond, Va.)

Keith P. Bohannon

Ambrose Wright Papers, Duke University

Augusta *Chronicle and Sentinel*, December 25, 1872.

Snead, Claiborne, *Address by Col. Claiborne Snead at the Reunion of the Third Georgia Regiment* (Augusta, Ga., 1874).

⚝ *Marcus Joseph Wright* ⚝

Marcus J. Wright's only known wartime portrait.
(Marcus J. Wright Papers, Southern Historical
Collection, University of North Carolina, Chapel
Hill)

Marcus J. Wright was born in Purdy, Tennessee, on June 5, 1831. After attending a local academy, Wright studied law and moved to Memphis where he served as clerk of the common law and chancery court. He also enlisted in a local militia unit, becoming lieutenant colonel of the 154th Tennessee Militia. When the Civil War began, state authorities mustered in the regiment and designated it the 154th Senior Tennessee Infantry.

The regiment later reported to Columbus, Kentucky, where Wright served as temporary military governor. On November 7, 1861, the 154th Tennessee fought in the Battle of Belmont. The regiment served in Bushrod Johnson's brigade at Shiloh (April 6–7, 1862), where Wright's wounds disabled him for several weeks.

Wright returned to the army in the late spring, serving on the staff of Major General Benjamin Cheatham as acting assistant adjutant general during the Kentucky Campaign and at the Battle of Perryville. On December 20, 1862, Wright was promoted to brigadier general to rank from December 13. He eventually was assigned to the former brigade of Daniel S. Donelson, comprised of the 8th, 16th, 28th, 38th, 51st, and 52d Tennessee.

Wright led the brigade throughout the campaigns of 1863. On September 19 at Chickamauga the brigade as a part of Cheatham's division launched three desperate attacks against a Union force, fighting for two hours and losing almost half its men. Two months later the brigade shared in the army's debacle at Missionary Ridge.

Following this campaign Wright was transferred to Georgia, where he served at Atlanta and Macon. Toward the war's end he commanded the District of North Mississippi and West Tennessee. Wright was paroled at Grenada, Mississippi, on May 19, 1865.

Wright practiced law again in Memphis postwar, but moved to Washington, D.C., where he was an assistant purser at the United States Navy Yard. In 1878 government authorities hired him as an agent to collect Confederate records for the *Official Records*. For the next four decades Wright devoted himself to this work. He wrote numerous articles for *Confederate Veteran*, and in 1911 his valuable *General Officers of the Confederate Army* was published. He retired in June 1917 and died in the nation's capital on December 27, 1922. He was buried in Arlington National Cemetery.

Jeffry D. Wert

Tucker, Glenn, *Chickamauga: Bloody Battle In The West* (Indianapolis, 1961).

⋆ *Zebulon York* ⋆

Born into a Polish family at Avon, Maine, on October 10, 1819, Zebulon York received an excellent education at Maine's Wesleyan Seminary and Kentucky's Transylvania University. Moving to Vidalia, Louisiana, after receiving a law degree from the University of New Orleans, he became one of the state's most prominent lawyers and richest planters. In 1861 it was claimed that the six plantations and seventeen hundred slaves owned by York and his business partner produced forty-five hundred bales of cotton. The two men reportedly paid the highest realty taxes in Louisiana.

At the beginning of the Civil War, York raised a company of infantry for a proposed "Polish Brigade." When the brigade failed to materialize, York's company became part of the 14th Louisiana Infantry, and York was elected major. Ordered to Virginia, the regiment was placed on the Peninsula outside Richmond. After being promoted to lieutenant colonel in February 1862, he experienced his first major fight on May 5 at the Battle of Williamsburg. Sent in to shore up Major General James Longstreet's right flank, the 14th Louisiana charged through an abatis of felled timber against Major General Joe Hooker's Yankees. Twice the regiment attacked but failed to carry the Union position. The third attempt succeeded, however, and York's men pushed the enemy back a mile. The regiment lost 194 men in the bloody fight and York fell wounded, but his actions were noted by superior officers. Longstreet wrote in his report, "Lieut.-Col. Zebulon York discharged his difficult duties with marked skill and fearlessness." In his first fight York had displayed a bravery that soon became famous in the regiment. One soldier later claimed York's daring in battle

"amounted to rashness." He also became known as one of the army's most profane swearers.

After the Seven Days' Campaign the 14th Louisiana's colonel resigned, and York was promoted to replace him on August 15. At Second Manassas he again was wounded but returned to fight at Antietam and Fredericksburg. In early 1863 York was sent to Louisiana to recruit for Major General Richard Taylor's army and to drill conscripts destined for the Louisiana brigades in Virginia. Some sources claim he returned to his command in time for Gettysburg, but official records show that his lieutenant colonel commanded the regiment during the campaign.

York was in the thick of the fighting at the Wilderness. The Louisiana troops suffered heavy casualties there, and on May 8, 1864, the 1st and 2d Louisiana brigades were consolidated and placed under Brigadier General Harry T. Hays. The two brigades kept their separate identities, however, and York was put in command of the 2d Brigade. During the vicious fighting around Spotsylvania, York was apparently absent, since Colonel Jesse Williams was killed at the "Mule Shoe" on May 12, reportedly while in command of the 2d Brigade. Hays was badly wounded during the Spotsylvania Campaign and left Virginia. On June 2 York was promoted to brigadier general, effective May 31, and was given permanent command of the consolidated brigade. He was the only soldier of Polish descent to become a Confederate general.

On June 13 York's brigade left the trenches at Cold Harbor to accompany Lieutenant General Jubal Early

The only known wartime portrait of General York in uniform, taken during the final year of the war. (Library of Congress)

on his raid against Washington. Now in Major General John B. Gordon's division, York saw heavy fighting at the Monocacy on July 19 when his brigade attacked a line of Federals holding a rail fence. The brigade was badly shot up but managed to break through the enemy position. When a second enemy line was cracked, York claimed the Yankees "ran like sheep without a Shepherd." He reported the assault cost him as much as half the brigade and that the fight was the bloodiest and most fierce he had ever witnessed. When the enemy fled, Early rode up and said, "General, you have handled your command well and it has done its duty nobly." York wrote a friend, "This I shall ever consider a complament [sic] of note coming from one of the most cross grained and faultfinding Gens. in the C.S. Army."

York's brigade contributed greatly to Early's victory at Kernstown on July 24 and fought well at the Third Battle of Winchester on September 19, 1864. At Winchester the brigade traded volleys with the Yankees at two hundred yards until the enemy broke and ran. York charged after them but had to stop and fall back when the rest of the division failed to keep up. The Yankees then crushed Early's left flank, and the Confederate line collapsed. During the fight York received his third wound of the war when he was hit in the wrist and had to have his arm amputated.

After recovering from his wound York was sent with two Catholic priests to a prison camp at Salisbury, North Carolina, in early 1865. There in a rather bizarre scheme he tried to recruit volunteers from the large number of Irish and German prisoners. At one time he claimed to have eight hundred Yankees ready to join the Confederacy, but apparently none actually enlisted.

After the surrender York was paroled in North Carolina and returned to Louisiana. Ruined financially by the war, he settled in Natchez, Mississippi, and operated the York House. He died there in August 5, 1900, and was buried in the city.

Terry L. Jones

Dmitry, John, *Louisiana*, Vol. X in Evans, *Confederate Military History*.

Jones, Terry L., *Lee's Tigers: The Louisiana Infantry in the Army of Northern Virginia* (Baton Rouge, 1987).

Uminski, Sigmund H. "Poles and the Confederacy," *Polish-American Studies*, XXII (1965), 99–106.

Brigadier General Young in 1863-64. (Library of Congress)

⭐ *Pierce Manning Butler Young* ⭐

Pierce Manning Butler Young was born at Spartanburg, South Carolina, on November 15, 1836. Young and his family moved to Bartow County, Georgia, when he was a small boy. He subsequently studied at the Georgia Military Institute until his appointment to the United States Military Academy in 1857. An outspoken Southern supporter at West Point, Young resigned from the academy during his senior year in March 1861, after Georgia's secession. On March 16 he was appointed a 2d lieutenant of artillery in the Confederate Army.

Young briefly served on the staff of General Braxton Bragg at Pensacola, Florida, before returning to Georgia in July and accepting a post as adjutant of Cobb's Legion, a unit of infantry, artillery, and cavalry under Brigadier General Thomas R.R. Cobb. By early 1862, Young was the command's major, but illness forced him to relinquish his post briefly. When he returned, he was promoted to lieutenant colonel and assigned command of the Legion's cavalry.

During the summer and fall campaigns of 1862, the mounted contingent of Cobb's Legion served in Brigadier General Wade Hampton's cavalry brigade. In August, Young suffered a wound in action at Burkittsville, Maryland, and on September 13, at Middletown, Maryland, he was hit in the chest. He was cited for "remarkable gallantry" during the Sharpsburg Campaign and promoted to colonel on November 1, 1862.

Young's skill as a cavalry officer shone during the operations of the Gettysburg Campaign in June and July 1863. At Brandy Station on June 9, Cobb's Legion spearheaded the counterattack of Hampton's brigade with a saber charge. Hampton called it a "gallant charge" and cited Young in his report. Major General J.E.B. Stuart described it as a "brilliant charge" and listed Young among other colonels who handled their regiments "admirably, and behaved with conspicuous daring."

Following the Battle of Brandy Station, the Confederate army marched north toward Pennsylvania, with Stuart's cavalry protecting the army's flank. Hampton's brigade counterattacked at Upperville on June 21, assisting in the repulse of the Union cavalry. Stuart's cavalry began their ride around the Union army four days later. On July 2 at Hunterstown, Pennsylvania, Young led Cobb's Legion in an unsupported charge and was routed. Young suffered a third wound after the army's return to Virginia in an August action south of the Rappahannock River.

Young's performance during the Gettysburg Campaign earned him promotion to brigadier general to rank from September 28. He was assigned to command of Hampton's former brigade, which had been under Colonel Matthew Calbraith Butler, who had lost a leg at Brandy Station. The brigade consisted of the 1st North Carolina, the 1st South Carolina, Cobb's Legion, the Jeff Davis Legion and Phillips' Legion. Young led the command during the Mine Run Campaign and the operations that fall. Before the beginning of the 1864 campaigns, Stuart reorganized the mounted units. Young's brigade then consisted of Cobb's Legion, Phillips' Legion, the 7th Georgia and the 10th Georgia Battalion.

Young's brigade fought with Stuart's cavalry throughout the spring, summer, and fall of 1864. He was wounded in the chest on May 30 in an engagement at Ashland. He led Hampton's division during part of the year when Hampton assumed command of the cavalry corps upon Stuart's death. Confederate authorities ordered Young to Georgia in November to secure remounts, recruit cavalrymen, and assist in the defense of the Augusta Powder Works from Union General William T. Sherman's Union forces. On December 30, Young was temporarily promoted to the rank of major general. He served under Hampton in the Carolinas during the war's final months.

After the war, Young returned to Georgia and farmed. In 1868 he was elected to the United States House of Representatives, serving three terms until 1875. He also attended the 1872, 1876, and 1880 Democratic national conventions as delegate. In 1885

President Grover Cleveland appointed the loyal Democrat consul-general to St. Petersburg, Russia. He remained in Russia for two years and in 1893, he was named United States minister to Guatemala and Honduras. He was serving in this diplomatic post when he died in New York City on July 6, 1896. He was buried in Cartiersville, Georgia, near his plantation.

Pierce Young was among that outstanding group of colonels and brigadiers who served in Stuart's cavalry corps. Wounded four times, he served with distinction and bravery at Brandy Station, Upperville, Hunterstown and the Petersburg operations.

Jeffry D. Wert

Derry, Joseph, *Georgia*, Vol. VI in Evans, *Confederate Military History*.

Freeman, Douglas Southall, *Lee's Lieutenants: A Study in Command* (New York, 1942–44).

Longacre, Edward G., *The Cavalry At Gettysburg* (Rutherford, N.J., 1986).

Young taken at a different sitting, again probably in
1863-64. (U.S. Army Military History Institute, Carlisle, Pa.)

⋆ William Hugh Young ⋆

William Hugh Young was born in Booneville, Missouri, on January 1, 1838. His parents moved to Red River County, Texas, when he was three and later relocated to Grayson County. Young attended Washington College, Tennessee, and McKenzie College, Texas, before entering the University of Virginia in 1859. Although he graduated in July of 1861, Young remained at the University of Virginia to study military tactics at a military academy that was affiliated with the university. While he prepared himself for military service, his father had already joined the Texas Reserves and would become a general in that organization.

When William returned to Texas in September of 1861, he promptly recruited a company, and its members elected him captain. As one of ten companies in the 9th Texas Infantry, Young led his men at the Battle of Shiloh, April 6–7, 1862, where the regiment formed part of Brigadier General J. Patton Anderson's brigade of Major General Braxton Bragg's corps. During the opening day of that engagement, the men of the 9th Texas were mown down by an Illinois battery. Those Texans who survived the artillery barrage ran. When the regiment was reorganized later that month, the members elected Young to be their new colonel, a selection that boded well for the Confederate army.

As part of Brigadier General Preston Smith's brigade of Major General Benjamin F. Cheatham's division, Young led the 9th Texas during the

Confederate invasion of Kentucky in the fall of 1862. Although Young's regiment participated in the Battle of Perryville on October 8, the limited number of casualties makes it apparent that the unit was not actively engaged.

Colonel A.J. Vaughan, Jr., led the brigade during the fighting at Murfreesboro, Tennessee, where, on December 31, Young had two horses shot from under him, and a Minié bullet struck him in his shoulder during the fighting near the Round Forest. Cheatham wrote of Young's performance: "...the Ninth Texas Regiment, under the command of that gallant officer, Col. W.H. Young, who did not hear the order [to withdraw], became detached and was farther to the left. It remained in the woods and continued to fight the enemy, and at last charged them on their flank and drove them from the woods on their entire right, losing very heavily."

Vaughan reported that he ordered Young to make the attack referred to by Cheatham, which Young "did in most gallant style, and succeeded in driving him, though with great loss, through the woods and open field on the other side...Colonel Young...seized the colors of his regiment in one of its most gallant charges and led it through."

On January 21, 1863, the 9th Texas was transferred to Brigadier General Matthew D. Ector's brigade. In

A damaged and faded portrait of William H. Young that is almost certainly postwar, with the uniform added by an artist. (Albert G. Shaw Collection, Virginia Historical Society, Richmond)

early May, Ector's brigade was one of the two that were transferred from Middle Tennessee to Central Mississippi. Although his were among the first troops to arrive in Jackson, Union forces had already effectively isolated Lieutenant General John C. Pemberton's men near Vicksburg. Ector remained in central Mississippi through the summer of 1863, while his brigade participated in General Joseph E. Johnston's unrealized efforts to relieve the Confederates besieged in Vicksburg. During the abortive fighting around Jackson, Young sustained a wound in the right thigh. He recovered in time to rejoin his regiment and accompany it, as part of Major General William H.T. Walker's division, to Georgia, where it arrived in time to participate in the Battle of Chickamauga, September 19–20. During that engagement, Young received yet another wound, this one in the chest.

On September 22, the brigade was ordered back to central Mississippi, where it remained until May of 1864, despite evidence indicating its relocation to Mobile in February. In May, the brigade now in Major General Samuel G. French's division, returned to Georgia with Lieutenant General Leonidas Polk to participate in the Atlanta Campaign.

On July 27, near the outskirts of Atlanta, a piece of shrapnel struck Ector above the left knee, rendering him unfit for further field duty. Young assumed command of the brigade that evening, French having detached him for special duty during much of the brigade during the ensuing weeks influenced French to report that he was "under obligations for valuable services" rendered by Young. He was promoted to brigadier general with temporary rank on August 16 to rank from August 15. The Confederate Congress did not approve his promotion until February 20, 1865.

When General John Bell Hood marched northward following his evacuation of Atlanta in September, French's division, which included Young's brigade, composed of four Texas and two North Carolina regiments, was detached and ordered to attack the Union forts that guarded Allatoona, Georgia. During the Confederate assault on October 5, Young had his horse shot from under him. He continued to lead his men on foot until his left foot was all but shot off by an artillery projectile. The Confederates had to leave him behind, and he was captured. Of Young, French reported: "Most gallantly he bore his part in action…I am indebted to…Young for [his] bravery, skill, and unflinching firmness."

During the next four months, Young was hospitalized at Marietta, Atlanta, Chattanooga, and Nashville. Federal authorities deemed him sufficiently recovered by February of 1865 to be confined to a prisoner of war camp. Young was sent to Johnson's Island, Ohio. He remained a prisoner there until July 24.

After the war, Young moved to San Antonio, Texas, where he became a conspicuous lawyer and a real estate operator until his death. He also operated a freight line, was affiliated with the Nueces River Irrigation Company, and edited the San Antonio *Express* prior to his demise on November 28, 1901. He is buried in Confederate Cemetery, San Antonio. In addition to the wounds enumerated above, he purportedly received two more, one in the neck and another in the jaw, either at Kennesaw Mountain or on July 27 at Atlanta. Whether these wounds or others were actually sustained by Young, his bravery on the battlefield is beyond reproach.

Lawrence L. Hewitt

Roberts, O.M., *Texas*, Vol. XI in Evans, *Confederate Military History*.

✴ *Felix Kirk Zollicoffer* ✴

Felix Kirk Zollicoffer, the son of John Jacob and Martha Kirk Zollicoffer, was born on May 19, 1812, at Bigbyville, Maury County, Tennessee. Of Swiss descent on his father's side, his grandfather, a revolutionary war soldier from North Carolina, had received a land grant in Tennessee.

After working on the family plantation, Felix attended Jackson College at Columbia for one year. At sixteen he went to work for a Paris, Tennessee, newspaper. In 1830, aged eighteen, he became a journeyman printer in Knoxville, and four years later was part owner and editor of the Columbia *Observer*. He also contributed to the *Southern Agriculturist* and the Hunts-ville, Alabama, *Mercury*. In 1835 he was named

Tennessee State Printer. That year he also married Louisa Pocahontas Gordon, by whom he fathered eleven children. In 1836 Zollicoffer volunteered for the military and served a one-year enlistment as a lieutenant in the Second Seminole War.

By the early 1840s, Zollicoffer was exercising considerable political clout statewide and was named editor of the Nashville *Republican Banner*. His mission was to champion the cause of Whig candidate James C. Jones in his forthcoming governor's canvass against Governor James Knox Polk. Zollicoffer headed Jones' successful campaign although plagued by an aneurysm. Following his inauguration as Tennessee's chief executive, Jones named Zollicoffer state comptroller and adjutant general, positions he held between 1845 and 1849. He was elected to the state senate in 1850 and held this office until his 1852

election to the 33d Congress to represent the 8th District.

Zollicoffer was a kingmaker and political czar, as he demonstrated in 1850 upon his return to the editorship of the *Banner*, where he plugged for first the nomination by the Whigs and then the election of William Bate Campbell as governor. In 1852 he was a delegate to the Whig National Convention. Although he opposed Major General Winfield Scott's nomination for president of the United States, afterward he toiled loyally for the Scott-Graham ticket. The campaign was bitter and led to a duel between Zollicoffer and John Leake Marling, editor of the rival Nashville *Union*. Zollicoffer was shot in his pistol hand and Martin was seriously injured by a shot in the head. Subsequently, the two editors became friends. Zollicoffer's efforts enabled General Scott to carry Tennessee.

Upon taking his seat in Congress. Zollicoffer resigned as editor of the *Banner*. A states rights Whig, he sought to calm sectional passions and, in 1856, supported Millard Fillmore and the American party "Know-Nothings". Four years later, he stumped for fellow Tennessean John Bell's candidacy for the presidency on the constitutional union party ticket. He had declined to stand for reelection to the 36th Congress in 1858, and in 1861 was a member of the Washington Peace Convention. He was addressing a rally called to

The uniform in this portrait of Zollicoffer is almost certainly an artist's addition. No other genuine uniformed photo has been found. (Barker Texas History Center, University of Texas, Austin)

oppose his state's secession when he learned of President Abraham Lincoln's April 15 call for seventy-five thousand volunteers. Soon thereafter, Governor Isham G. Harris tendered Zollicoffer the command of the Tennessee state troops, with the rank of major general. He declined, citing lack of experience, but soon changed his mind. On July 9 he was commissioned a brigadier general in the Confederate states army. On the 26th, he was ordered by the War Department to proceed to Knoxville, assume command of the District of East Tennessee, "preserve the peace, protect the railroad, and repel invasion." Some five weeks after Zollicoffer reached Knoxville, he was notified by the War Department that "The neutrality of Kentucky has been broken by the [Union] occupation of Paducah..." and he was directed to take action to hold Cumberland Gap.

To achieve his mission, Zollicoffer ordered three regiments to cross into Kentucky and, on the 17th, he departed Knoxville en route to Cumberland Ford (present-day Pineville). He reached Cumberland Ford on the 19th, and learned that only that morning an eight hundred-man column from his command had advanced to Barbourville, destroyed Camp Andrew Johnson, and killed twelve Yankees. An expedition sent out by Zollicoffer in late September scored more successes—a pro-Union Home Guard camp was broken up at Laurel Bridge and two hundred barrels of salt were secured at the Goose Creek Salt Works. These actions were followed by a rebuff when Zollicoffer, with forty-five thousand men, advanced to attack a Union force led by Brigadier General Albin Schoepf at Camp Wildcat, on the Rockcastle River. There was sharp fighting on October 21, and the Confederates fell back, first to Cumberland Ford and then to Cumberland Gap.

Zollicoffer was concerned about the threat of a Union advance into East Tennessee from Kentucky by way of Jacksboro or Jamestown. After strengthening the Cumberland Gap earthworks, he marched south and then west with five infantry regiments, a company of artillery, a large baggage train, and several companies of cavalry. The column, traveling by way of Clinton and Wartburg, reached Jamestown on November 22, and Mill Springs on the Cumberland River on the 29th, having marched 250 miles since leaving Cumberland Ford.

Early in December, General Schoepf took position at Somerset with orders to keep Zollicoffer south of the river. He failed in his mission, for Zollicoffer, in the face of orders to the contrary, crossed the Cumberland and occupied and fortified a bridgehead at Beech Grove. On December 10, Brigadier General William H. Carroll (then at Knoxville) was ordered to reinforce Zollicoffer with his brigade, but did not reach Beech Grove until January 15, 1862. Meanwhile, President Jefferson Davis had directed Major General George B. Crittenden, the hard-drinking son of Kentucky U.S. Senator John A. Crittenden, to proceed to the Bluegrass State and take command of Zollicoffer's and Carroll's brigades. Crittenden reached Mill Springs on January 3, and was surprised to find Zollicoffer and his troops still north of the Cumberland River, which was at flood stage because of heavy rains.

By the night of January 17, a second Union column, led by Brigadier General George H. Thomas, had arrived in the area and had gone into camp at Logan's Cross Roads, eight miles north of Beech Grove. The Confederate generals, with their backs to the river, determined to attack Thomas at dawn on Sunday the 19th, and rout him before Schoepf, marching from Somerset, could intervene.

Zollicoffer's brigade led as the Confederates took up the march at midnight. Soon thereafter a cold rain set in. The first shots were fired at daybreak and the Confederates deployed and pressed ahead, gaining about four hundred yards. Union resistance stiffened, to be followed by a lull as both sides called up reserves. General Zollicoffer, very near-sighted and clad in a raincoat without insignia, had ridden out in front to reconnoiter, but lost his bearings. He called out to the 4th Kentucky Union and commanded its leader, Colonel Speed Fry, to order his people to cease fire. Fry, satisfied that the stranger was a brother officer, obeyed. Zollicoffer was about to turn and ride off when his aide galloped out of the woods, and, shooting at Fry shouted, "It is the enemy, General!" Fry pulled his revolver and shot at Zollicoffer, while calling to his soldiers to resume fire. Zollicoffer fell from his horse, pierced by several balls, one of which struck him in the chest near the heart and killed him. The Battle of Mill Springs lasted another three hours before the Confederates abandoned the field and retreated. Zollicoffer's body fell into the hands of the Federals, but was turned over to the Confederates at Bowling Green. After lying in state in the Hall of the House of Representatives at the Tennessee state capitol, he was buried on February 2 in the Nashville City Cemetery.

Edwin C. Bearss

Myers, Raymond E., *The Zollie Tree* (Louisville, 1964).

Porter, James, *Tennessee*, Vol. VIII in Evans, *Confederate Military History*.

✸ The Trans-Mississippi Generals ✸

By 1864, General Edmund Kirby Smith was hard-pressed in the Trans-Mississippi Department, cut off as he was from the capital in Richmond it sometimes took literally months for a letter or dispatch to reach President Davis or the War Department. In such a state of affairs, he had to act on his own responsibility more than any other Confederate department commander, including such matters as promotions. Repeatedly Smith pleaded with Richmond to send him more brigadiers, or else to grant him authority to create his own generals to fill vacancies. Davis would never do so, jealously guarding his sole prerogative to elevate men to general rank. He did sometimes confirm by official appointment and nomination the informal "promotions" that Smith had to make in the interim, but several other such "generals" were never appointed by Davis, nominated to the Senate, nor confirmed by that body. Yet these men acted as generals in the field, with commensurate command, wore the full uniforms of generals so far as their surviving photographs can suggest, and were paroled at war's end at their general rank. Thus, while they are not strictly speaking generals within the definition of Confederate statute, they are included here in the sketches that follow.

✫ Arthur Pendleton Bagby ✫

Born May 17, 1833, in Monroe County, Alabama, at Claiborne, Bagby matured while his father served his home state as governor and as a United States senator and represented the nation as its diplomatic representative in Russia. Thus the son acquired his education in the national capital, followed by an appointment to the United States Military Academy in 1848. He graduated in his nineteenth year, 1852.

As a 2d lieutenant in the 8th Infantry, he served at Fort Columbus in New York before being assigned to Fort Chadbourne on the Texas frontier. There he relinquished his commission in the fall of 1853. Back in Alabama he pursued legal studies and received his official acceptance into that profession in 1855. After three years as an attorney at Mobile, he joined the westward migration and settled in Gonzales, Texas, by 1858. Two years later he wedded Frances Taylor.

When the Civil War began in 1861, Bagby formed a company in the neighboring counties of Lavaca and Victoria. In October he became major of the 7th Texas Cavalry in the brigade of Henry H. Sibley. From December 1861 to February 1862 Bagby marched with four companies from San Antonio to El Paso to join the invasion of New Mexico while most of the brigade advanced north to capture Albuquerque and Santa Fe. Bagby remained with his battalion guarding the Mesilla Valley in southern New Mexico. He became lieutenant colonel of the regiment on April 4, 1862. Later that month a captain charged Bagby with threatening acts

while drunk, but a court-martial absolved him.

After being driven out of New Mexico, the brigade returned to Texas in the summer of 1862 and received two months' leave. When the regiments regrouped that fall, Bagby had been advanced to colonel of the 7th Texas. Major General John Bankhead Magruder, new commander of the District of Texas, ordered the brigade to Houston in December to participate in an effort to recapture Galveston. Bagby led volunteers from his regiment aboard the cottonclad river steamer *Neptune*, one of two vessels that surprised the Union naval squadron on the morning of January 1, 1863. The successful attack, supported by land force, captured one Federal ship and drove the others from the harbor, though Union fire disabled the *Neptune*.

In February Bagby's regiment marched with the brigade to Louisiana and joined Major General Richard Taylor in April along Bayou Teche. On April 12 and 13 Bagby's regiment formed the left of Taylor's line that halted a Union advance in the Battle of Bisland. A Federal turning movement forced a withdrawal westward on the 13th and 14th past Franklin toward Niblett's Bluff on the Sabine. In the fighting on the 13th Bagby suffered a wound in his right arm. Taylor reported that Bagby "merits the highest consideration."

Arthur Bagby as colonel of the 7th Texas Cavalry, sometime prior to April 1864. (Museum of the Confederacy, Richmond, Va.)

Bagby commanded the Confederate post at Shreveport in May while recovering from his wound. By late summer he had returned to duty and had become commander of the brigade, including the 4th, 5th, and 7th Texas Cavalry as well as Waller's battalion. He successfully directed his regiments during the Confederate victory at Stirling's Plantation, east of the Atchafalaya River on September 29. When Brigadier General Tom Green again attacked a Union camp on Bayou Bourbeau close to Grand Coteau on November 3, Bagby led his men dismounted in the center of the Confederate line and made a "brilliant" charge. They achieved a second success by capturing over seven hundred prisoners and driving the Federal forces from the field. Following the battle, Lieutenant General Edmund Kirby Smith, commander of the Trans-Mississippi Department, requested promotion for Bagby to brigadier general, along with other colonels directing brigades.

During December Bagby and his brigade returned to Texas to defend against Union occupation of the coast. They camped at Virginia Point, near Galveston, in January 1864 but moved to Brazoria County at Columbia during February. While Bagby recovered from an illness, the brigade started for Louisiana in March to oppose a new Federal advance up the Red River. He returned to duty at the beginning of April as the brigade rejoined Taylor south of Mansfield. By slowing Union progress Bagby earned from Taylor the comment that, "His conduct was, as always, that of a brave and skilled soldier."

When Taylor successfully counterattacked at Mansfield on April 8, Bagby's brigade fought dismounted on the left flank. The next day at Pleasant Hill Bagby and his men again advanced dismounted as part of the left wing, but the Federal lines held. On April 11 Taylor directed Bagby to attack the Union river fleet at Grand Bayou, but the ships passed before he arrived. To trap the Federals, Taylor then ordered Brigadier General H.P. Bee to cut off their retreat with cavalry at Monett's Ferry on the Cane River. Bagby on the 23d formed the right of the Confederate line that led until outflanked from the left. In late April and early May Bagby harassed the Union army in Alexandria and on its retreat to the Mississippi River. By May 10 he was commanding a cavalry division in place of the less-experienced Bee. Amidst the fast-moving campaign Kirby Smith on April 13 appointed Bagby a brigadier general, officially dated March 17.

In the following months Smith continued to press President Davis for confirmation of the promotion, which never came.

During the summer and fall of 1864 Bagby continued to direct a cavalry division that defended the Atchafalaya River, then fell back into western Louisiana in the spring of 1865. As the conflict drew to an end, Kirby Smith in March declared to a Confederate senator, "Bagby (won his promotion), should be a major-general, commanding division of Texas and Louisiana cavalry of two brigades." In a last act of recognition Smith promoted Bagby to major general on May 16, to rank from May 10, three weeks before the department surrendered, though like the previous promotion, this had no official sanction.

When the war ended, Bagby became an attorney at Victoria, where he briefly helped edit the Victoria *Advocate*. By the 1870s he was living in Hallettsville, where he died February 21, 1921.

Alwyn Barr

Hall, Martin Hardwick, *The Confederate Army of New Mexico* (Austin, 1978).

Handbook of Texas Staff, *Handbook of Victoria County* (Austin, 1990).

Noel, Theophilus, *A Campaign From Santa Fe to the Mississippi* (Shreveport, 1865; reprinted Houston, 1961).

Winters, John D., *The Civil War in Louisiana* (Baton Rouge, 1963).

✶ *Xavier Blanchard Debray* ✶

Born during 1819, in Epinal, France, a youthful Debray achieved his schooling in the military academy of his native country. After a short time as a French diplomat, he became an immigrant to America in 1848, landing September 25 at New York. He migrated westward and received his citizenship April 5, 1855, at San Antonio, Texas. There he began to publish *El Bejareno*, a Spanish-language newspaper. By 1856 he had moved to Austin, where he first translated Spanish documents for the General Land Office of Texas through 1857. Later he helped form an academy and directed a band in the Texas capital. During 1859 he narrowly lost the election for mayor.

After the secession of Texas in 1861 Debray joined a Travis County company, the Tom Green Rifles, as 1st lieutenant. During the summer Governor Edward Clark made him a staff officer to help form new military units. His appointment to be major in the 2d Texas Infantry came August 10. When a cavalry battalion lost its commander, however, Debray replaced him with the rank of lieutenant colonel on December 7. With the addition of three companies in January 1862 the battalion became the 26th Texas Cavalry. Debray won election as colonel on March 17.

During the spring of 1862 a directive came for Debray to lead his regiment east across the Mississippi River, but new orders soon altered the direction westward to New Mexico. Before he could move far, word arrived that Confederate forces had begun to withdraw from the territories, which left him and his regiment camped near the vulnerable Texas coast.

On July 8, 1862, Debray received appointment as the commander of the Military Sub-district of Houston. In the weeks that followed he shifted units rapidly to meet Union naval raids from Matagorda to Sabine Pass. When a Federal squadron occupied Galveston harbor in early October, he agreed with the decision to withdraw Confederate forces from Galveston Island, yet he opposed any retreat from the coast.

In December Debray assisted the new commander of the District of Texas, Major General John Bankhead Magruder, with plans for the recapture of Galveston. When Magruder launched his land and water assault on the morning of January 1, 1863, Debray led part of the troops who recaptured the island. Magruder in his report commended Debray's "coolness and courage" as well as his leadership.

Debray continued to direct what had become known as the Eastern Sub-district of Texas until February 13, when he received command of the Galveston defenses. On May 30 Magruder made him an acting brigadier general while seeking confirmation of the promotion from the Confederate government. For most of June Debray temporarily directed the Eastern Sub-district. As commander at Galveston, Debray in mid-August disarmed men of two regiments who mutinied over supply and pay problems, but he also began an investigation into the causes. When Federal troops occupied the Texas coast from the Rio Grande to Matagorda Bay in the fall, Debray led a Texas cavalry brigade of three or four regiments as part of Magruder's defense force. His men held various

X.B. Debray sat for his portrait in 1864-65 after Kirby Smith made him a brigadier. (Courtesy of Larry Jones)

positions near Indianola, Lavaca, and Columbia during November and December.

When the Union army under Major General Nathaniel P. Banks began to advance up the Red River in the spring of 1864, Confederate commanders shifted troops from Texas to meet the invasion in Louisiana. Debray and his brigade reached Pleasant Hill on April 2 to assist in slowing the Federal movement. Major General Richard Taylor, the Confederate district commander, declared that his effort "deserves great credit."

At Mansfield on April 8 when Taylor drove back Banks' army, Debray's men fought in the Confederate right wing. The following day at Pleasant Hill he led a "gallant" but unsuccessful charge on the left in which he suffered an injury and lost a boot when Confederate fire killed his horse. As he limped back to the Confederate lines, he met Taylor, who asked, "Are you wounded?" Debray replied, "No, General…but as you may see, I was sent on a bootless errand." "Never mind your boot," Taylor responded. "You have won your spurs." Lieutenant General Edmund Kirby Smith, commander of the Trans-Mississippi Department, agreed and appointed Debray a brigadier general on April 13, to rank from April 8. President Davis never made the appointment official.

Following the major battles Debray and his brigade served in the cavalry division of Brigadier General H.P. Bee as it harassed the Union retreat and tried unsuccessfully to surround Banks at Monett's Ferry on April 23. Debray continued to lead forays against Banks at Alexandria and during the Federal withdrawal to the Mississippi River in May. He and his brigade moved about in western Louisiana during the summer, camping at points where forage and food could be found. While guarding the Atchafalaya River in October and November, Debray's men labored under illness and shortages. During the fall Kirby Smith continued to urge confirmation of Debray as a brigadier.

In December Debray led his brigade across the Sabine River and slowly moved through east Texas to the Richmond area and then to Hempstead in the spring of 1865. Debray kept his men together and protected Houston as other units began to disband. Briefly Magruder shifted command of the Military District of Texas to Debray in June, just before the final Confederate surrender.

After the war Debray settled at Houston, where he unsuccessfully promoted a *Texas Monthly Review* that would publish accounts of Lone Star units in the Civil War. In 1867 he went to Galveston, where he performed accounting for the Produce Exchange and later served as secretary. Island citizens elected him in 1871 one of their delegates to the Tax Payers Convention at Austin that urged lower taxes. During 1874 he won election to one year as an alderman. By 1877 he had moved to the Texas capital, again as a translator of Spanish documents for the General Land Office of Texas. He died January 6, 1895, and received burial in Austin.

Alwyn Barr

Debray, X.B., *A Sketch of the History of Debray's (26th) Regiment of Texas Cavalry* (Austin, 1884).

Hayes, Charles W., *Galveston, History of the Island and the City* (Austin, 1974).

Lonn, Ella, *Foreigners in the Confederacy* (Chapel Hill, 1940).

⋆ B. Frank Gordon ⋆

The first record of Gordon's service in the Confederate army shows him as the adjutant of Colonel John R. Graves' 1st Brigade, 2d Division, Missouri State Guard. He was serving in this capacity during the Battle of Wilson's Creek on August 10, 1861, where he was severely wounded. Graves praised the "great courage" he showed during that battle. Gordon apparently assisted Colonel Joseph O. Shelby in raising the latter's cavalry regiment in Lafayette County, Missouri, in mid-August 1862. Shelby and his recruits left the county on August 18 on their return to Arkansas. On August 24, a detachment of the 6th Kansas Cavalry attacked the Confederate's camp at Coon Creek, but they were driven off. Shelby's regiment was mustered into service as the 5th Missouri Cavalry on September 9, 1862, on Elk Horn Creek near Pineville, Arkansas, and Gordon was elected lieutenant colonel. Two other regiments were mustered in at the same time and placed in a brigade with the 5th Missouri under Shelby.

Gordon thus led the regiment from that point until the end of the war, except when absent on leave or detached duty. The brigade soon established Camp Kearney, south of Newtonia, Missouri, and Gordon's men were engaged in several skirmishes with Union troops near there at Carthage and Mount Vernon during the month of September. On September 30, a Federal force attacked Colonel Douglas H. Cooper's Indian brigade at Newtonia. Cooper asked Shelby to send him reinforcements, and the latter sent Gordon and his regiment. The Missourians charged and overran the 9th Wisconsin Infantry Regiment but soon had to fall back under heavy fire from other enemy troops. Gordon's losses in this engagement were four men killed and eleven wounded.

Several days later, the Confederate forces returned to northern Arkansas from Newtonia to go into winter quarters. Gordon's regiment again fought the enemy in an engagement at Cane Hill, Arkansas, on November 28, where they were stationed on the right flank of the Confederate line. Late in the action, Gordon led portions of his and another regiment in a counterattack that drove the Federals back in confusion. He distinguished himself again in the Battle of Prairie Grove on December 7. In Shelby's after action report, Gordon was described as "there among his men, ever where the fire was heaviest and hottest, leading them to glory."

As part of Brigadier General John S. Marmaduke's division, Shelby's brigade raided into southern Missouri from December 31, 1862, to January 25, 1863. Gordon led his men in actions at Springfield on January 8 and Hartville on January 11. The Missourians fought dismounted, which they often did during the war. In the attack on Hartville, heavy Union fire threw the regiment into momentary confusion. Gordon rallied his men, as one soldier later wrote, "even in the jaws of death," and helped drive the Federals from the town. Shelby's brigade wintered at Batesville, Arkansas.

Marmaduke led another raid into Missouri from April 17 to May 2, 1863, Gordon had little opportunity to distinguish himself, and his regiment suffered only a handful of casualties in light skirmishing. The brigade acted as rear guard during the retreat from Missouri. At the Battle of Helena on July 4, the 5th Missouri again had few men killed and wounded even though Shelby's brigade led the attack on one of the Union fortifications. Gordon commanded Shelby's brigade during the early part of the Federal campaign against Little Rock (August 1–September 14), because Shelby was suffering from a wound received at Helena. Gordon did not accompany the brigade during Shelby's raid into Missouri in September and October, but remained behind in Arkansas with rest of the regiment.

When Shelby was promoted brigadier general on December 15, Gordon became colonel of the 5th Missouri. Shelby received orders to follow the rear of Union Major General Frederick Steele's army when it began its advance from Little Rock toward Shreveport, Louisiana (the Camden Expedition) in late

March 1864. Shelby's men attacked the Union rear guard near Spoonville on April 2. About dark, Gordon led a "desperate and daring" charge that pushed the enemy back. Shelby wrote that Gordon had behaved "with undeviating courage" in the fight. The Confederates could do little more than harass the numerically superior Federal army. Gordon's regiment fought in the Battle of Marks' Mill on April 25, where the men captured two artillery pieces.

Following the conclusion of the Camden Expedition, Shelby took his brigade into the White River valley to recruit and gather supplies. Gordon stationed his regiment near Augusta, where he had orders to suppress jayhawking and stealing, arrest absentees, and picket nearby ferries on the river. Shelby instructed him to "shoot down all persons caught jayhawking." On July 12, Shelby sent Gordon to destroy a portion of the railroad between Little Rock and Devall's Bluff. Gordon's men routed the 10th Illinois Cavalry in an engagement on Bayou Des Arc on July 14. Later in the month, the regiment assisted Colonel Archibald S. Dobbin's troops in operations against plantations south of Helena being run by Federal leasees. Shelby's whole force made another raid on the Little Rock to Devall's Bluff railroad on August 24. Gordon commanded the rear guard after the raid and successfully blunted the Union pursuit. Shelby called him "a brave and skillful officer."

He led his regiment during Major General Sterling Price's Missouri Expedition, August 29–December 2, driving the Federals out of Lexington on October 13 and holding the town for several days. In an engagement at the Big Blue River on October 22, Gordon's regiment was broken by a Union counterattack, but he rallied his men and joined the army in its retreat into the Indian Territory. Gordon's men were in the second defensive line at the Battle of the Little Osage on October 25 and helped cover the retreat of the army's wagon train. The 5th Missouri again helped save the train in an engagement at Newtonia in November. This was the last battle Shelby's brigade fought during the war.

Gordon and his men spent the winter of 1864–65 in camp at Pittsburg, Texas. The brigade was at Corsicana, Texas, when it disbanded upon hearing of the impending surrender of the Trans-Mississippi Department. General Edmund Kirby Smith appointed Gordon a brigadier general on May 16, 1865, to replace Shelby, whom he appointed a major general, as brigade commander. Gordon accompanied Shelby and others to Mexico rather than surrender.

Arthur W. Bergeron, Jr.

Edwards, John N., *Shelby and His Men: The War in the West* (Cincinnati, 1867).

O'Flaherty, Daniel, *General Jo Shelby: Undefeated Rebel* (Chapel Hill, 1954).

✦ Sidney D. Jackman ✦

Thought to have been born in Kentucky, Jackman was living in Missouri when the Civil War started. After the war, one of Jackman's men wrote that initially Jackman was "a Union man...but was forced to organize a company of Confederate soldiers to protect his people from the jayhawkers." Jackman was reported to be in Bates County, Missouri, in early 1862 trying to recruit. The Federals reported his "band of robbers and desperadoes" at about five hundred strong. On June 1, Union sources said that he was in the Indian Territory cooperating with regular Missouri troops and Colonel Stand Watie's Indians.

Jackman and his men participated in an engagement at Lone Jack, Missouri, on August 16, 1862. There the Confederates routed a force of Union Missouri militiamen and captured two artillery pieces. Jackman's 7th Missouri Infantry Regiment was reportedly organized on August 31 but soon broke up. Some of the officers and men of this unit went into the 16th Missouri Infantry Regiment. Jackman remained in Missouri with a small band of men through the fall of 1863. On several occasions, Union troops moved against him and temporarily broke up his force. Colonel Joseph O. Shelby led a cavalry raid into Missouri in September and October 1863, and Jackman accompanied Shelby back into Arkansas with a small number of men.

In early 1864, Union correspondence placed Jackman back in Missouri recruiting men for the Confederate army. His command at this time stood at about 125 men. One dispatch stated, "He evades all posts and public roads and commits no depredations, and has moved since crossing the Arkansas about forty miles a day." Major General William S. Rosecrans ordered his subordinates to track down and "kill the robbers." By early May, Jackman was back in Arkansas. On May 3 his force attacked and captured the wagon train of the 2d Arkansas (Union) Cavalry Regiment near Richmond on the Buffalo River. Two days later, a Federal force attacked Jackman's camp and drove his men off. The Union commander reported that Jackman had been slightly wounded in the brief engagement.

On May 19 Shelby, now a brigadier general and commanding Confederate forces in Arkansas north of the White River, ordered Jackman into the Boston Mountains to recruit men for Confederate service, return all absentees to the ranks, and arrest all Jayhawkers. Shelby instructed him concerning the latter: "Deal with them as murderers and robbers, and punish them with death wherever found."

By June 11 Jackman had succeeded in raising a small regiment that was called Jackman's Missouri Cavalry. Shelby assigned the regiment to Colonel Thomas H. McCray's brigade, but within a couple of months Jackman had become brigade commander. His men attacked the railroad between Little Rock and Devall's Bluff on August 4. They tore up some track but were forced back by Union troops. A small Federal cavalry brigade attacked and drove them back at Hickory Plains on August 7. During Major General Sterling Price's Missouri Expedition, Jackman's

Sidney D. Jackman served as colonel of the 7th Missouri Infantry, and only got his "promotion" to brigadier on May 16, 1865, along with several of the other Trans-Mississippi "generals." A postwar view. (Museum of the Confederacy, Richmond, Va.)

brigade consisted of two Missouri regiments and two Missouri battalions, and was part of Shelby's division. In an engagement near Boonville on October 11, Jackman's men repulsed a Union attack with heavy losses. Shelby wrote, "This brilliant fight stamped him a fine cavalry officer, brave and skillful in action, with everything requisite to make him a dashing commander." Four days later, Jackman's brigade assisted in the capture of the garrison at Glasgow. Again Shelby's report praised his conduct, saying he "displayed his usual courage and made a most brilliant and successful charge, driving everything before him." The brigade played a prominent part in the Battle of the Big Blue on October 22, holding its ground successfully against several Union assaults.

During the army's retreat into Kansas, Jackman's troopers guarded the wagon train. On October 25, at the Battle of Charlot (or Charlot Prairie) near the Marmaton River, Jackman rushed his men to support the troops being driven back by the enemy. He "came rushing up to avenge his fallen comrades" and "charged down upon the rushing enemy like a thunderbolt, driving them back and scattering their front line badly." His quick action saved the day and allowed the train to escape to safety. The Missourians fought their last engagement at Newtonia on October 28, and Price's army then proceeded unmolested to northern Texas.

By November 30 Jackman's brigade was in camp at Clarksville. The men remained in Texas until disbanded just before the surrender of the Trans-Mississippi Department. On May 16, 1865, General Edmund Kirby Smith appointed Jackman a brigadier general to rank from the same date. One of Shelby's staff officers provided the following assessment of Jackman after the war: "part Guerrilla and part regular, [he] carried over to the line the circumspection of the ambuscade. He fought to kill, and to kill without paying the price that ostentatious fighting invariably costs. Patient, abiding as a rock in the tide of battle, satisfied with small gains, but not carried away by large ones; serene under any sky, and indomitable to the end of the play...."

Jackman settled in Texas after the war. After serving one term in the state house of representatives, he was appointed by President Grover Cleveland as a United States marshal in the western part of the state. He remained in this position until his death, which occurred prior to 1911.

Arthur W. Bergeron, Jr.

"Col. Sidney Jackman," *Confederate Veteran*, XIX (1911), p. 436.

Edwards, John N., *Noted Guerrillas, Or the Warfare of the Border* (St. Louis, 1880).

Edwards, John N., *Shelby and His Men: The War in the West* (Cincinnati, 1867).

Embree, D.A., "Fighting the Kansas Jayhawkers," *Confederate Veteran*, XIX (1911), p. 73.

Scroghem, Elkana, "Border Warfare in Missouri," *Confederate Veteran*, XXII (1914), p. 39.

⋆ *Wilburn Hill King* ⋆

King was born in Cullondenville, Georgia, on June 10, 1839. He was educated at Americus, Georgia, where he studied medicine and law. In 1856, he visited Texas, and he settled there in Cass County four years later. King was in Missouri during the secession crisis and in February 1861 enlisted in the Johnson Guards at Warrensburg. He soon was promoted to sergeant and later 1st lieutenant. The unit became Company E, 3d Missouri State Guards Regiment and was ordered to Jefferson City. There the regiment was reorganized, and King became captain of his company. He led his men in the Battle of Wilson's Creek, August 10, and was seriously wounded. King later resigned when the Missouri State Guard failed to become accepted into regular Confederate service. He went to Texas and enlisted in what became Company B, 18th Texas Infantry Regiment. When that regiment was organized on May 13, 1862, King was elected its major.

The regiment received orders on June 12 to march to Little Rock, Arkansas. Near that town, the 18th Texas was placed in a brigade of a division commanded by Brigadier General Henry E. McCulloch. Major General John G. Walker assumed command of the division in January 1863. After remaining in camp near Little Rock for several months, Walker's division was ordered on April 22 to proceed to Alexandria, Louisiana, and join Major General Richard Taylor's army in the District of West Louisiana. By this time, King had been promoted to lieutenant colonel of his regiment.

The division reached Alexandria on May 27 and was immediately sent to the northeastern part of the

state to help relieve the Vicksburg garrison. Taylor ordered Walker to attack Union posts at Milliken's Bend and Young's Point. Brigadier General James M. Hawes led the 1st Brigade against the latter position. King's regiment did not become engaged because Hawes found the Federals too strongly posted and supported by several gunboats. The men saw their first action in a skirmish near Richmond, Louisiana, on June 15. There the regiment held back attacks by the 5th Minnesota Infantry Regiment until outflanked and forced to retreat. The 18th Texas soon rejoined the division, which had abandoned Richmond in the face of superior odds. Taylor shifted his attention to south Louisiana after the fall of Vicksburg, and Walker's division joined him there in August.

King was now colonel of the regiment, and got his first chance to command the men in action at an engagement at Bayou Bourbeau on November 3, 1863. In this battle, King's regiment formed part of a temporary brigade with the 11th and 15th Texas Infantry regiments, all under Colonel Oran M. Roberts. The brigade had been thrown together to support Brigadier General Tom Green's cavalrymen as they harassed the rear guard of a Union army retreating from Opelousas toward New Iberia. Roberts' infantrymen bore the brunt of the battle against two enemy brigades and eventually routed the Federals after hard

Wilburn H. King appears in a brigadier's blouse, though without the collar insignia, and with the distinctive gauntlet showing the Texas Lone Star. This may be a postwar image from his years as adjutant general of the state. (*Confederate Veteran*, XVI)

fighting. King led his men on foot "with undaunted firmness." Of the 320 men from the 18th Texas who went into this action, approximately 60 became casualties.

Brigadier General Thomas N. Waul replaced Hawes as commander of Walker's 1st Brigade in late February 1864. The brigade formed on the center of the division's line at the Battle of Mansfield on April 8. Taylor's army assaulted and overran two Federal divisions before hitting a third one and pushing it back. King was severely wounded during the final Confederate attack about dark and spent several months recovering. General Edmund Kirby Smith appointed King a brigadier general on April 16, to rank from April 8. The Confederate Congress, however, never acted on this appointment. After the war, a former comrade ascribed King's rapid rise in rank to his "military skill, courage, and hard fighting." King assumed command of his old brigade after his recovery because Waul had resigned.

On June 10 Walker replaced Taylor as district commander, and King took over the division. He continued to lead it until September 3 when Major General John H. Forney arrived to take command. King then assumed command of a Texas infantry brigade in Major General Camille J. Polignac's division. This brigade occupied camps at Camden and Walnut Hill, Arkansas, and Minden, Louisiana, until it was broken up in February 1865.

King was assigned to a new brigade in Forney's Texas division. When Forney was relieved before the surrender of the Trans-Mississippi Department, King once again took over the division. He disbanded it at Hempstead, Texas, on May 21–22, 1865. One of King's subordinates remembered him as a skillful and intrepid regimental commander. Those qualities would undoubtedly have carried over had he had an opportunity to lead his brigade or division in combat.

King went to Mexico at the end of the war, and lived briefly in Central America. After his return to the United States, he practiced law in Jefferson, Texas. He moved to Sulphur Springs in 1875 and later became mayor of the town. He served in the state legislature from 1878 to 1881, when he was appointed state adjutant general, and remained in that post until January 23, 1891. He retired to his home in Sulphur Springs, where he died on October 12, 1910. King was buried in Corsicana, which was the residence of a relative.

Arthur W. Bergeron, Jr.

Barr, Alwyn, *Polignac's Texas Brigade* (Houston, 1964).

Blessington, J.P., The Campaigns of Walker's Texas Division (Austin, 1968).

King, W.H., "Early Experiences in Missouri," *Confederate Veteran*, XVII (1909), pp 502–503.

"L.M.M." "Service of Brig. Gen. W.H. King," *Confederate Veteran*, XVI (1908), p. 395.

Webb, Walter Prescott, ed., *The Handbook of Texas*, Vol. II (Austin, 1952).

Wheeler, L.T., "Gen. Wilbur Hill King," *Confederate Veteran*, XIX (1911), pp. 173–73.

☆ *Levin M. Lewis* ☆

Lewis was born on January 6, 1832, in Baltimore, Maryland. At a young age, he went to live with an uncle in Vienna, Maryland, and was schooled there and in Washington, D.C. He attended the Maryland Military Academy, 1848–49, and the Wesleyan University, 1850–51. Lewis studied law under a judge and then read law for four years in Cambridge, Maryland. He was admitted to the Missouri bar in 1855 and practiced in Liberty, Clay County, for a few years. He soon became a minister in the Methodist church, and from 1858–60, he served as principal of the Plattsburg High School.

In April 1861, Lewis was appointed by Governor Claiborne F. Jackson as colonel of the 3d Missouri Infantry Regiment, 5th Division, Missouri State Guard. He acted as a volunteer aide-de-camp to Major General Earl Van Dorn at the Battle of Pea Ridge, March 7–8, 1862. The 3d Missouri's term of enlistment expired shortly afterwards and Lewis entered regular Confederate service as captain of what became Company A., 7th Missouri (Jackman's) Infantry Regiment, in June 1862. As major of that regiment, he accompanied a small force that moved into Missouri in August to recruit. The Confederates attacked and defeated a unit of the Union Missouri militia at the Battle of Lone Jack on August 16. There Lewis received four wounds: "two on the head, one of which is on the forehead and will show in a portrait, another which disfigures his hand, and one across the breast." The regiment was mustered in on August 31 but soon broke up. Lewis then became major of Colonel Josiah H. Caldwell's 7th Missouri Infantry Regiment (later redesignated the

16th Missouri), and Lewis' men became part of the brigade commanded by Brigadier General Mosby M. Parsons.

Lewis participated in the Battle of Prairie Grove on December 7 and became lieutenant colonel shortly afterwards while at Camp Mazard, south of Fort Smith, Arkansas. Caldwell resigned in January 1863 and Lewis was promoted to colonel. He led his men in the Battle of Helena, Arkansas, on July 4, in which the regiment assaulted a line of Union fortifications on Graveyard Hill and was thrown back with heavy losses. Lewis was wounded by a shell fragment, left on the field, and captured by the Federals. Taken at first to Alton, Illinois, Lewis later was imprisoned at Johnson's Island, Ohio, where he was a leader in an abortive plot to break out of the prison.

Lewis was exchanged in September or October 1864 with the assistance of Missouri Governor Thomas C. Reynolds, and went to Richmond, Virginia. There he learned that Reynolds had nominated him for a seat in the Confederate Senate. Lewis chose, however, to return to his regiment, and joined his men at camp at Camden, Arkansas, in November. The 16th Missouri at that time formed a part of the 2d Missouri Brigade of Parson's division. They remained in various camps in Arkansas through the winter.

In March 1865, the division received orders to march to Shreveport, Louisiana, the headquarters of the Trans-Mississippi Department. The news of General Robert E. Lee's surrender and the fall of

---

Levin M. Lewis has not left behind a uniformed portrait that has been found. This is a postwar image. (*Confederate Veteran*, XV)

Richmond reached Shreveport during the third week of April. A mass meeting was held on April 19 and several speakers encouraged continued resistance to the Federals. Lewis reportedly stated that he would never surrender. When he learned shortly afterwards that Major General Sterling Price contemplated arresting department commander General Edmund Kirby Smith to prevent him from negotiating a surrender to the Federals, Lewis informed Smith that a plot was under way. His action was probably motivated by his "personal and political obligations" to Governor Reynolds, who was an enemy of Price's and who had already spoken to Smith about the possibility of establishing contact with Union authorities. On May 16 Smith appointed Lewis a brigadier general to rank from the same date, and Lewis took command of the 2d Missouri Brigade. The department was surrendered on May 26, and on June 2, Price went to their camp to inform Lewis' men of the terms. Lewis was paroled at Shreveport later in the month.

After the surrender, Lewis served as a minister in Shreveport for a year and then took over Ryland Chapel (later St. John's Church) in Galveston, Texas. Three years later, poor health caused him to give up that position and move back to Missouri, where he became president of Arcadia College and held that post for two years. After two years as pastor of a church in St. Louis, Lewis became president of the Arkansas Female College at Little Rock in 1874. He became a professor of English at Texas A & M University in 1878. In 1880 he was elected president of Marvin College in Waxahachie, later becoming pastor of the First Methodist Church in Dallas. His health failing again, Lewis went to Los Angeles, California, where he died in 1887.

Arthur W. Bergeron, Jr.

Cassell, T.W., "Gen. Levin M. Lewis," *Confederate Veteran*, XV (1907), pp. 346–47.

Castel, Albert, *General Sterling Price and the Civil War in the West* (Baton Rouge, 1968).

Speer, William A., *Encyclopedia of the New World: Texas, Arkansas, Colorado, New Mexico and Indian Territories* (Marshall, Tx., 1881).

Thrall, Homer S., *Brief History of Methodism in Texas* (Nashville, 1894).

⭐ *Robert Plunket Maclay* ⭐

Maclay was born February 19, 1820, at Armagh, Mifflin County, Pennsylvania, and acquired his early education at the Lewiston Academy. He graduated 32d in the class of 1840 at West Point, where his classmates included future Confederate generals John P. McCown, Richard S. Ewell, and Bushrod R. Johnson. He was brevetted a 2d lieutenant in the 6th U.S. Infantry. On October 1, 1840, he was promoted 2d lieutenant in the 8th U.S. Infantry.

Maclay took part in the closing stages of the Second Seminole War in Florida. From 1843–45, he was stationed at Forts Brooke and Marion, Florida, and became a 1st lieutenant on December 31, 1845. He served under General Zachary Taylor in the Mexican War and was wounded at the Battle of Resaca de la Palma on May 9, 1846. Promoted to captain on January 22, 1849, Maclay served at Fort Worth and other posts in Texas until December 31, 1860, when he resigned his commission.

Several sources state that Maclay entered Confederate service as a major of artillery. He was named assistant adjutant and inspector general with the rank of major on the staff of Major General John G. Walker on January 2, 1863. Walker had just assumed command of a division of Texas infantrymen near Little Rock. Maclay became Walker's chief of staff and acted in that capacity until the spring of 1864. The division remained in Arkansas until April, when Walker received orders to report for duty with Major General Richard Taylor in the District of West Louisiana.

During the next several months, the division participated in an ill-fated campaign in northeastern Louisiana to try to relieve the Vicksburg garrison. Taylor ordered the men into south Louisiana shortly after the surrender of the Mississippi town. The Texans occupied several camps south of Alexandria and in late September joined Taylor's army at Washington, Louisiana. They participated in several minor campaigns in November and December but saw little fighting. By early 1864, the division was stationed near Marksville.

The Red River Campaign began in mid-March, and the division had to fall back toward Shreveport. Walker's men formed the right wing of Taylor's infantry forces at the Battle of Mansfield on April 8 and helped rout the Union army, and fought again the next day in the Battle of Pleasant Hill. Walker was slightly wounded during that engagement, and Maclay persuaded him to dismount and be placed on a litter.

General Edmund Kirby Smith then ordered the division into Arkansas to oppose a Union army under Major General Frederick Steele. At the Battle of Jenkins' Ferry on April 30, Maclay accompanied Walker as the latter rode "along the lines, cheering his men forward" in an assault on the Federal position. The division marched back to Louisiana in May. On May 13 Smith appointed Maclay a brigadier general to date from April 30. Maclay replaced Brigadier General Thomas N. Waul, who had received a disabling wound at Jenkins' Ferry.

It is unclear how long Maclay actually commanded this brigade. His appointment "caused very great dissatisfaction" among the men, and in late October Smith considered transferring another general to take over the brigade. Maclay apparently soon went on leave. On January 31, 1865, Smith wrote to him that the legality of his promotion had been challenged and stated that he did not want Maclay to return to command until a decision on the appointment was received from Richmond. Maclay's leave was extended for sixty days to await this report. There is no record that Maclay ever resumed his position.

After the war, he became a planter in Pointe Coupee Parish, Louisiana. Maclay died of pneumonia on May 20, 1903, at his daughter's home, Levy Plantation, near New Roads, Louisiana. His burial place remains unknown.

Arthur W. Bergeron, Jr.

Blessington, J.P., *The Campaigns of Walker's Texas Division* (Austin, 1968).

Eliot, Ellsworth, Jr., *West Point in the Confederacy* (New York, 1941).

Maclay, Edgar Stanton, *The Maclays of Lurgan* (Printed by the author, 1889).

✶ *Horace Randal* ✶

Randal was born in McNairy County, Tennessee, probably on January 1, 1833, according to his tombstone, although his United States Military Academy records indicate he was born in 1831. In 1839 his family settled near San Augustine, Texas. In 1849 Randal was one of the first two Texans appointed a cadet at West Point, where he spent five years because of deficiencies in mathematics and English. He graduated on July 1, 1854, ranking forty-fifth in a class of forty-six, and was brevetted 2d lieutenant, 8th Infantry. On March 3, 1855, he was promoted to 2d lieutenant, 1st Dragoons. His service was mainly on the southwestern frontier, with stations at Fort Washita, Indian Territory; Fort Davis, Texas; and Fort Union, Las Lumas, and Fort Buchanan, New Mexico Territory. He was engaged against the Apaches in the surprise of their camp near Fort Bliss, Texas, July 22, 1855, and near the Almagre Mountains, New Mexico, in April 1856, and again near the Gila River, November 30, 1856.

When Texas seceded from the Union, Randal resigned from the army on February 27, 1861. According to the reminiscences of Captain T.W. Blount, a Confederate veteran, and of General Randal's family as recorded by Reverend George L. Crocket of San Augustine, while in Washington, D.C., to settle his accounts he declined Senator Charles Sumner's offer to command the cavalry in President Abraham Lincoln's inauguration parade. Sumner returned a few days later with the assurance that if Randal would remain in the Union, he would shortly be advanced to the rank of major general. (The rank of major seems more plausible.) Randal "emphatically declined" the offer and went to Montgomery, Alabama, to tender his services to the Confederacy. He was promised a commission as captain in the Regular Army and was ordered to Pensacola, Florida, to serve under General Braxton Bragg. When he received instead a commission as a 1st lieutenant in the Regular Army, according to Reverend Crocket, "He at once returned to Montgomery, and finding that the slight had been intentional, expressed his opinion in a forcible manner to the Adjutant General, tore up his commission and left the room."

Randal went to Virginia as a private citizen. The Dallas *Herald* of October 16, 1861, cited a report that he would "be made colonel of the 1st regiment of Texas infantry in Virginia." He acted as a voluntary assistant to Major General Gustavus W. Smith at Fairfax Court House without rank or pay. President Jefferson Davis refused Smith's request that Randal be appointed Inspector-General of the II Corps of the Confederate Army of the Potomac, because he had offered no explanation of his resignation from the Regular Army. Davis later admitted to Smith that an error had been made in Randal's case but pleaded his inability to promote him captain over men who had outranked him in the United States Army. On November 16, 1861, Randal was named Smith's aide-de-camp with the rank of 1st lieutenant in the provisional army. On December 21 Davis nominated Randal to the rank of 1st lieutenant of cavalry in the Regular Army, to rank from March 16, 1861.

"My chief on General Smith's staff was Colonel Horace Randal, in some respects the most remarkable man I met during the war," South Carolinian John Cheves Haskell noted in his memoirs. "He was, when I first met him, a year or two under thirty, of a handsome carriage, and a most remarkable horseman. He never spared his horse, but rode always at half speed, day or night. I have seen his horse go down with him many times, but he was always up as soon as the horse was, on him and off again in the time that most men would take to pick themselves up. He was a classmate of Stuart at West Point, but had more physical dash than Stuart. His other classmates, Hood among them, always predicted that he would be the cavalry leader of the war if he got a chance." Haskell added that Randal was "a most diffident, modest man in speaking of himself...."

After the army went into winter quarters, Randal resigned as A.D.C. and returned to Texas to raise the

28th Cavalry Regiment in east Texas. He was commissioned colonel on February 12, 1862. The Marshall, Texas *Republican* predicted that "Col. Randal's regiment will be perhaps the finest cavalry regiment that has ever been sent from Texas to the seat of war. The history and reputation of the Colonel for ability and gallantry has drawn towards him the best material in the State." On July 9, 1862, the regiment left Marshall for Arkansas, where it was dismounted and later joined as infantry what became the 2d Brigade of Major General John G. Walker's Texas Greyhound Division. Randal was appointed brigade commander on September 3, 1862, and served in Arkansas and Louisiana. "Col R[andal] is very popular with both men & his superior officers," wrote Dr. Edward W. Cade, a surgeon in the 28th Texas. "Col Randal is the finest, most military-looking man of them all," Kate Stone noted in her journal, after meeting a number of officers of Walker's division at Monroe, Louisiana.

Randal's brigade was in reserve at the Battle of Milliken's Bend, Louisiana, June 7, 1863, during Grant's siege of Vicksburg. On November 8, 1863, Lieutenant General E. Kirby Smith, commander of the Trans-Mississippi Department, wrote to Richmond, asking for Randal's promotion to brigadier general; but the War Department took no action because, in Adjutant General Samuel Cooper's opinion, "the want of proper returns from the Trans-Mississippi Department makes it impossible to determine here the wants of general officers for the various commands there, consistent with a proper organization agreeably to acts of Congress."

After the Battle of Mansfield (Sabine Cross Roads), April 8, 1864, in the Red River Campaign, Lieutenant General Richard Taylor said of Randal: "In vigor, energy, and daring Randal surpassed my expectations, high as they were of him and his fine brigade." This high opinion was strengthened by Randal's gallant performance on the 9th at Pleasant Hill. Kirby Smith on his own initiative promoted him to brigadier general, to rank from April 8, 1864; but the Confederate government never confirmed the appointment.

Randal was mortally wounded in the Battle at Jenkins' Ferry, Arkansas, April 30, 1864, and died on May 2, an hour after the burial of Brigadier General William R. Scurry of Texas, a fellow brigade commander in Walker's division. Randal was buried at the hamlet of Tulip, near the battlefield, and later his remains were removed to the Old Marshall Cemetery at Marshall, Texas. A state marker was erected at his grave in 1962. Randall [sic] County, Texas, created in 1876, was named for him.

Norman D. Brown

Anderson, John Q., *A Texas Surgeon in the C.S.A.* (Tusacaloosa, 1957).

Blessington, Joseph P., *The Campaigns of Walker's Texas Division* (New York, 1875).

Crocket, George L., *Two Centuries in East Texas: A History of San Augustine County and Surrounding Territory from 1685 to the Present Time* (Dallas, 1932).

Smith, Gustavus W., *Confederate War Papers: Fairfax Court House, New Orleans, Seven Pines, Richmond and North Carolina* (New York, 1884).

⋆ *Alexander Watkins Terrell* ⋆

Terrell was born on November 3, 1827, in Patrick County, Virginia. His father moved the family to Boonville, Missouri, in 1832. He was educated in primary schools and attended the University of Missouri. He studied law in Boonville and was admitted to the bar in 1849. Terrell practiced law in St. Joseph until 1852, and then moved to Austin, Texas, in the latter year hoping to improve his wife's health. In 1857 he was elected judge of the 2d Judicial District, and sat on that bench until 1862.

Terrell was a good friend of Sam Houston and initially opposed secession. In November 1861, Terrell declined the offer of a commission as colonel of the 8th Texas Infantry Regiment. Governor Francis R. Lubbock sent him to Richmond in February 1862 to carry a letter to Secretary of War Judah P. Benjamin. On June 12, 1862, Brigadier General Henry E. McCulloch named Terrell as captain and volunteer aide-de-camp on his staff. Terrell accompanied McCulloch to Little Rock, Arkansas, and remained on his staff until McCulloch was replaced by Major General John G. Walker in January 1863. Major General John B. Magruder commissioned Terrell as a lieutenant colonel on March 31 and appointed him commander of a cavalry battalion being raised for possible service either in New Mexico and Arizona or in northern Texas and the Indian Territory. Organized as Terrell's Texas Cavalry Battalion on May 30, the unit was soon increased to a regiment. It was mustered in as Terrell's Texas Cavalry Regiment at Navasota on June 20 and ordered to train at Camp Groce near Hempstead. Colonel Terrell's unit is frequently misidentified as the 34th Texas Cavalry.

In September the regiment moved to Galveston and was temporarily dismounted. General Edmund Kirby Smith, commander of the Trans-Mississippi Department, wanted to make Terrell head of the Texas branch of the department's cotton bureau, and Terrell traveled to Houston to speak to the bureau chief. While he was away, several officers led a mutiny, and nearly one hundred men left Galveston for their homes. The officers feared the permanent loss of the regiment's horses. Though he turned down Kirby Smith's offer to head the Texas cotton bureau, Terrell did agree to sit on a committee formed to investigate the "management, purchase, and transportation of Government cotton." Terrell submitted the committee's report on March 3, 1864, and ended his association with the cotton bureau.

In November 1863, Terrell's regiment saw duty at Sabine Pass, LaVaca, and Velasco. By the end of the year, it was assigned to Colonel Xavier B. Debray's brigade of Brigadier General Hamilton P. Bee's division and was stationed at Camp Wharton on Jones' Creek. Magruder ordered the men back to Galveston in late February 1864. The Union Red River Campaign, which began in March of that year, caused Kirby Smith to order reinforcements to Major General Richard Taylor's army, and Bee's division was one of the units that was sent to join Taylor near Pleasant Hill. Bee reached Taylor on April 5 with only Terrell's

Alexander W. Terrell has not left a uniformed portrait that can be located. This image dates from probably the 1880s. (*Confederate Veteran*, XX)

and two other regiments of the division. On the morning of April 8, these units skirmished with the advancing Federal army south of Mansfield and held it back while Taylor's infantry units formed a line of battle. The cavalrymen fell back to the army's right flank, but Taylor soon ordered Terrell to reinforce other cavalry units on the army's left. The regiment participated in the battle fought that afternoon, fighting dismounted alongside the infantrymen. Terrell chose to remain mounted as he led his men in the assault. After the Federals were routed, Terrell's men quickly retrieved their horses so that they could conduct a pursuit. They had acquitted themselves well in their first engagement with the enemy.

At the Battle of Pleasant Hill on April 9, Terrell led his men in an attack on the Union army's left flank. The rough terrain and confused battle lines resulted in Terrell and one of his companies being cut off from the rest of the army. It took them most of the night to make their way back to their own lines. Because of the severe fighting they had seen on those two days, the men of the regiment were not heavily engaged in the Battle of Blair's Landing on April 12 but acted as flank guards. The remaining regiments of Bee's division had reached the army by this time, and Terrell's regiment formed part of a brigade with the 1st and 35th (Likens') Texas Cavalry regiments. Terrell frequently acted as brigade commander during the succeeding weeks of the campaign. He and his men missed participating in the Battle of Monett's Ferry on April 23 because Bee sent them to the rear to guard his wagon train.

The regiment fought in several skirmishes as the army pursued the Federals down the Red River. In an engagement at Bayou Lamourie on May 7, Terrell led an attack that ran into a hidden force of Federals and was thrown back with dozens of casualties. Terrell's men were in reserve when the Battle of Yellow Bayou (May 18) began but later reinforced the right flank in time to cover its retreat. Terrell became permanent brigade commander after the conclusion of the campaign. His troopers performed picket duty along the Atchafalaya River during the fall and early winter and fought several skirmishes with Union soldiers stationed at Morganza. The brigade remained near Alexandria until April 1865, when it moved to Grand Ecore. During this period, the 7th Texas Cavalry Regiment replaced the 35th Texas in Terrell's brigade. Terrell received orders in May to take his brigade to

Marshall, Texas. From there, the men were sent toward Austin. They were disbanded on May 14 at Wild Cat Bluff on the Trinity River. Kirby Smith appointed Terrell a brigadier general on May 16 to rank from the same day. Terrell rode to Austin to join a group of officers and governmental officials who had decided to go to Mexico rather than surrender. In Mexico, in July, he was appointed a "chef d'batallion" (colonel) in the French occupation army. He resigned in November 1865 and returned to Texas.

After practicing law at Houston for a short time, he retired to his plantation in Robertson County. Terrell moved to Austin in 1871 and resumed his practice. He was elected reporter of the Texas Supreme Court in 1874 and to the state senate the next year. Serving in the senate until 1882, he was then elected to the state house of representatives. President Grover Cleveland appointed him minister plenipotentiary to Turkey in 1893, a post he held until 1897. Terrell died in Mineral Wells, Texas, on September 9, 1912, and was buried in the State Cemetery in Austin.

Arthur W. Bergeron, Jr.

Chamberlain, Charles K., "Alexander Watkins Terrell, Citizen, Statesman." Doctoral dissertation (University of Texas, 1956).

"Judge Alexander Watkins Terrell," *Confederate Veteran*, XX (1912), pp. 575–76.

Spencer, John W., *Terrell's Texas Cavalry* (Burnett, Tex., 1982).

Terrell, Alexander Watkins, Papers, University of Texas Archives.

Wallis, Mary Ella, "The Life of Alexander Watkins Terrell, 1827 to 1912." Master's thesis (University of Texas, 1937).

⭐ *The Generals Who Weren't* ⭐

While in the ideal, every brigade in an army would have been commanded by a general—hence the title "brigadier"—in practice the exigencies of the service, disease, and battle casualties often resulted in brigades being commanded temporarily and even permanently by colonels, even lieutenant colonels. The Confederate government never caught up with this backlog, and President Davis, who held exclusive power to create general officers, may not have wished to do so, for he often declined to recognize a permanent brigade commander with a general's stars.

Nevertheless, this did not stop a number of colonels from literally promoting themselves, styling themselves brigadier general or "temporary brigadier" in their correspondence, and even going to the trouble and expense of having uniforms made with the insignia of a rank they never received. Perhaps it was just wishful thinking, or maybe they felt they were simply readying themselves for a permanent rank that, in the end, never came.

Then there were other state militia generals in almost every Confederate state who never transferred into the Confederate service. They could not exercise rank over Confederate troops, and rarely took part in campaigns or battles except in Georgia, but still some of them adopted wearing the Confederate uniform and insignia of general officers.

Finally, there were a few mysterious characters who were neither militia generals, nor colonels commanding brigades, who simply wore the uniform anyhow.

All three categories of men left behind photographs of themselves in such uniform, thereby confusing historians and buffs ever since about their true rank and status. On the following pages appear a number of these bogus "brigadiers" in their uniforms and insignia. Quite certainly not one of them was a genuine general; chances are all of them deserved to be.

Archibald S. Dobbin was colonel of an Arkansas cavalry regiment, and from 1863 onward was frequently in brigade command in the Trans-Mississippi. (Museum of the Confederacy, Richmond, Va.)

In spite of his affecting the uniform of a full brigadier, and often being called "General Dobbin" in reports, chiefly by the enemy, he never got the promotion and was paroled as a colonel. An unpublished image. (Alabama Department of Archives and History, Montgomery)

One of the mysteries of generals' photography, the man seated in the center is identified as the guerilla and later outlaw Frank James, and the man standing at right as his brother Jesse. Both identifications are highly questionable. Nevertheless, the seated man is wearing what appears to be a general officer's blouse, with the collar insignia quite distinct. The buttons, though artistically retouched, appear to be in threes, such as worn by some major generals. (State Historical Society of Missouri)

A real mystery is the identity of the Confederate officer seated beside Federal General Joseph Hayes. It would appear to be either an individual parole scene, or else some surrender formality staged for the camera. The Confederate wears a colonel's stars, but a brigadier's buttons on his tunic. His sleeve braid also appears to be that of a brigadier. (Courtesy of James C. Frasca)

Julius Caesar Bonaparte Mitchell certainly had the name for a general, but he never rose higher than colonel of the 34th Alabama. He disappears from the record in July 1864. (Alabama Department of Archives and History, Montgomery)

Another view of Mitchell showing him in his proper uniform as a colonel. (Medford Historical Society, Medford, Mass.)

Colonel Thomas Munford led the 2d Virginia Cavalry through the last three years of the war, often temporarily commanding a brigade. Nevertheless, Munford, though often recommended for a brigadiership, never got one, and was not entitled to wear the uniform he sports in these images. (Cook Collection, Valentine Museum, Richmond, Va.)

Munford sat repeatedly for his portrait, perhaps to validate on a glass plate a promotion that he never got on paper. (William A. Turner Collection)

Another variant image of Munford. (Museum of the Confederacy, Richmond VA)

Colonel Thomas P. Ochiltree wears both the sleeve braid and the buttons of a brigadier general, but never rose to that rank. (Medford Historical Society, Medford, Mass.)

He sat at least twice for the camera, looking a little less dapper in this later war image. (Medford Historical Society, Medford, Mass.)

Francis H. Smith was colonel of the 9th Virginia at the beginning of the war, but soon reverted to his true life's calling, the superintendency of Lexington's Virginia Military Institute, where he held the rank of brigadier general in the Virginia state forces. Hence his donning the Confederate brigadier's uniform. (U.S. Army Military History Institute, Carlisle, Pa.)

M.S. Stokes commanded the 1st North Carolina Infantry from May 1861 until his mortal wounding at Ellerson's Mill on June 26, 1862. His collar being turned down, no insignia can be seen. (Medford Historical Society, Medford, Mass.)

Nevertheless, Stokes' blouse buttons and sleeve braid are clearly correct for a brigadier. Being a senior colonel, he may have been in line for a promotion when he fell in battle. (Western Reserve Historical Society, Cleveland, Oh.)

M. Jefferson Thompson was lieutenant colonel of the 3d Missouri Infantry. By 1864, however, he was styling himself brigadier, as his buttons here suggest. (Museum of the Confederacy, Richmond, Va.)

Thompson, a flamboyant character, loved to sit for the camera, leaving behind many more portraits than most genuine generals. (Atlanta Historical Society, Atlanta, Ga.)

There was often a hint of a smile on his wiry features. (Confederate Museum, New Orleans, La.)

Thompson still appears to wear the collar stars of a colonel in this image, a Confederate rank which he seems never to have attained. (Albert G. Shaw Collection, Virginia Historical Society, Richmond)

⋆ *Addendum* ⋆

Inevitably in a project of this scope sources will be missed or overlooked, resulting in photographs not located in time to include them in their proper place in the series. Also, happily, the appearance of the earlier volumes of *The Confederate General* has stimulated collectors and buffs to bring their images to the attention of the editors, creating much new material.

As a result, the portraits that follow represent an addendum of more photographs received too late to include in the earlier volumes. We can be certain that even more will continue to come to light in the days and years ahead, and perhaps at some future date circumstances will allow for a complete revision of this series to include them, and these as well, in their proper places within the series.

P. G. T. Beauregard posed for the camera more than any other Confederate general, though most of his portraits come from only about three sittings. This portrait and several that follow date from early 1861. (Museum of the Confederacy, Richmond, Va.)

Some of his portraits are only the slightest variants of other poses. This one, for example, is very close to... (Museum of the Confederacy, Richmond, Va.)

At the same sitting Beauregard changed his pose for this.
(Museum of the Confederacy, Richmond, Va.)

...this one. (William A. Turner Collection)

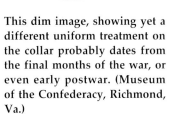

This dim image, showing yet a different uniform treatment on the collar probably dates from the final months of the war, or even early postwar. (Museum of the Confederacy, Richmond, Va.)

Taken in a different uniform sometime later in the war, this moody pose comes from Beauregard's other most productive sitting for the camera. (National Archives)

A previously unpublished portrait of Albert Blanchard, taken while colonel of the 1st Louisiana, judging from his buttons and the absence of a wreath around his collar stars, which appear to be unusual brass pin-ons. (William A. Turner Collection)

(Publisher's Note: Since the original publication of this volume, the subject of the photograph shown here has been identified, not as Albert Blanchard, but as Colonel Winchester Hall of the 26th Louisiana Infantry Regiment. Thanks to Arthur W. Bergeron, Jr., of Baton Rouge, Louisiana, for the identification.)

Milledge L. Bonham seems to have had only one wartime sitting, of which this is a variant pose. (Museum of the Confederacy, Richmond, Va.)

This vignette is yet another variant from the same sitting.
(Museum of the Confederacy, Richmond, Va.)

Another early war image of Simon Buckner which, though artistically retouched, appears to be genuine. (Albert G. Shaw Collection, Virginia Historical Society, Richmond)

An unpublished portrait of John Bullock Clark, Jr., when he was colonel of the 6th Missouri prior to March 1864. (Courtesy of Dr. and Mrs. Tom Sweeney)

Richard M. Gano as a lieutenant colonel in the Kentucky cavalry
in 1861–62. (Courtesy of Steve Mullinax)

Fitzhugh Lee sitting comfortably next to a friend in a studio in Richmond, Virginia. (Valentine Museum, Richmond, Va.)

A profile of R.E. Lee showing, as usual, his colonel's stars on his collar. (William A. Turner Collection)

Probably taken at the same sitting, this portrait is only the slightest of variants from others. (William A. Turner Collection)

A portrait of William Gaston Lewis probably taken near the close of the war. (William A. Turner Collection)

A previously unpublished portrait of Robert D. Lilley taken during the final year of the war after the loss of his arm at Winchester. (William A. Turner Collection)

General George E. Pickett, probably taken late in the war, though his insignia is indistinct, and his blouse buttons appear to be arranged as for a colonel, which might argue for an 1861 date. (William A. Turner Collection)

A standing view of General Francis R.T. Nicholls taken at Anderson & Blessing studio in New Orleans. (Courtesy of Vann R. Martin)

✬ *Contributors* ✬

Anne J. Bailey: *Assistant Professor of History,*
Georgia Southern University, Statesboro, GA

C. Alwyn Barr: *Professor of History,*
Texas Tech University, Lubbock, TX

Edwin C. Bearss: *Chief Historian,*
National Park Service, Washington, D.C.

Arthur W. Bergeron: *Historian,*
Louisiana Office of State Parks, Baton Rouge, LA

William A. Blair: *Department of History,*
Pennsylvania State University, University Park, PA

Keith S. Bohannon: *Department of History,*
University of Georgia, Athens, GA

Norman D. Brown: *Professor of History,*
The University of Texas at Austin, TX

Charles F. Bryan: *Director,*
Virginia Historical Society, Richmond, VA

Peter S. Carmichael: *Department of History,*
Pennsylvania State University, University Park, PA

Albert Castel: *Department of History,*
Western Michigan University, Kalamazoo, MI

Thomas W. Cutrer: *Associate Professor,*
Arizona State University, Phoenix, AZ

William C. Davis: *Writer/Historian,*
Mechanicsburg, PA

Gary Gallagher: *Head, Department of History,*
Pennsylvania State University, University Park, PA

Walter Griggs: *Associate Professor of Decision Sciences
and Business Law,*
Virginia Commonwealth University, Richmond, VA

Lowell H. Harrison: *Department of History,*
Western Kentucky University, Bowling Green, KY

Herman Hattaway: *Professor of History,*
U.S. Military Academy, West Point, NY

Lawrence L. Hewitt: *Associate Professor of History,*
Southeastern Louisiana University, Hammond, LA

Terry L. Jones: *Assistant Professor of History,*
Northeast Louisiana University at Monroe, LA

Robert K. Krick: *Chief Historian,*
Fredericksburg and Spotsylvania National Military
Park, Fredericksburg, VA

Robert E.L. Krick: *Assistant Historian,*
Richmond National Battlefield Park, Richmond, VA

Archie P. MacDonald: *Regents' Professor of History,*
Stephen F. Austin State University, Nacogdoches, TX

Richard M. McMurry: *Writer,*
Decatur, GA

Michael Parrish: *Writer/Historian,*
The Jenkins Rare Books & Manuscripts Company,
Austin, TX

Donald C. Pfanz: *Historian,*
Fort Sumter National Monument, Sullivans Island, SC

Brian C. Pohanka: *Writer/Historian,*
Alexandria, VA

James I. Robertson, Jr.: *C.P. Miles Professor of History,*
Virginia Polytechnic Institute and State University,
Blacksburg, VA

Charles P. Roland: *Emeritus Professor of History,*
University of Kentucky, Lexington, KY

Benjamin E. Snellgrove: *Professor of History (Part time),*
Southeastern Louisiana University, Hammond, LA

Richard J. Sommers: *Archivist,*
U.S. Army Military History Institute, Carlisle, PA

Bryce A. Suderow: *Writer,*
Washington, D.C.

W. Davis Waters: *Assistant Site Manager,*
Bennett Place, Durham, NC

Jeffry D. Wert: *Writer/History Teacher,*
Penns Valley High School, Spring Mills, PA

Steven Woodworth: *Department of Social Science,*
Toccoa Falls College, Toccoa Falls, GA

Mitch Yokelson: *Researcher,*
National Archives, Washington, D.C.

⋆ *Photograph Credits* ⋆

The editors would like to thank the following individuals and
institutions who generously permitted the use of their photographs.

Alabama Department of Archives and History,
Montgomery

Arthur W. Bergeron, Jr.

Chicago Historical Society

Civil War Times Illustrated Collection, Harrisburg, PA

Confederate Military History, Clement A. Evans

Confederate Museum, Charleston, SC

Confederate Museum, New Orleans, LA

Confederate Veteran

Dale S. Snair

Dave Mark

Dementi Studio, Richmond, VA

Don Tiedeken

Duke University Library, Durham, NC

Evans J. Casso

Generals in Gray, Ezra Warner

Herb Peck, Jr.

Hunt-Morgan House, Lexington, KY

Jack T. Greer

Kentucky Historical Society, Frankfort

Lawrence T. Jones

Lee-Fendall House, Alexandria, VA

Lee Wallace, Jr.

Library of Congress, Washington, D.C.

Louisiana State University, Baton Rouge

Mansfield State Commemorative Area, Louisiana
Office of State Parks

Mark Katz

Medford Historical Society, Medford, MA

Mike Miner

Mississippi Department of Archives and History,
Jackson

Missouri Historical Society, St. Louis

Museum of the Confederacy, Richmond, VA

Museum of New Mexico, Sante Fe

National Archives, Washington, D.C.

New York Historical Society, New York

North Carolina Division of Archives and History, Raleigh

Oakly Park, Edgefield, SC

Old Courthouse Museum, Vicksburg, MS

Photographic History, Francis T. Miller

Robert J. Younger

Russell W. Hicks, Jr.

South Caroliniana Library, University of South Carolina, Columbia

Southeastern Louisiana University, Hammond

Steve Mullinax

Ted R. Rudder

Texas State Archives, Austin

Tulane University, New Orleans, LA

University of Arkansas Archives, Little Rock

University of Georgia Library, Athens

University of North Carolina, Chapel Hill

U.S. Army Military History Institute, Carlisle, PA

U.S. Military Academy Archives, West Point, NY

Valentine Museum, Richmond, VA

Vann R. Martin

Virginia Historical Society, Richmond

William A. Albaugh

William A. Turner

William C. Davis

Western Reserve Historical Society, Cleveland, OH